The Railways of
BRISTOL &
SOMERSET

The Railways of

BRISTOL

& SOMERSET

Martin Smith

IAN ALLAN
Publishing

Half title page:
Class 37 No 37206 pulls Orient Express stock into Wapping Wharf, Bristol, on 12 July 1984. Author

Previous pages:
The coaches being loaded on board the SS Beljeanne by a floating crane at Avonmouth Docks on 13 June 1930 are for a South American railway. The bodies were separated from the bogies for transportation. Port of Bristol Authority

Right:
The Somerset & Avon Railway Association has acquired the former GWR yard at Radstock for its headquarters. This forlorn notice near the old engine shed typifies all too clearly the task which it and all other preservation organisations have, or have had, to face. Author

First published 1992

ISBN 0 7110 2063 9

All rights reserved. No part of this book may be reproduced or transmitted in any form or by any means, electronic or mechanical, including photo-copying, recording or by any information storage and retrieval system, without permission from the Publisher in writing.

© Martin Smith 1992

Published by Ian Allan Ltd, Shepperton, Surrey; and printed by Ian Allan Printing Ltd at their works at Coombelands in Runnymede, England.

Contents

Acknowledgements

Above all, thanks are due to my wife, Micky. Although she once had trouble differentiating between a Pannier tank and a lavatory brush, she is now learning fast. I spent countless hours throwing bits of paper in the air in fits of desperation trying to convince Micky that I was writing a book and, bless her, she never once mentioned the words 'legal separation'.

Thanks are also due to four people who are probably unaware of the publication of this book, but, without whose help, encouragement and advice over the years, it would probably never have been written. The foursome are: Captain David Games, Peter Herring, Keith Nelson and Dave Saunders.

In addition, I would like to express my sincere gratitude to the following people who helped with the preparation of this book:

Mr I. P. Arnold (Fisons PLC, Glastonbury), Peter Barnfield (West Somerset Steam Railway Trust), David Bromwich (Local History Library, Taunton), Mr S. Cole, (ARC Southern Ltd), Mr I. C. Dunford (St. Ivel, Chard), Ken Goodway (Avon Valley Railway), Mrs J. Gough (Port of Bristol Authority), Roger Hateley (Industrial Railway Society), Pete Keenleyside, Andy King, (Bristol Industrial Museum), John Knott, Robin Linsley (British Railways Board), Frank Lismore, Peggy Rowe (Radstock & District Museum), Adrian Spence (Ordnance Survey), Bill Sweet (Somerset & Avon Railway Association), Mr I. P. Thornell (British Fuel Company, Filton), Mike Vincent, Mike West.

Also, the staff of Bristol Central Library, Taunton and Frome Libraries and the Public Record Office, Kew.

Martin Smith
Coleford
Somerset.
September 1991

Bibliography

Several standard reference works have been used during the preparation of this book. They are:

History of the Great Western Railway, (E. T. MacDermot, C. R. Clinker, O. S. Nock). Ian Allan.
Locomotives of the Great Western Railway, Railway Correspondence & Travel Society.
History of the Southern Railway, (C. F. Dendy Marshall, R. W. Kidner). Ian Allan.
History of the Somerset Coalfield, (C. G. Down, A. J. Warrington). David & Charles.
Industrial Locomotives of South Western England, (ed R. K. Hateley). Industrial Railway Society.

Clinker's Register, (C. R. Clinker). Avon Anglia.
British Locomotive Catalogue (B. Baxter, D. Baxter). Moorland.
The British Steam Railway Locomotive 1825-1925, (E. L. Ahrons). LPC.
Among the other publications which have been consulted are:
An Historical Survey of Great Western Engine Sheds, (E. Lyons, E. Mountford). OPC.
The Weston, Clevedon & Portishead Light Railway, (C. Redwood). Sequoia.
The Midland Railway, (C. Hamilton Ellis). Ian Allan.
The Somerset & Dorset Railway, (R. Atthill). David & Charles.
Somerset & Dorset Locomotive History, (D. Bradley & D. Milton). David & Charles.

Lines to Avonmouth, (M. Vincent). OPC.
Reflections on the Portishead Branch, (M. Vincent). OPC.
Preserved Locomotives of British Railways, (P. Fox, N. Webster). Platform Five.
Studies in the Business History of Bristol, (ed C. Harvey, J. Press). Bristol Academic Press.
Bridgwater Docks and the River Parrett, (Brian J. Murless). Somerset County Council Library Service.

Much information has been picked from a variety of periodicals and these include:
Great Western Echo, Railway Observer, Railways, Railway Magazine, Trains Illustrated, Railway World, Bristol Evening Post, Bradshaw's, various public and working timetables.

1 The Main Lines

The early railway history of the Bristol area is closely associated with the Great Western, but 'God's Wonderful Railway' was not quite as quick off the mark as is often believed. By the time the first GWR train left Bristol's Temple Meads station for Paddington in 1841, the Bristol & Exeter Railway was already running its own scheduled passenger services from the same station. Furthermore, apart from the B&E, other railway passenger services had operated from Bristol since 1835 and the first freight line in the area had been open to traffic since 1831.

The true pioneer was the Avon & Gloucestershire Railway which, on 5 June 1831, completed its 5¼-mile colliery tramway between a riverside wharf near Keynsham and the village of Mangotsfield. In a bout of exhibitionism, the company had shown off the first completed section of its line on 30 December the previous year, and the horse-drawn wagon which was used achieved fame as the first railway movement in the area. Sadly, the reaction of the horse, the wagon and the load of coal is unrecorded. The A&G's dream of steam haulage did not materialise, and, throughout its existence, the company did not progress beyond horse power; that, no doubt, did not help the A&G's claim to a place in the history books.

The plan of campaign was for the Avon & Gloucestershire to link up with the Bristol & Gloucestershire Railway at Mangotsfield, the latter company having been authorised to construct a 10-mile railway from a wharf at Cuckold's Pill in Bristol to the romantically named village of Coalpit Heath. With rather more chumminess than many neighbouring railways were to display elsewhere, the two concerns agreed to joint use of the line between Mangotsfield and Coalpit Heath. This section was opened in July 1832 but was, at first, of more use to the A&G than the B&G. The A&G had an exit route for its coal on the river but the B&G's target, Bristol, could only be reached by transhipping coal at Mangotsfield into road vehicles. It was 6 August 1835 before the entire B&G line was opened throughout. The unveiling

Above:
This picture of Bristol Temple Meads station was taken in 1889. The original Brunel GWR terminus is the turreted building on the left of the station incline, while the Bristol & Exeter's grandiose office building is on the right of the frame. It is tempting to speculate that the figure behind the horse-drawn cab which is descending the incline is an MOT tester checking for traces of illegal exhaust emission. Photomatic

ceremony involved seven wagons, each horse-drawn, which left Bristol at 10.30am and rendezvoused with two carriages at the eastern end of Staple Hill tunnel. The procession arrived at Coalpit Heath at 1.30pm and, after the invited guests indulged in the customary spa water and sticky buns, they left at 5pm for the 3½hour journey back to Bristol. The guests had claimed the distinction of being the first official railway passengers in Bristol, over five years before the Great Western sold its first tickets at Temple Meads.

The southern terminus of the Bristol & Gloucestershire line was at Cuckold's Pill Wharf, on the opposite bank of the Avon to where the Great Western's massive goods depot was to be built in years to come. From the wharf, the line ran through the suburbs of Lawrence Hill and Fishponds on its way to Mangotsfield; like the Avon & Gloucestershire, it was built to a gauge of 4ft 8in. The A&G had anticipated that it would become the premier of the two lines as it had enjoyed three years consolidation of its position before the B&G had reached Bristol, but the corporate smugness was due for a jolt. Within a year of the B&G's opening, the significance of its riverside outlet at Bristol was emphasised by the fact that three times more coal was going on the B&G than on the A&G and the

former became, unsurprisingly, well aware of its superior status. The B&G was keen to progress to locomotive power but, apart from the cost of buying a suitable beast, the line had been built only to tramway standards and upgrading would involve considerable outlay. It is known, however, that the company tried out an engine at some stage but it did not present the directors with the predicament of whether to pursue upgrading for further locomotive haulage. Before it had got under way, the contraption exploded.

The Bristol & Gloucestershire had not underestimated its potential. It was situated in a key position for an extension northwards and, although the company itself had neither the wish nor the means to strike out for the city of Gloucester and beyond, others were waiting in the wings. On 1 July 1839, assent was given for the similarly named Bristol & Gloucester Railway to build a 22-mile line from Westerleigh, near Coalpit Heath, to Standish, near Gloucester, and an essential part of the new company's Act was the absorption of the old Bristol & Gloucestershire and its upgrading for locomotive-hauled trains.

Meanwhile, the Great Western was getting its act together, but almost 10 years were to elapse between the demonstration train on the Avon & Gloucestershire and the first GWR departure from Temple Meads. When the section of the GWR's Paddington line had been completed between Bristol and Bath, the company's hierarchy was eager to play with the new toy. A special train carrying five directors and the Great Western's chief engineer, the diminutive but flamboyant Isambard Brunel, made a trial trip between the two cities on 21 August 1840. The 11¾-mile run took 33 minutes, which included an eight minute wait at Keynsham station and a further stop near Newton St Loe to pick up George Frere, the company's resident civil engineer. Ten days later, the first public train left Temple Meads at 8am; even without the delays experienced by the earlier 'trial' train it, too, took 33 minutes. The train consisted of three first class and five second class carriages and was hauled by outside-framed 2-2-2 locomotive *Fireball*, one of the first of a class of 62 locomotives.

On that first day, 10 trains ran in each direction between Bristol and Bath, and carried a total of 5,880 passengers. Keynsham was the only intermediate stop at that time as the stations at Saltford and Twerton were not opened until December 1840. It was 7o'clock on the morning of 30 June 1841 when the inaugural train left Temple Meads on the service to Paddington.

Bath station was, much to the chagrin of the directors, not fully completed in time for the first public train. Bristol Temple Meads had only narrowly beaten the clock as the last rail into the station had been laid just half an hour before the scheduled departure of that train! Both stations, despite their differing stages of completion, boasted impressive over-all roofs, the one at Bath having a 50ft span and that at Temple Meads a 72ft span. Bath station was built in the local limestone and stood on a 73 arch viaduct; it was to remain virtually unaltered until 1897. Its original goods yard, which was to the west of the station and at right-angles to the line was, however, resited west of the station in 1877 and, three years later, the single-road engine shed to the east of the station was replaced by a structure of similar size, albeit minus its turntable, just beyond the new goods yard.

Temple Meads housed the company's board room and residential premises for the station superintendent; the massive goods shed, which did not open until 1842, was to the north-east of the station but was on a lower level than the main railway line. The little matter of a 12ft drop was overcome by means of a series of hydraulic lifts and wagon turntables. About half a mile to the west of Temple Meads was a three-road engine shed which had a small yard with a 40ft turntable and, on the opposite side of the line, were the coke ovens where Rhondda coal was prepared for the locomotives.

The entire line between Temple Meads and Paddington was, of course, built to the broad gauge of 7ft 0¼in which Brunel had championed despite the fact that 4ft 8½in had been adopted as standard by almost all of the other railways in the rest of the country.

Conveniently for all concerned, the other company which was initially accommodated at Temple Meads station, the Bristol & Exeter Railway, also used the broad gauge. The B&E had been formally incorporated on 19 May 1836, and it had its sights set on traffic from the coalfields around Nailsea and Backwell in North Somerset and the potential of the harbour at Uphill, near Weston-super-Mare, as a steamer port serving Ireland and South Wales. But, ironically, these two sources of revenue were never to be pursued by the company. The B&E's staff suggestion box came up with two ideas which would reduce expenditure; the first was to abandon the idea of an independent Bristol terminus at Pylle Hill and, instead, to use Temple Meads station at least for the time being. The second idea was to lease the line to the GWR in order to avoid the expense of locomotives and rolling stock; the alternative form of motive power, horses, was considered not altogether suitable for the 76 miles from Bristol to Exeter. By this time, three of the B&E's directors were gentlemen who also sat on the GWR board and this no doubt helped to overcome any opposition to the idea. The working agreement was signed on 14 August 1840.

Ever mindful of the pennies, the Bristol & Exeter decided to settle for opening as far as Bridgwater and then worrying about the rest at a later date. The 33½-mile line between Bristol and Bridgwater was almost ready for opening by the end of May 1841 and, on 1 June, the obligatory 'Directors' Special', which carried 400 guests, completed the journey in 1¾ hours. The eight-coach train was hauled by 2-2-2 *Fireball*, the same locomotive which had been in charge of the inaugural Bristol-Bath train the previous

year. Stops were made at all of the five intermediate stations, Nailsea, Clevedon Road, Banwell, Weston Junction and Highbridge. Of those stations, Nailsea was to be renamed Nailsea & Backwell in 1905, Clevedon Road became Yatton in 1847 and Banwell had a history of an identity crisis ahead of it; it was renamed Worle in 1869, Puxton in 1884 and, in 1922, Puxton & Worle. Weston Junction was abandoned in 1884.

The ceremonial train on the Bristol & Exeter was two weeks in advance of the official public opening. Despite the economy of using Temple Meads station, it was a laborious procedure as a reversing manoeuvre was required for each B&E train. This inconvenience was finally circumvented in 1845 when the B&E opened its own station at right-angles to the GWR's at Temple Meads. The new B&E terminus fell a little short of the grandeur which had once been envisaged for it, and its unfinished state on opening day did not add to appearances. Local railwaymen were quick to note that it was in close proximity to Bristol's cattle market and so the station became known, irreverently, as the 'cowshed'. The new arrangement at Temple Meads incorporated an express platform situated on the curve between the entrances of the two stations so that through trains from Paddington to Exeter would not have to cope with the tedium of reversing.

Exeter was finally reached on 1 May 1844. It had been a piecemeal opening of the line south of Bridgwater, with Taunton seeing its first train on 1 July 1842. Taunton station was just to the north of the main part of the town, and both its up and down platforms and buildings were on the same side of the track and almost 100 yards apart. There was a loading bay and wagon turntable between the two platforms but the main goods traffic was dealt with in a traverser-equipped shed on the opposite side of the line. The unorthodox layout of passenger facilities lasted until the station was extensively rebuilt in 1868. A further rebuilding in 1895 resulted in the platform length being trebled, and the provision of an avoiding loop to the south of the main line. Wellington was reached on 1 May 1843, and the B&E's only tunnel, at Whiteball on the Somerset/Devon border, was completed in February the following year.

While the Bristol & Exeter was inching its way southwards, the fledgling Bristol & Gloucester Railway saw its future as an ally of the Great Western and, no doubt influenced by its engineer, a certain Mr Brunel, abruptly decided to use the broad gauge. Subsequently, those nice people at the GWR kindly offered the use of Temple Meads station to the B&G and, as the latter had not even started thinking about a site for a separate passenger terminus, this was welcomed. The relatively minor expense of constructing a spur to the GWR at Lawrence Hill was considered to be well worth it. Elsewhere on the B&G, engineering work on upgrading the line was well in hand, but was only to standard gauge dimensions. With extremely careful calculations, it was decided that the works would just about accommodate the broad gauge, but some structures such as Staple Hill tunnel left only inches to spare.

The Bristol & Gloucester's sudden change of heart over gauge matters did not amuse the old trendsetter, the Avon & Gloucestershire. It retained running powers over the B&G between Mangotsfield Junction and Coalpit Heath, and was not overwhelmed at the prospect of converting its own rolling stock just because of its neighbour's dalliance with the Great Western. The B&G, however, agreed to pay the A&G £240 compensation and to lay a third rail to the A&G's 4ft 8in gauge over the jointly-used section and this became the very first mixed gauge line in the country. Thus, a further innovation was to be credited to the unsung pioneers. In theory, the mixed gauge arrangement was sound but, in practice, it didn't account for different types of motive power being operated by each of the users. The B&G's locomotives, with speeds of 40mph, were to prove rather faster than the A&G's horses and so, in order to avoid delays to the former's trains, the latter had to undertake to leave a 90 minute gap between its departures and those of its neighbour.

By the spring of 1844, the Bristol & Gloucester's line was completed and, on 13 June, a directors' special left Bristol for Stonehouse. The ceremonial passenger train to Gloucester ran on 6 July; 10.00am had been the scheduled departure time but, as some of the directors who had insisted on being present set a wonderful example by arriving late, the double-headed train did not leave Temple Meads until 12.26pm. The scheduled public passenger service of six trains in each direction, with 90 minutes allowed for the 37 miles, commenced two days later; it was the mid-1840s before the journey time was reduced to 65 minutes. On the same day as the line was opened to the public the old pioneer, the Bristol & Gloucestershire Railway, was formally absorbed by the new B&G.

Although quite happy with the cosy arrangements with the Great Western at Bristol, the Bristol & Gloucester had not completely forgotten its earlier aspirations of getting to Birmingham and, on 14 January 1845, amalgamation was agreed with the Birmingham & Gloucester Railway. Hiccups in the formalities prevented the early incorporation of the Bristol & Birmingham Railway, and so the two constituents continued, for the time being, to wear their own separate hats. The Great Western liked the sound of the new company but, despite negotiations for amalgamation, the B&B became betrothed to the great adversary, the Midland, on 8 February 1845. The marriage took place on 3 August 1846.

The arrival of the Midland in Bristol challenged the Great Western's pride and joy, the broad gauge. Although the GWR succeeded in forcing the Midland to retain the broad gauge northwards from Bristol, the latter converted the line to mixed gauge in 1848 and, six years later, removed its greatest embarrassment, that of broad gauge workings, from its schedules. The broad gauge rails were not removed between Westerleigh and Gloucester until 1872 but the Bristol to Westerleigh section retained the mixed gauge until 1882 for the benefit of a daily Bristol & Exeter coal train which continued, until that year, to have authorised access to Parkfield Colliery.

When the Midland took over the Bristol & Birmingham Railway, the only station in the Bristol area to be inherited was the one at Yate. Immediately after the absorption, the Midland built a primitive station at Mangotsfield which was replaced, in 1860, by a better-equipped station about a ¼-mile to the southwest of the original. Stapleton station opened in 1866 only to be renamed Fishponds the following year and, on 2 May 1870, a small station opened in Bristol at Waterloo Road, Old Market and was called, confusingly, St Philip's. This station was intended to relieve congestion at Temple Meads by handling the Midland's local trains although, by that time, final preparations were in hand for the commencement of work on the joint Great West-

Table One
Locomotive Stock of the Bristol & Gloucester Railway

2-4-0 — Driving wheels: 5ft 0in; cylinders: 15in x 18in; weight: 17½ tons

No	Name	Built	Works No	Wdn	Disposal
1	Tugwell	Sept 1844	268	1856	Scrapped
2	Industry	Sept 1844	269	Mar 1854	Sold to Thomas Brassey
3	Pilot	Sept 1844	270	Sept 1851	Scrapped

2-2-2 — Driving wheels: 6ft 6in; cylinders: 15in x 18in; weight: 18 tons

No	Name	Built	Works No	Wdn	Disposal
4	Bristol	July 1844	260	Sept 1853	Sold to Thomas Brassey
5	Gloucester	July 1844	261	Mar 1855	Sold to Thomas Brassey
6	Berkeley	July 1844	262	Sept 1853	Sold to Thomas Brassey
7	Wickwar	July 1844	263	Jan 1853	Boiler exploded
8	Cheltenham	July 1844	264	Sept 1853	Sold to Thomas Brassey
9	Stroud	Dec 1844	265	Mar 1854	Sold to Thomas Brassey

0-6-0 — Driving wheels: 4ft 6in; cylinders: 16in x 21in; weight: 26 tons

No	Name	Built	Works No	Wdn	Disposal
10	Dreadnought	July 1844	266	May 1856	Sold to Thomas Brassey
11	Defiance	Dec 1844	267	Aug 1857	Sold to Thomas Brassey

Notes
1. Thomas Brassey was the contractor for the North Devon Railway.
2. The Midland renumbered all ex-B&G locomotives at least twice. Numbers given above are those first carried.
3. No 4 Bristol hauled the first directors' special on 13 June 1844.

Right:
The Midland Railway's station at Fishponds, on the outskirts of Bristol, was previously named Stapleton. In this picture, which was taken around the turn of the century, an unidentified locomotive struggles up the incline from Bristol with a mixed freight train. Behind and to the left of the station building is the familiar landmark of Parnall's factory chimney.
Lens of Sutton.

ern/Midland/Bristol & Exeter expansion of Temple Meads. The only other Midland station to appear on the old B&B line was at Staple Hill but this was not opened until 1888.

The Midland's St Philip's station was adjacent to the line running to the Avonside goods depot which had opened in 1866 and, just a stone's throw from the station, a new locomotive shed was opened in 1873. The old Bristol & Gloucester shed, although well-equipped for its time, had been outgrown by the early 1870s; the replacement, which took the less confusing title of Barrow Road, was a roundhouse with a 42ft turntable. A four-road fitting shop was added to the shed in 1874. Although Barrow Road had no allocation of express locomotives until the 1900s, many representatives of other well-known Midland classes became Bristol-based. These included ten of the Neilson-built 6ft 8in '800' class 2-4-0s and, later, Johnson '1282' class 2-4-0s. Remarkably, several members of both classes were to survive until the 1930s. From the late 1880s, the famous Johnson 4-2-2s were introduced for passenger services on the Midland, and a number of these had Barrow Road as home. Four of the shed's singles were to last until 1926, all of 10 years after the Great Western had dispensed with its last single-driver.

The local trains which were destined for St Philip's station from 1870 were not only those on the Gloucester line. On 4 August 1869, the Midland had extended to Bath by means of a branch from its main line at Mangotsfield and the services from Bristol to Bath via the Midland line were often earmarked for the new station. The route from Mangotsfield towards Bath was, for the first few miles, almost parallel to the old Avon & Gloucestershire tramway, but there was no likelihood of speed contests between Midland locomotives and A&G horses on adjacent lines. The tramway had become a victim of mechanical competition and had been formally abandoned in 1865, although it was to have occasional bursts of activity in future years with traffic from California Colliery in Longwell Green, which reopened in 1876 for a period of 28 years. The grand old Avon & Gloucestershire, the com-

pany which had opened the first railway in the Bristol area and had also been party to the country's first mixed gauge line, was to see its last usage on 30 January 1904 when 66 tons of coal left Tramway Junction for Willsbridge Wharf.

Four years after the Great Western had seen the Bristol & Birmingham Railway snatched from its grasp, it lost its working agreement with the Bristol & Exeter. The opening of the B&E's own terminus and the completion of its main line throughout seemed to restore thoughts of self-sufficiency in the boardroom, and on 1 May 1849, the company reverted to full independence. In preparation for this, it had established coke ovens and a carriage workshop at Bridgwater the previous year and it was felt that these facilities could share the workload with a repair depot at Exeter. But, Exeter was not to become the Swindon of the south-west.

The Bristol & Exeter's locomotive superintendent, James Pearson, favoured Exeter in his home county as the site for the B&E's main works, but his directors overruled him and plumped for Bristol. The works were built at Pylle Hill adjacent, coincidentally, to the proposed site of the original B&E terminus, and were completed in September 1851; next door to the works was a six-road engine shed and sizeable yard. Four months before the completion of the works, the B&E had opened its own goods sheds near Pylle Hill. There was a depot on each side of the line, one for goods inwards, one for outwards and the availability of these facilities released the B&E from having to squeeze part of its traffic into the congested GWR goods depot. The

final piece in the jigsaw which emphasised the B&E's restored independence was the completion of its impressive office building at Temple Meads in October 1854.

By the mid-1850s, services on both the Great Western and the Bristol & Exeter had reached a degree of routine. During the first year of the service between Bristol and Paddington, the fastest train was the 'Night Mail' which, with 10 stops, took four hours and 10 minutes. One run of only two hours and 40 minutes was recorded from Paddington to Bristol on 19 July 1842 by a four-coach train hauled by 'Firefly' class 2-2-2 *Damon* but this was hardly a regular service; it was not every day that Prince Albert travelled to Bristol to see the launching of Brunel's floating miracle, the S S *Great Britain*. By 1845, the GWR was keen to do its bit of public relations for the broad gauge and, on 10 March that year, introduced a service taking just three hours between Bristol and Paddington. That was the fastest scheduled train in the world at the time but, just 20 months later, even that was improved on by half an hour when Gooch's famous 'Iron Duke' 4-2-2s were introduced for express passenger duties. In 1845, the fastest run between Paddington and Exeter took 4½ hours for the distance of marginally under 194 miles but this was a punishing schedule. Although a five minute reduction was introduced in 1847, the more realistic time of five hours and 10 minutes had crept into the timetables 15 years later.

Almost a year after the Bristol & Exeter departed from the Great Western fold, the latter made its first significant acquisition in the Somerset area when, on

Above:
Between 1868 and 1873 the Bristol & Exeter renewed four of its celebrated broad gauge 4-2-4Ts and, when they were inherited by the GWR as a result of the absorption, they were renumbered 2001-04. On 27 July 1876, however, No 2001 was involved in a serious accident at Long Ashton and this prompted Swindon to rebuild the three survivors as 4-2-2 tender engines. The former No 2004 took the number of the withdrawn locomotive, No 2001, and continued to perform well on express duties southwards from Bristol until its retirement in 1889. This photograph is undated but, judging from the posed nature of the view, it was almost certainly taken soon after rebuilding in 1877. Photomatic

Centre left:
In the late 1840s Daniel Gooch designed his famous 8ft 'Iron Duke' class broad gauge locomotives, which enabled an acceleration of services to and from Bristol. This rare view shows Lightning, *which was built in 1847.* Photomatic

Left:
An unidentified GWR 'Metro' 2-4-0T arrives at Frome station on a service from Bath. Frome was a key point on the Wilts, Somerset & Weymouth line which, although taken over by the GWR in 1850, did not actually reach the town until just after the absorption. In this late-19th century photograph the longitudinal sleepers are clearly seen; the line diverging to the left led to a single-road goods shed but the main goods yard was behind the platform in which the train stands. Lens of Sutton

Above:

The village of Limpley Stoke, between Bath and Bradford-on-Avon, straddled the Somerset/Wiltshire border. The railway arrived in 1857 when the final section of the former Wilts, Somerset & Weymouth Railway was completed under GWR ownership, and this picture shows the state of affairs circa 1910. The small goods yard was to the south of the station and it can be seen that the main commodity handled is Bath Stone for the building industry.
Lens of Sutton

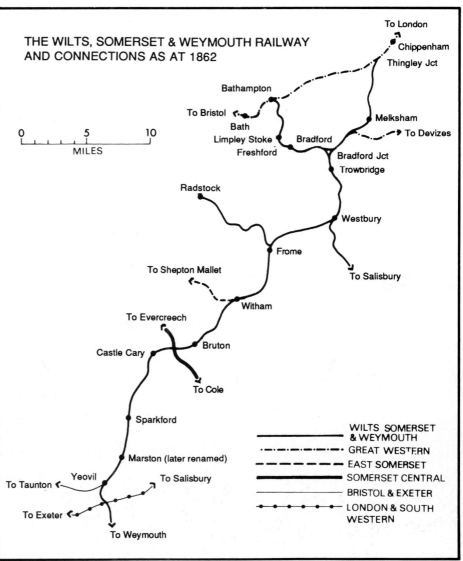

THE WILTS, SOMERSET & WEYMOUTH RAILWAY AND CONNECTIONS AS AT 1862

———————	WILTS SOMERSET & WEYMOUTH
—·—·—·—	GREAT WESTERN
— — — —	EAST SOMERSET
━━━━━	SOMERSET CENTRAL
—————	BRISTOL & EXETER
·•·•·•·	LONDON & SOUTH WESTERN

14 March 1850, the Wilts, Somerset & Weymouth Railway was formally taken over. In its entirety, the WS&W was to leave the main Bristol to Paddington line west of Chippenham at Thingley Junction and continue through Westbury, Frome, Castle Cary, Yeovil and into Weymouth. Also planned was a branch from Westbury to Salisbury, a link from Bathampton to Bradford Junction and a colliery branch from Frome to Radstock. The Act for this GWR-backed broad gauge line and its branches was obtained in 1845 but, after acquisitions of the necessary land and the letting of contracts, the corporate piggy-bank was embarrassingly empty. The first section, the 13½ miles between Thingley Junction and Westbury, opened on 5 September 1848, but that was as far as the WS&W got and, consequently, that was all that existed to pass to the GWR in 1850.

Construction of the uncompleted parts of the Wilts, Somerset & Weymouth Railway was restarted by the Great Western. Frome was reached on 7 October

Above:
Drummond's 'T9' class 4-4-0s handled many of the crack expresses on the L&SWR through southern Somerset, and even when the 'T14' class 4-6-0s started to appear in 1905, the 4-4-0s were not completely ousted from their familiar duties. Although this view of No 122 at Yeovil Junction is undated, it could well have been taken around 1907-09 during the rebuilding of the station. Lens of Sutton

1850 and Warminster, on the Salisbury branch, almost a year later but, on arriving at those towns, the GWR did a fair impersonation of its predecessor, the WS&W, and stopped work amidst pleas of poverty. The hiatus in the completion of the line was not popular, particularly as the GWR blatantly attached greater importance to the coal line from Frome to Radstock, which looked like a potential winner. Despite the threat of the archrival, the London & South Western, intruding into south Somerset and into Dorset, it took much cajoling and threats of legal action to get the GWR to recommence work on the original sections.

On 1 September 1856, the 26 mile extension from Frome to Yeovil was opened, four months ahead of the final section to Weymouth. The other line which was part of the scheme, the link between Bathampton and Bradford Junction, was opened on 2 February 1857 to provide direct through running from Bath and Bristol to Weymouth and Salisbury. The station at Yeovil was Pen Mill which was also to become the town's home for the Bristol & Exeter Railway. A two-road engine shed was provided to the south-west of Pen Mill station and, apart from the addition of a single-road annexe in 1877, was to remain almost unaltered during its 102-year life. Between Frome and Yeovil, the engineering works had allowed for a double track but the line laid was single; doubling throughout was not completed until 1881, seven years after conversion to standard gauge. In the meantime, the little matter of allowing

trains to pass was taken care of by the provision of loops at the intermediate stations at Witham, Bruton, Castle Cary and Sparkford; Marston station was the only one on the line not to be built with a passing loop.

After conversion to the standard gauge, the majority of duties on the former Wilts, Somerset & Weymouth line were handled by 2-4-0s of the '56' and '481' classes although the ubiquitous 0-6-0STs did their share of freight turns. When the Great Western eventually got round to building 4-4-0s early this century, members of the 'Duke' class were drafted to the line and were succeeded by 'Bulldog' 4-4-0s in the years prior to the grouping. Most of the motive power for the line was provided by the sheds at Bristol, Weymouth and Westbury. Apart from the shed at Yeovil, the only other one on the Somerset section of the line was the 60ft long single-road shed at Frome which opened in 1854. At the time of the grouping in 1923, Frome's allocation comprised seven 0-6-0STs, one 'Dean Goods' 0-6-0, a 'Bulldog' 4-4-0 and three railmotors.

The Great Western's plans for further expansion to the south were obstructed with predictable regularity by the London & South Western Railway. In 1848, the L&SWR had received assent to extend westwards from Salisbury but this was little more than a blocking measure as not one blade of grass was cut in preparation for the work. By 1855, the Board of Trade showed exasperation with the London & South Western's inactivity and ordered the company to start work on its line. Fearful of the outlay involved, the L&SWR enlisted the help of the contractor, Thomas Brassey, to construct the nominally independent Salisbury & Yeovil Railway. With uncharacteristic boldness, the L&SWR undertook to construct the line between Yeovil and Exeter itself. The Salisbury & Yeovil Railway was to be leased to, and worked by, the L&SWR from the outset with the agreement that, although built initially with a single track, double-width trackbeds would be provided so that, when gross receipts of £40,000 had been maintained for three consecutive years, doubling would be undertaken. Formal absorption of the Salisbury-Yeovil section by the L&SWR did not take place until 1878.

Yeovil was reached on 1 June 1860, and the London & South Western's trains used temporary facilities in the Bristol & Exeter's station at Hendford for a year until the town's joint station was ready. Between Salisbury and Yeovil, the line passed through Wiltshire and then crisscrossed the Dorset/Somerset border; in Somerset, stations at Templecombe and

Milborne Port were opened for the start of services. On 19 July, the extension from Yeovil to Exeter was opened, which included stations at Sutton Bingham, Crewkerne and Chard Road. The transfer of freight between the gauges at Yeovil was eased on 1 June 1864 by the opening of a broad gauge spur from Hendford to a goods depot at Clifton Maybank which was adjacent to the Exeter line. It was not until the Great Western's line was converted to standard gauge in 1874 that a physical connection to the London & South Western was established. At Templecombe, a single-road shed was constructed in 1870 to house the shunters in the exchange yard and, although never having had an allocation of its own, the shed went on to have a life of over 80 years.

While the London & South Western was the major obstacle in any Great Western attempt to expand southwards, the Midland Railway played a similar role to the north. However, on 1 August 1868, the GWR gained a small but very significant foothold to the north of Bristol on the fringe of Midland territory. On that date, it absorbed the 11½-mile line from Bristol to New Passage, on the banks of the River Severn. The line, which had opened to the public on 8 September 1863, was acquired from the Bristol & South Wales Union Railway but had been engineered in its early days by Brunel and, from the outset, worked by the GWR. Its purpose was to provide a link across the Severn; New Passage was the point from which ferries left for Portskewett, on the foreign side of the river.

On 25 August 1863, some two weeks before the public opening, a ceremonial train hauled by Swindon-built GWR 0-6-0 *Pyracmon* left Temple Meads for New Passage from where its passengers were treated to a dose of Severn ozone on the ferry crossing from the unfinished landing stage. When regular public services commenced, the trip to New Passage was scheduled to take 40 minutes and three of the five daily trains in each direction called at all five intermediate stations. These were Lawrence Hill, Stapleton Road, Filton, Patchway and Pilning with Ashley Hill being opened in July 1864. By 1869, the weekday service was six trains each way but the journey time was 45 minutes.

Under the Great Western, the line did well and was converted to standard gauge in August 1873; its eventual demise was only brought about by the opening of the £2-million Severn tunnel on 1 December 1886. The GWR's route to the tunnel was over the former Bristol & South Wales Union line to a point half a mile east of Pilning station and, from there, it used a newly-completed line to the tunnel and on to South Wales. To cope with the coal traffic which used the tunnel route, the line between Pilning and Bristol was doubled in 1887 and this involved providing a second tunnel at Patchway to augment the existing one there. The decision not simply to widen the original bore at Patchway was taken because a new one could be laid on an easier gradient to assist the heavy coal trains.

The Great Western was very aware of the importance of the new link to South Wales and constructed a loop at Dr Day's Junction, to the east of Temple Meads, to enable through running from Wales to London without any tedious reversing in Bristol. It was, of course, freight traffic which predominated on the Severn tunnel route and so a large marshalling yard, Bristol East depot, was established near St.Anne's. Its construction, which was completed in 1889, involved the demolition of No 1 tunnel on the Bristol-Paddington main line and, conveniently, made space for a future station at St Anne's Park which was eventually to be built in 1898.

On 1 August 1876, some eight years after the Great Western had acquired its link to South Wales, its route mileage received a major boost with the formal absorption of the Bristol & Exeter Railway. A most useful inheritance was the B&E engine shed and workshop in Bristol. The Great Western's original shed east of Temple Meads had long since outgrown itself, even before the intrusion of a four-road standard gauge shed in the

same yard in 1872, and the GWR wasted no time in converting the former B&E works into a twin-turntable roundhouse for standard gauge locomotives with broad gauge stock enjoying the extra space of the existing six-road shed. This depot, Bath Road, was to remain largely unaltered until the early 1930s although it was augmented by new engine sheds at St Philip's Marsh in July 1910. St Philip's Marsh depot was a standard twin-turntable roundhouse and, for many years to come, no official differentiation was made in respect of which shed was home to which locomotives. Although the shed's repair shop was to be extended in later years, the roundhouse buildings remained little altered until their closure in July 1964.

A single-road shed at Weston also came into the GWR fold, as did the two-road depot at Taunton, the latter structure having had peripatetic tendencies. It had started life at Bridgwater when the B&E terminated there but was dismantled, transported to Taunton and reassembled on a site west of the station in 1842. When Taunton station and yard were rebuilt in 1868, the shed was once again uprooted and resited facing the opposite direction. It was replaced, in 1896 by a standard GWR single-

turntable roundhouse which was to survive for 68 years.

Apart from the stations which had opened simultaneously with the B&E's line to Exeter, seven others had materialised by the time the company came into the Great Western fold. Ashton station had opened in 1854, but was swiftly renamed Bedminster; it was to be replaced by a new station some 200 yards to the west in 1884. Bourton station, which had been opened in 1860, was to be renamed Flax Bourton in 1888 and, five years later, resited slightly to the west. The station at Uphill, to the south of Weston, at least stayed put but, like the above pair, had a change of identity; opened in 1871, it became Bleadon & Uphill the following year. Further south, Durston station had opened in 1853, while Norton Fitzwarren and Dunball stations did not materialise until 1873. Brent Knoll station was added two years later.

The Bristol & Exeter's independent life ceased a little too early for the company to see the completion of the new station at Temple Meads. The master plan for extending Bristol's main station had first surfaced in 1861 and the logical approach was for the three companies which used it, the Bristol & Exeter, the Great Western and the Midland, to share the cost of new joint premises equally.

However, the general atmosphere which prevailed between, in one corner, the two broad gauge companies and, in the other corner, the Midland, was not exactly conducive to decisions which involved logic. It was March 1871 before work commenced on the project, and, on 6 July 1874, the new down side was opened. It was 1 January 1878 before the up side and the roof were completed. Apart from the addition of the bay line in 1892 and an island platform in 1898, the new station was largely unaltered until 1935.

The broad gauge finally came to an end in May 1892, but the next new standard gauge line in the Bristol area was not opened until 5 February 1900. This was the Avonmouth & Severn Tunnel Railway between Pilning Junction and Avonmouth, a 7¾-mile heavy duty freight

Below:
When they were introduced in 1891, Williams Dean's 7ft 8in Singles enabled an improvement of express schedules to and from Bristol. These locomotives represented the final development of Singles on the GWR, as the production of numerous 4-4-0s was only a little way off. No 3009 Flying Dutchman was one of the 30 members of the class which were built as 2-2-2s and, like its chums, was rebuilt as a 4-2-2 in 1894.
Photomatic

Above:
A further 50 locomotives were built as 4-2-2s between 1894 and 1899 and one of these was No 3067 **Duchess of Teck**. *Both of these locomotives were frequent visitors to Bristol until their respective withdrawals in February and December 1914.* Photomatic

line intended to serve the dock at Avonmouth which, since its opening to shipping in 1877, had been served only by the Bristol Port Railway and Pier line and, latterly, the Clifton Extension Railway. For the first 1¾ miles from Pilning Junction, the A&ST was laid on the trackbed of the old Bristol & South Wales Union Railway; it then curved southwards towards the dock. A boost to the line's fortunes was not far away as, in 1908, the larger Royal Edward Dock was opened adjacent to the old dock at Avonmouth and the added facilities attracted not only more freight trade, but also more passengers on trans-Atlantic sailings. There had, however, been one flaw with the plans for the new dock. It was designated to occupy land which was crossed by the A&ST and so a realignment of the line between Holesmouth and Gloucester Road was required. This two mile diversion was completed in 1903 to clear the way for work on the dock.

The Great Western was quick to see the potential of the new dock at Avon-

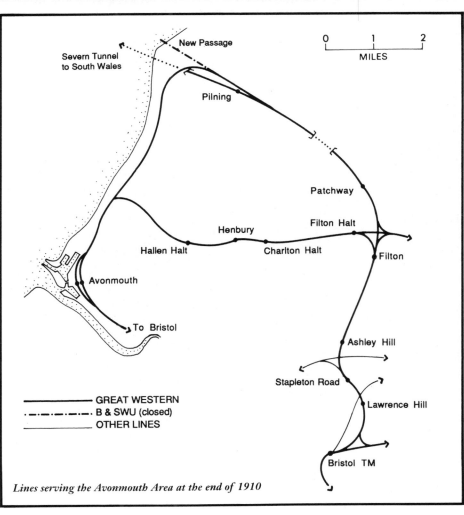

Lines serving the Avonmouth Area at the end of 1910

Top:

This photograph of Castle Cary station looking eastwards was taken circa 1910, and shows the ex-WS&W line to Weymouth disappearing in the centre foreground. The tracks off to the left are the GWR's direct route to Taunton, which opened in 1906. Lens of Sutton

Above:

The spacious Royal Edward passenger terminus at Avonmouth Docks was used not only by the GWR but also the Midland, the latter having access to the port by means of a joint agreement concerning the line via Clifton Down. In this 1922 photograph the inscriptions on the walls provide clear evidence of the dual-use of the terminus. Port of Bristol Authority

mouth and the usefulness of the line from Pilning. On 1 May 1903, it opened its new, faster line between Patchway and Swindon via Badminton which would enable both dock and Severn tunnel traffic bound for London to miss Bristol and Bath completely and save 10 miles into the bargain. In order to keep gradients to no more than 1 in 100, the Badminton line had required extensive earthworks and these included the Sodbury tunnel which, at over 2½ miles long, still remains as one of the longest railway tunnels in the country. Opening to passengers did not take place until 1 July, and there were seven stations including those at Winterbourne, Coalpit Heath and Chipping Sodbury.

The distance between Avonmouth and Paddington was reduced to just 120 miles on 9 May 1910 with the opening of a direct line from Stoke Gifford to Holesmouth. Although intended primarily as a cut-off route for freight, the new line also helped the acceleration of schedules for passenger trains from Avonmouth's Royal Edward passenger terminus. On 13 July 1910, a boat train was recorded as taking just two hours eight minutes from Avonmouth to Paddington via the new route. Loops were provided at Filton, where the new line crossed the South Wales line, to enable through running in three out of four possible directions. This meant that Filton and Patchway stations had to be resited.

In the south of its area, the Great Western eventually opened its shorter route to Taunton on 11 June 1906. For 46 years, the company had scrapped ferociously with the London & South Western for traffic from London to Exeter and beyond; the latter's 172-mile line to Exeter had had a 22-mile advantage but, with the new route, the GWR reduced the difference to just two miles. The cut-off line left the Savernake line west of Pewsey; it proceeded to Westbury and then used the old Wilts, Somerset & Weymouth line as far as Castle Cary. From there, a new section had been built to link up with the former B&E Yeovil branch at Langport. It was first used by passenger trains on 2 July; between Castle Cary and Langport, there were stations at Keinton Mandeville, Charlton Mackrell, Somerton and Langport East while an additional one, Long Sutton & Pitney, was opened in 1907.

The London & South Western was quick to counter the Great Western's attack. The much-heralded Drummond 4-6-0s of 1905 were earmarked for West of England expresses, and, in order to accommodate them on the route west of Salisbury, over £37,000 was allocated for upgrading the line. Part of the general

outbreak of World War 1 saw them drafted to military trains and services on the West of England line were then taken over by older 4-4-0s which, more often than not, were used double-headed. The standard of haulage on the West of England trains was raised again in 1918 with the introduction of Urie's 'King Arthurs'. The last summer timetable before the grouping shows that the fastest L&SWR train from Waterloo to Exeter took three hours 24 minutes, but the GWR had the edge. Between Paddington and Exeter, it could take passengers via Frome in three hours flat.

Throughout the histories of the Great Western and the Bristol & Exeter, train services benefited from remarkably fast schedules. The first recorded ton-up in

Below:
Yate station was opened by the Midland Railway on its line between Bristol and Gloucester. The general cheerfulness of the World War 1 soldiers waiting for a southbound train suggests that it is a case of well-deserved leave. Lens of Sutton

Above:
Langport East station on the GWR's Taunton cut-off line was photographed circa 1910, with an unidentified steam railmotor arriving on a Taunton train. These units were much in vogue at this time, and, between 1903 and 1908, more than 100 were introduced by the GWR for short-haul services; they were, however, found to have their limitations and only a few survived to see the 1930s. It took British Railways some time to repeat the exercise in the form of diesel multiple-units. An older station in the town was on the Taunton-Yeovil branch which was unveiled in 1853 but, when the line in the picture opened in 1906, the old branch station was renamed Langport West. East station closed on 10 September 1962 and West on 15 June 1964. Lens of Sutton

improvement in southern Somerset included the rebuilding of Yeovil Junction station between 1907 and 1909. The main lines through the old station curved around two island platforms, and this meant a speed limit of 20mph for through trains; the new station layout incorporated two through lines which were much straighter, thus dispensing with the speed limit. Other features of the new station were a bay platform for Yeovil Town branch trains and an extended goods yard.

By the turn of the century, the fastest train between Waterloo and Exeter had been scheduled for 3½ hours but the improvements around Yeovil enabled the time to be reduced by 18 minutes by 1909. Although the Drummond 4-6-0s were useful performers on the line, the

Britain is credited to GWR 4-4-0 No 3440 *City of Truro* which, in 1904, was timed at 102.3mph on Wellington Bank south of Taunton when in charge of a Plymouth to London mail train. The true speed was hushed up until 1922 as it was felt that it could alarm not only the authorities, but also some passengers and, although the accuracy of the timing has often been questioned, the clockwatcher was C. Rous Marten to whom the word 'inaccuracy' was foreign. Considering that Pearson's singles were known to reach speeds of over 80mph on the B&E in the 1850s, the feat of *City of Truro* is perfectly feasible. By 1912 the journey time from Bristol to Paddington was down to two hours, and the trains on these crack expresses were usually hauled by Churchward's 'Star' class 4-6-0s; the same locomotives were used on the fastest trains on the Taunton to Paddington service and were allowed 420 tons behind the tender.

Despite the quest for speed, the express lines in the Bristol and Somerset area were relatively free from serious acci-

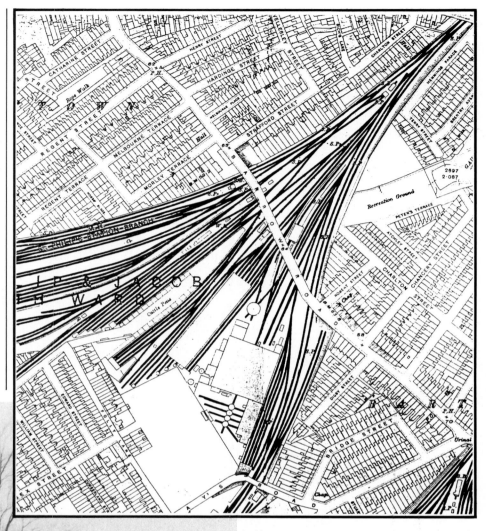

Above:
The size of the site of the Midland Railway's shed at Barrow Road in Bristol is evident in this 25in/mile Ordnance Survey map of 1918. The line from Temple Meads station enters from the south and disappears northeast, while the spurs to St Philip's station and Avonside Wharf exit west. Virtually all of the terraced housing vanished in the 1960s and the shed followed suit in 1965. Today, some of the shed site is used for a waste transfer depot, but a sizeable proportion of the area still remains empty. Crown copyright

dents, and the only two incidents of note both occurred south of Bristol on the former Bristol & Exeter line. On 27 July 1876, the London-bound 'Flying Dutchman' express consisting of five coaches and a van became derailed at 60mph at Long Ashton; the crew perished and 14 passengers were seriously injured. In the early hours of 11 November 1890, a signalling error at Norton Fitzwarren resulted in a special express from Plymouth Docks colliding with a stationary train. Ten passengers were killed and 11 people, including the crew, were seriously hurt.

The Somerset section of the London & South Western's main line was almost

Above:
This view of Yate station looks northwards, and is believed to have been taken circa 1920. Only two members of the station staff seem prepared to brave the winter wind and rain to pose for the camera. Lens of Sutton

completely free from mishaps. The only significant accident occurred on 4 July 1914 when an eastbound freight train broke its couplings to the west of Yeovil Junction. An attempt to divert the leading wagons into the loop at the station was, in theory, sound but, in practice, it was not foreseen that the escapees would catch up and collide with the leading ensemble. The collision resulted in 22 wagons being destroyed and part of the West signalbox being demolished.

The outbreak of World War 1 in 1914 put an end to the activities of the racers on the footplates. Services were decelerated for reasons of economy, while unscheduled troop train movements made predictable timetabling difficult. The Bristol area played its part in the campaign, with the docks at Avonmouth assuming strategic importance and the Severn tunnel route proving vital for the 'Jellicoe Specials', the trains which got the Rhondda coal to the Fleet. The war caused great disruption of the country's railways, and, in order to restore a semblance of order, the newly formed Ministry of Transport instigated the Grouping which altered things irreversibly from 31 December 1922.

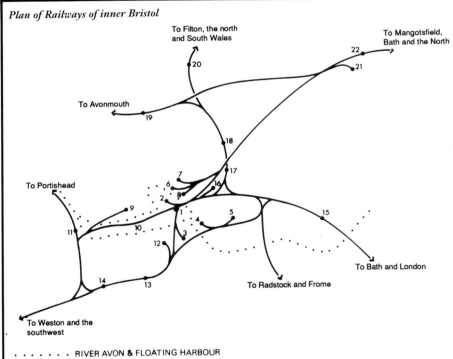

Plan of Railways of inner Bristol

. . . . . . RIVER AVON & FLOATING HARBOUR

1 *Temple Meads Station*	13 *Bedminster Station*
2 *Temple Meads Goods*	14 *Parson Street Station*
3 *Bath Road Locomotive Depot*	15 *St Anne's Park Station*
4 *St Philip's Marsh Locomotive Depot*	16 *Former Broad Gauge Locomotive Depot*
5 *Marsh Junction Diesel Depot*	17 *Lawrence Hill Station*
6 *Avonside Wharf*	18 *Stapleton Road Station*
7 *St Philip's Station*	19 *Montpelier Station*
8 *Barrow Road Locomotive Depot*	20 *Ashley Hill Station*
9 *Canons Marsh Goods Depot*	21 *Deep Pit Colliery and Atlas Locomotive Works*
10 *Wapping Wharf*	22 *Fishponds Station*
11 *Ashton Gate Platform*	
12 *Pylle Hill Goods Depot*	

2 The Branches

When Brunel engineered his broad gauge railways, he often preferred to serve towns which were only a few miles from the lines by means of branches instead of diverting the main lines themselves. In Somerset, the first manifestation of this policy was at Weston-super-Mare, where the townspeople found themselves one and a half miles from the Bristol & Exeter main line. Although the population of Weston in 1841 was only 2,100, civic leaders and prominent businessmen were aware of the town's potential as a holiday resort and, understandably, they felt a little miffed at being stuck at the end of a branch rather than having their own main line station.

The branch to the centre of Weston was opened simultaneously with the main line to Exeter on 14 June 1841. It left the Exeter line at Weston Junction, terminating at Alexandra Parade station, and the service was initially provided by four-wheel coaches, each of which was drawn by three horses. Locomotive traction soon appeared and one daily through train each way between Bristol and Alexandra Parade was introduced. It is known that the Bristol & Exeter's unique railmotor, No 29 *Fairfield*, was used on the branch in the early 1850s. On 20 July 1866, the branch was doubled and was truncated at a new station, Locking Road, situated a few hundred yards short of the original terminus. This arrangement survived until the laying of a through loop from the main line in 1884.

Clevedon also had aspirations towards tapping the holiday trade, but the town did not get its railway until 28 July 1847. The three and a half mile branch left the Bristol & Exeter main line at Yatton station, which had, until the opening of the branch, been called Clevedon Road. At Clevedon, the station yard was relaid and the platform length trebled to 600ft when the branch was converted to standard gauge in September 1879 and, at the same time, the single-road engine shed and 35ft turntable were dispensed with. It has been suggested that the shed was reassembled at Yatton but, considering the disparity in sizes of the two struc-

tures, that theory is most unlikely. By the early 1920s, the summer timetables for the Clevedon branch showed around 15 daily trains each way and one through service from Bristol. Immediately prior to the Grouping, the allocation for Yatton shed, from where the branch was serviced, comprised '517' class 0-4-2T No 1428, 'Metro' 2-4-0T No 630 and one steam railmotor, but these were used

Below:
This photograph of the GWR station at Radstock looking towards Bristol dates to the early years of this century. The light engine is almost certainly a 'Metro' class 2-4-0T, which has quite probably been sent along from the shed simply to join in the posing routine. The level crossing can be seen immediately beyond the station and, just behind the signalbox, was another level crossing though which the Somerset & Dorset line ran.
Lens of Sutton

on the Wells and Blagdon branches as well as the Clevedon line.

One of the Bristol & Exeter's success stories was in the field of excursion trains. The company had the advantage of operating in an area which appealed to trippers and, in the days when long-distance travel was a lifetime's event to most people, the lure of the mud at places such as Weston and Clevedon proved overwhelming for many town and city dwellers. The B&E was not the least class-conscious of railway companies and, while the profits from excursion traffic were not to be sniffed at, the company's directors remarked that thronging masses of uncultured day excursion oiks could deter the genteel and sensitive regulars. With a bout of lateral thinking, the board came up with the idea of segregated excursion platforms. At the dispatching end, such platforms were provided at Bedminster and Pylle Hill in Bristol and, at the receiving end, both Weston and

Clevedon were equipped with excursion platforms. Although Clevedon's closed in 1879, the one at Weston did a roaring trade and a larger replacement at Locking Road station was provided in 1914.

In the 1870s, excursion fares from Bristol were one shilling (5p) to Clevedon and one and sixpence (7½p) to Weston. Although the coming of the railway helped to boost Clevedon's holiday trade, improved communications had a greater effect on the community's status as a dormitory town for Bristol. Before the 1840s, Clevedon was the prime seaside resort and Weston was definitely second division but, with rail connections, the standing of the towns reversed.

The Bristol & Exeter completed its hat-trick of broad gauge branches with the opening of the line from Taunton to Yeovil. The earthworks between Yeovil and Martock had been completed in 1849, but work between Martock and Durston did not commence until June

1852 and, considering the delays due to floods the following winter, it was a remarkable achievement to have the entire line ready for the opening on 1 October 1853. Flooding was to prove a regular hazard at the Taunton end of the line but the trackbed was not raised above the flood level until 1906, when that section became part of the Great Western's fast cut-off route through southern Somerset.

When the Yeovil branch opened, there were intermediate stations at Durston, Athelney, Langport and Martock. In 1882, a further station was provided at Montacute, and, in 1906, Langport station was renamed Langport West when the new fast cut-off line was opened. At Yeovil, the branch originally terminated at Hendford station, but it was extended to Pen Mill in February 1857 to link up with the Great Western line from Westbury and Frome. Hendford was subsequently pressed into use as a goods depot and it filled this role until 1967. In pre-Grouping years on the Yeovil branch, seven trains were timetabled each way on weekdays, but it was not the speediest journey known to mankind; none was scheduled to take less than one hour for the 20-mile journey.

The next branch to open in Somerset was yet another broad gauge effort but, this time, a Great Western freight line. After formally taking over the Wilts, Somerset & Weymouth Railway in 1850,

the GWR procrastinated furiously over the completion of the predecessor's proposed main line and, instead, attached greater urgency to constructing a branch from Frome to Radstock. The expansion of the North Somerset coalfield promised revenue from the colliery traffic, and Radstock was the town at the hub of the mining industry.

On 14 November 1854, the 8½-mile Radstock branch was opened for coal traffic but passenger services did not commence until 5 July 1875. Leaving Radstock for Frome, the line was on a 1 in 69 gradient as far as Mells, where the only intermediate station was opened in 1875. It was not until 1898 that the station was renamed Mells Road in recognition of the fact that station and village were over two miles apart, even for athletic crows. The branch was serviced from Frome shed, but a single-road shed was provided at Radstock in 1866; a 42ft turntable was added at Radstock in 1894 although, of the locomotives which are known to have been allocated to the shed, few were tender engines.

Below:
This turn-of-the-century view of Yatton station shows a small crowd waiting for a southbound train. Behind the down platform, a locomotive-less train waits in the bay for the Wells and Witham branch, while almost hidden behind the buildings on the up platform is the bay platform for the Clevedon branch train. Lens of Sutton.

In June 1874, the Frome-Radstock branch was converted to standard gauge so that it could provide a continuous link with the Bristol & North Somerset Railway's line from Bristol to Radstock which had opened nine months previously. The provision of a through run from Bristol to Frome without a break of gauge was tactically timed by the Great Western as the Somerset & Dorset Railway was about to open its standard gauge extension across the North Somerset Coalfield to Bath. The unveiling of the 16-mile B&NS on 1 August 1873 took many locals by surprise as, since the formation of the company in 1862, most corporate activity had seemed to be on paper. Shareholders had become concerned at the company's lack of urgency and, as a result of investigations into the management in 1867, one prosecution and several embarrassingly hasty resignations had followed. The BN&S was blatantly underfinanced and, in 1878, its directors offered it for sale to the Great Western but the sibling's debts ruled out any appeal. Two years later, the GWR decided that it really wanted the B&NS after all but, with a display of symbolic nose-thumbing, the B&NS refused. The GWR waited in the wings until the B&NS's finances grew more desperate and, on 1 July 1884, the inevitable absorption took place.

Between Bristol and Radstock, the intermediate stations were at Brislington,

Pensford, Clutton, Hallatrow, and Welton; the last named station was renamed Welton & Midsomer Norton in 1898, only to have the title reversed in 1904 to Midsomer Norton & Welton. Right up to the 1920s, services between Bristol and Frome usually consisted of between five and seven trains daily with a journey time of around an hour and a quarter for the trip.

Back on the broad gauge, the first section of the East Somerset Railway opened on 9 November 1858. It left the Frome-Yeovil line at Witham and terminated at Shepton Mallet; the first train was hauled by the Great Western's 'Bogie' class 4-4-0ST *Homer*. The decision to use a tank engine for inaugural duties was because the directors had undertaken not to use tender locomotives unless turntables were provided at both Witham and Shepton Mallet. A locomotive hiring fee was far more acceptable than the cost of two turntables. Cranmore station was opened simultaneously with the first section, and an unstaffed halt at Wanstrow was added in 1860. Despite its elevation to the status of a station in 1909, Wanstrow was not provided with freight facilities until after the grouping. Just five months after the opening to Shepton Mallet, preparatory work was commenced on an extension to Wells and this additional section was opened on 1 March 1862 to complete the 14-mile branch.

The East Somerset branch was steeply graded with several sections of around 1 in 50, but the sharpest climb was the 1 in 37 on the approach to Wanstrow station from the east. It was only at the Wells end that any reasonable amount of level running could be undertaken. The original station at Wells was closed on 31 December 1877, and passenger traffic was transferred to Tucker Street station as a result of rationalisation by the Great Western which had, by then, taken over not only the ESR but also the Bristol & Exeter. The B&E had arrived in Wells on 5 April 1870 when its 17½-mile branch from Yatton was opened throughout. This line took some of the ESR's traffic, and, consequently, the ESR courted the GWR with a view to absorption. Wedlock took place on 2 December 1874.

The Bristol & Exeter's branch from Yatton to Wells had, in fact, been promoted by the Somerset & Dorset Railway as a blocking measure against a broad gauge proposal for a line from Bleadon to Wells. Unlike many other rival companies, the two combatants agreed to a sensible arrangement whereby the B&E should take over the S&D's plans and construct the line from Yatton. The section between Yatton and Cheddar was opened on 3 August 1869, some eight months before the extension to Wells, and it had intermediate stations at Congresbury, Sandford, Woodborough and Axbridge; Woodborough was renamed Winscombe on 30 October the same year. When the section between Cheddar and Wells opened, there were stations at Draycott and Lodge Hill, an additional one at Wookey being added in 1871. In time, the branch became known as the 'Strawberry Line' as it proved very popular with pickers who fancied a paid holiday during the summer months.

In Wells, the original East Somerset Railway station was one third of a mile from Tucker Street station, and, when the Bristol & Exeter first started operating into Tucker Street, the timing on many 'connections' with trains at the ESR station left all of one minute for passengers to sprint from one station to the other. Even when the two lines were linked on 1 January 1878, the railway arrangement at Wells remained somewhat unorthodox as the link line ran through Priory Road station, which was the terminus of the Somerset & Dorset

Below:
In the GWR working timetable of 1886, the weekday passenger service between Yatton and Wells comprised five trains each way with a journey time averaging a little under an hour. Only one of the passenger trains is shown to run beyond Wells to Witham. By the summer of 1922, six trains plied each way between Yatton and Wells daily but four of these continued to Witham. The journey time from Yatton to Wells was little different from 1886.

WELLS BRANCH. (Single Line.) **Narrow Gauge.**

Down Trains. YATTON TO WELLS.—Week Days. Sundays

Miles from Yatton.	STATIONS.	1 Bristol and Wells Goods. A arr.	1 dep.	2 Passenger. arr.	2 dep.	3 R R Goods. dep.	4 Passenger. arr.	4 dep.	5 R R Goods. dep.	6 Passenger. arr.	6 dep.	7 Bristol Goods. arr.	7 dep.	8 Passenger. arr.	8 dep.	9 Passenger. arr.	9 dep.	10	10	Sundays 1 Passenger. arr.	Sundays 1 dep.
		A.M.	A.M.	A.M.	A.M.	A.M.	A.M.	A.M.	P.M.	P.M.	P.M.	noon.	P.M.	P.M.	P.M.	P.M.	P.M.			A.M.	A.M.
	Yatton	5 40	6 0	....	9 55	....	....	11 45	*12 50*	—	1 15	12 0	1 25	—	4 0	....	7 5	....	....	10 0	10 10
1½	Congresbury	6 8	6 21	9 59	10 0	..	11 49	11 50	—	1 19	1 20	1 32	1 40	4 4	4 5	7 8	7 9	..	..	10 14	10 15
4½	Sandford	6 31	6 42	10 6	10 8	....	11 56	11 57	—	1 26	1 27	1 50	2 0	4 11	4 12	7 14	7 15	....	....	10 21	10 22
5¾	Winscombe	6 50	7 5	10 12	10 13	..	12 1	12 2	—	1 30	1 31	C R		4 15	4 16	7 19	7 20	..	..	10 25	10 26
8	Axbridge	7 13	7 25	10 18	10 20	....	12 6	12 8	—	1 35	1 37	2 15	2 25	4 21	4 22	7 24	7 25	....	....	10 30	10 32
9¾	Cheddar	7 35	X8 0	10 24	X10 26	..	12 12	X12 14	*1 20*	1 41	1 43	2 30	X3 5	4 26	4 28	7 30	7 32	..	..	10 36	10 38
11¾	Draycott	8 6	8 12	10 32	10 33	....	12 21	12 22	*Weds. only.*	1 47	1 48	—	—	4 33	4 34	7 38	7 39	....	....	10 42	10 43
14	Lodge Hill	8 19	8 25	10 38	10 39	..	12 29	12 30		1 52	1 53	—	—	4 39	4 41	7 44	7 45	..	..	10 47	10 48
16½	Wookey	8 31	8 55	10 46	10 47	*11 35*	12 37	12 39		1 59	2 1	3 20	3 45	4 48	4 50	7 52	7 55	....	....	10 54	10 56
17½	**Wells**	9 0	..	10 52	..	*11 40*	12 45	12 55		2 5	—	3 50	4 10	4 55	—	8 0	—	..	..	11 0	—
31¾	Witham	—	—	—	—	—	1 40	—		—	—	5 30	—	—	—	—	—	....	....	—	—

Up Trains. WELLS TO YATTON.—Week Days. Sundays

Miles from Wells.	STATIONS.	1 Passenger. arr.	1 dep.	2 Passenger. arr.	2 dep.	3 R R Goods. dep.	4 Passenger. arr.	4 dep.	5 Passenger. arr.	5 dep.	6 R R Cattle. dep.	7 Bristol Goods. arr.	7 dep.	8 Passenger. arr.	8 dep.	9	9	10 Bristol Goods. arr.	10 dep.	Sundays 1 Passenger. arr.	Sundays 1 dep.
		A.M.	A.M.	A.M.	A.M.	A.M.	A.M.	A.M.	P.M.	P.M.	P.M.	P.M.	P.M.	P.M.	P.M.			P.M.	P.M.	A.M.	A.M.
14¼	Witham	—	—	—	—	—	—	—	—	—	*Wednesdays only.*	—	12 55	—	—	....	....	—	6 10	—	—
	Wells	....	7 20	....	10 0	*10 55*	—	11 50	—	2 35		2 10	5 0	—	5 40	..	..	7 20	8 5	—	11 20
1	Wookey	7 23	7 24	10 3	10 4	*11 0*	11 51	11 55	2 38	2 39		5 5	5 20	5 43	5 44	....	....	8 10	8 20	11 23	11 24
3½	Lodge Hill	7 30	7 31	10 11	10 12		12 0	12 1	2 45	2 46		C R		5 50	5 51	..	..	—	—	11 30	11 32
5¾	Draycott	7 35	7 36	10 16	10 17	..	12 4	12 6	2 50	2 51		—	—	5 57	5 58	....	....	8 31	8 38	11 36	11 37
7¾	Cheddar	7 40	X7 41	10 22	X10 24	....	12 11	X12 14	2 55	X2 56	*3 5*	5 50	•6 14	6 3	•6 6	..	..	8 45	8 50	11 42	11 44
9½	Axbridge	7 47	7 48	10 28	10 30	..	12 18	12 20	3 1	3 3	*3 20*	6 19	6 35	6 11	6 13	....	....	C R		11 48	11 50
11¾	Winscombe	7 53	7 54	10 36	10 37	....	12 26	12 27	3 8	3 9	*3 30*	C R		6 19	6 20	..	..	9 5	9 15	11 55	11 57
13	Sandford	7 57	7 58	10 41	10 42	..	12 31	12 32	3 12	3 13	*3 40*	—	—	6 24	6 25	....	....	9 21	9 35	12 0	12 2
16	Congresbury	8 4	8 5	10 48	10 50	....	12 38	12 40	3 19	3 20	—	—	—	6 31	6 33	..	..	9 44	9 55	12 8	12 10
17½	**Yatton**	8 10	8 13	10 55	..	..	12 45	..	3 25	..	*3 50*	6 55	7 10	6 38	..	....	....	10 0	10 20	12 15	....

A Goods and Passengers from Cheddar.

CROSSING ARRANGEMENTS BETWEEN YATTON AND WELLS.

The 6.0 a.m. Train from Yatton will cross the 7.20 a.m. from Wells at Cheddar.
The 9.55 a.m. Train from Yatton will cross the 10.0 a.m. Train from Wells at Cheddar.
The 11.45 a.m. Train from Yatton will cross the 11.50 a.m. Train from Wells at Cheddar.
The 1.25 p.m. Goods from Yatton will cross 2.35 p.m. ex Wells at Cheddar.

Single Line worked by Train Staff. The Staff Stations are Yatton, Cheddar and Wells.

TRAIN STAFF AND TICKETS:—

SECTION.	COLOR OF STAFF AND TICKETS. *Staff.*	*Tickets*	SHAPE OF STAFF AND TICKETS. *Staff.*	*Tickets.*
Wells and Cheddar	Green	Green	Square	Square
Yatton and Cheddar	Red	Red	Round	Round

branch from Glastonbury. When the B&E arrived in Wells, it wanted to use the ESR station, but the Board of Trade considered that the practice of running through the yard of the S&D station would compromise on safety. The only solution was for the B&E to build its own station and provide exercise for passengers changing trains. After its closure to passengers, the original ESR station became the GWR's goods depot.

The engine shed situation at Wells was no simpler. The Somerset & Dorset had its own shed which, until the 1870s, still retained the mixed gauge road that had been laid in the dark and distant past when the S&D's predecessor, the Somerset Central Railway, was worked by the Bristol & Exeter. When the B&E was absorbed by the Great Western, the original shed at Tucker Street was demolished and the locomotives rehoused at the East Somerset shed. This was, itself, demolished in September 1879 to facilitate the building of a 75ft long twin-road shed on the same site. Both the ESR and the B&E sheds originally had 40ft turntables but, although the 'new' shed of 1879 had a turntable of a similar size, it is not known which, if either, of the two older turntables was re-used in the city.

By the 1870s, the population of Wells was well under 5,000, but it had been served by five different railway companies, and three of those had operated in the city simultaneously. Furthermore, its three stations had each had a locomotive depot, but all this railway activity was centred on the junction of three single-track rural branches. At the end of 1921, the GWR shed at Wells had an allocation of just three 0-6-0STs, a pair of 'Dean Goods' 0-6-0s and a 'Metro' 2-4-0T.

In August 1859, the Bristol & Exeter took over a ½-mile long branch from the Bridgwater Corporation, and the railway company saw it as a useful acquisition as the line was suitable for extending across the River Parrett to the Canal Dock. The Corporation had used horse-power on the original line, but the B&E upgraded it for mixed gauge locomotive haulage and reopened it in November 1867. The extension across the river was by means of a telescopic bridge which cost £8,000 to build, and was opened in March 1871. Although not unique in Britain, telescopic bridges are, nevertheless, extremely rare and Bridgwater's example was manually operated until the end of 1871. Even after the provision of an engine for the bridge movement, the option of manual override was retained until 1913.

The arrival of a locomotive-operated railway in the dock area provided a boost to trade, and sidings were laid to a brewery, a timber yard and saw-mills, but the cramped nature of the area meant that the prolific use of wagon turntables could not be avoided. The coal wharves did good business, and, by 1876, Bridgwater had become the fifth largest coal-importing port in Britain, with 160 vessels registered in the town. The opening of the Severn tunnel in 1886 changed the face of coal transportation and many ports on the English side of the Bristol Channel saw their sea-borne imports of the dark stuff decimated almost overnight. Bridgwater dock, however, was well enough established to diversify to secure a reasonable future. A major modernisation of the quays in 1907 necessitated the realignment of several of the existing railway lines in the dock area.

At Dunball, two miles to the north of Bridgwater, a wharf and a horse-operated tramway were acquired by the Bristol & Exeter from a local coal merchant in 1867; the wharf was extended and the ½-mile tramway was upgraded for mixed gauge locomotive haulage in November 1869. Apart from the coal merchant, a brick manufacturer also used the wharf branch and dispatched an average of 10,000 tons annually by means of the B&E. At Dunball, the locomotives which worked the coal trains usually had to perform their own shunting, but at Bridgwater, a dock shunter was provided. In 1893, the Bridgwater engine was treated to a single-road shed which had originally formed part of the B&E carriage workshop just to the south of the station.

The staunchly standard gauge London & South Western had two branches emanating from its Salisbury-Exeter line. At Yeovil, a Brunelesque policy was adopted and, instead of laying the main line through the centre of the town, it was planned to run to its south. Until the line was completed beyond Yeovil towards Exeter, a 2½-mile spur was provided to take trains into Hendford station, Yeovil's original Bristol & Exeter Railway terminus. When the L&SWR's main line to Exeter was opened, the spur into Yeovil was officially relegated to branch status. The branch was opened simultaneously with the Salisbury & Yeovil main line on 1 June 1860, and, for part of the way between Yeovil Junction and Yeovil Town, it ran almost parallel with the Great Western's line from Yeovil to Weymouth. In the town itself, Hendford was superseded by Yeovil Town joint station on 1 June 1861, and this reduced the length of the L&SWR's branch to 1¾ miles. Despite the construction of Yeovil Junction station, the practice of starting and finishing a number of trains at Yeovil Town station was to continue for over a century right until the closure of the branch.

Table One
Gauge Conversion of Branch and Freight Lines

From	To	Original Co	Length (m.ch)	Conversion To MG	SG
Weston Junction	Weston-s-Mare	B&E	1.38	1875	1879
Yatton	Clevedon	B&E	3.45		1879
Durston	Yeovil(PM)	B&E	20.35	1867/8	1879
Frome	Radstock	GWR	8.19		1874
Witham	Wells	ESR	13.65		1874
Yatton	Wells	B&E	17.43		1875
Bridgwater	Bridgwater Dock	B&E	0.76*	*	1892
Dunball	Dunball Wharf	B&E	0.36*	*	1892
Creech Junction	Chard	B&E	12.61		1891
Norton Fitzwarren	Minehead	WSR/MR	22.60		1882
Bedminster	Portishead	B&PP&R	9.49		1880
Norton Fitzwarren	Barnstaple	D&S	42.50		1881
Bristol (TM)	Bristol Docks	GWR/B&E	1.24*	*	1892

Note:
* Laid as mixed gauge.

24

Right:
This photograph of Williton station was taken in the late 1870s and, despite the disappearance of the tracks beneath the flood water, it can be clearly seen that the locomotive and its three-coach train are operating on the broad gauge. Compare this picture to the later one of the same station and the water cranes are conspicuous by their absence, although a supply of the wet stuff does not seem to be a major problem in this scene. Lens of Sutton

The London & South Western's engine shed at Yeovil was not at the Junction but at the Town station. It was a three road structure with a separate arched entrance to each road, and was accompanied by a 43ft turntable. The 50ft turntable at Yeovil Junction was of more use and, consequently, the one at Yeovil Town fell into disuse and was dismantled in 1917. Yeovil Town's stud usually numbered around 20 locomotives which ranged from main line passenger locomotives to tank engines for the branch duties to Yeovil Junction. Just before the Grouping, there were over 20 push-pull trains making the five minute trip each way over the branch on weekdays.

The main line between Yeovil Junction and Exeter was opened on 19 July 1860, and, on 8 May 1863, a 3½-mile branch to Chard, complete with a canal tramway, was opened by the nominally independent Chard Railway Co. This necessitated renaming Chard Road station on the main line as Chard Junction, while the terminus of the branch was given the title of Chard Town. Chard was reached by the Bristol & Exeter's broad gauge branch from Taunton on 11 September 1866. This ran into Chard Joint station, which was operated as a L&SWR/B&E concern, the former railway company having officially taken over the Chard Railway in 1864. The 13-mile B&E line from Creech Junction, near Taunton, to Chard had been promoted by the Chard & Taunton Railway, a subsidiary of big brother, and there were stations at Hatch and Ilminster with a further one at Thorn being opened in 1871 only to be renamed Thornfalcon in 1901.

At Chard Joint, the dual occupation of the station did not extend to the camaraderie of mixed gauge facilities as the two railway companies were kept distinctly separate, each with their own gauges, platforms, signalboxes and staff. The Great Western and the London & South Western were not ideal bedfellows, and this was well illustrated in 1884. By that year, much of the GWR had been converted to the standard gauge, but east of Exeter, the only line on which the GWR retained the broad gauge was the

Chard branch. The GWR felt that by keeping to the broad gauge, the possible threat of the L&SWR obtaining running powers to Taunton would be obviated. Conversion to standard gauge did not take place until 19 July 1891, just 10 months before total extinction of the broad gauge.

During World War 1 both the Great Western and the London & South Western had to make economies and, much though it must have hurt, the two companies entered into negotiations to simplify operations at Chard. The result was that, from 1 January 1917, the L&SWR abandoned passenger services into Chard Town and the GWR took over the working of the line between Chard Joint and Chard Junction. After the war, the two rival companies reverted to working their own lines into Chard Joint. By the summer of 1922, the London & South Western's Chard branch was served by nine daily trains each way, with a journey time of nine minutes, and locomotives working this branch had access to the Great Western's 70ft long single-road shed. The 41ft turntable near the shed was jointly owned by the GWR and the L&SWR, but it was the former which maintained an official allocation, the latter using it basically as a stabling point. In 1901, the GWR allocation at Chard comprised '517' class 0-4-2T No 544 and '1076' class 0-6-0ST No 1145. In the summer before the Grouping, GWR services between Taunton and Chard had stabilised at six trains each way on weekdays with an extra one from Taunton on Saturdays; the journey time was around 40 minutes

The single-road sub-shed at Templecombe was administered from Yeovil, and housed the locomotive engaged on exchange shunting duties between the L&SWR and the Somerset & Dorset. In the early 1920s, Templecombe's resident was usually a 'G6' 0-6-0T although a 'K10' or 'T9' 4-4-0 was sometimes retained for main line duties. Despite the limited sphere of operations conducted from Templecombe shed, four sets of engine crews were allocated to the depot in the mid-1920s.

It was the turn of the Bristol & Exeter to open the next branch line in Somerset. Work on the broad gauge line from Taunton to Watchet had been started by an independent company, the West Somerset Railway, but it took three years and the drainage of the corporate coffers to complete the 15-mile line which, in places, was engineered over gradients of up to 1 in 80. The WSR did the sensible thing and accepted terms for a lease from the B&E, and it was the new proprietor which had the privilege of seeing the line opened to passengers on 31 March 1862 with four trains, each taking 50 minutes, advertised each way. Intermediate stations were at Bishop's Lydeard, Crowcombe Heathfield (shortened to Crowcombe in 1889), Stogumber and Williton, but none had freight facilities until five months after the line was unveiled. At Crowcombe, a siding was laid to Triscombe quarry, where quartzite and sandstone were extracted. An additional station was opened at Norton Fitzwarren, where the branch diverged from the main line, on 1 August 1873.

Watchet was a logical target for the company as the town's harbour had been much improved for the coming of the independent West Somerset Mineral Railway some 15 years earlier. There was always a degree of speculation about whether the WSMR would strike out for Minehead itself or whether the Bristol & Exeter would try to take it over, but the two railway companies remained completely separate concerns with neither interchange facilities nor friction. At Watchet, the WSMR concentrated on exporting the ore it had transported from the hills, leaving the B&E, and, later the Great Western, free to play with imports which included wood pulp from Scandinavia and esparto grass from North Africa.

The 8¼-mile extension from Watchet to Minehead was constructed by another independent company, the Minehead Railway, and opened on 16 July 1874. It was worked by the Bristol & Exeter from the outset but the Minehead Railway retained its separate identity until 1897. This section had stations at Washford, Blue Anchor and Dunster. The town of Minehead offered good potential for traffic as its status as a seaside resort was growing and it was a convenient base for exploring Exmoor. When motor tours came into their own in the early 1900s, Minehead's popularity as a holiday centre expanded rapidly and, between 1874 and 1923, its population more than trebled to over 6,000. The town and the railway had been mutually beneficial.

In the early 1890s, the service between Taunton and Minehead was, usually, four trains each way on weekdays with an additional one on Saturdays, and the journey time was around 70 minutes. By the time of the Grouping, seven trains ran each way daily with an extra one on Fridays but the journey time remained the same as 30 years previously. In the late 1800s, the 'Metro' 2-4-0Ts and various classes of 0-6-0STs provided the usual forms of motive power, but by the early 1920s, smaller 4-4-0s started to be used. The sole locomotive allocated to Minehead in 1921 was, however, one of the old guard: 'Metro' No 456. The engine's home was a 70ft single-road shed which, along with a turntable, had previously lived at Watchet. The shed and turntable had been installed at Watchet in March 1862, not only because that town was, at that time, at the

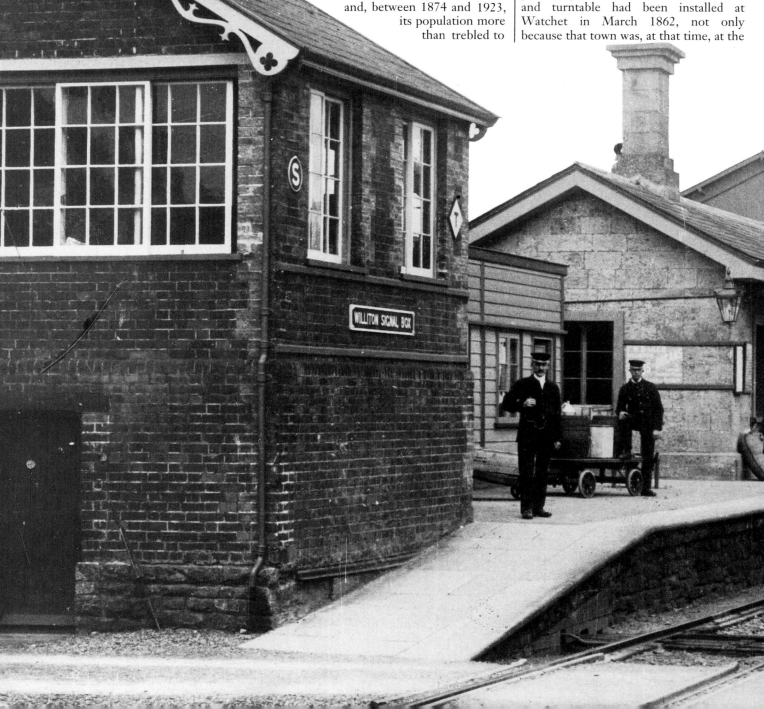

end of the line, but also because the Bristol & Exeter had to provide a shunter for its lines at the eastern end of the harbour. The relocation of the facilities to Minehead took place with the opening of the extension in July 1874.

After Watchet, Portishead was the next town on the Bristol Channel to get a branch line. On 18 April 1867, the 9½-mile broad gauge line from Bristol was opened and, although worked by the Bristol & Exeter, had been built by the Bristol & Portishead Pier and Railway Co which continued to maintain the line until absorption by the GWR in 1884. Plans for a tramroad to a dock at Portishead had been around since 1800, the

Below:
This picture of a somewhat drier Williton station looking towards Minehead is believed to have been taken not long after the 1882 conversion of the line to the standard gauge. The substantial goods shed can be seen adjoining the down platform just beyond the footbridge. In later years, the delightful footbridge was replaced by a wrought-iron structure which was re-sited nearer to the water crane in the foreground. Lens of Sutton

BRISTOL AND EXETER RAILWAY

Opening of the West Somerset Railway

TAUNTON to WATCHET

On Monday, 31st March, this line will be opened for
PASSENGER TRAFFIC
and the following trains will run:—

	DOWN TRAINS			
LEAVING	Class 1 & 2 a.m.	Class 1, 2 & 3 p.m.	Class 1 & 2 p.m.	Class 1, 2 & 3 p.m.
Taunton	9.50	2. 5	5.00	7.30
Bishops Lydeard	10.5	2.19	5.14	7.44
Crowcombe Heathfield	10.19	2.33	5.28	7.58
Stogumber	10.26	2.40	5.35	8. 5
Williton	10.35	2.49	5.44	8.20
Watchet (arrival)	10.40	2.55	5.50	8.20
	UP TRAINS			
Watchet	8.45	12.30	3.30	6.15
Williton	8.52	12.36	3.36	6.21
Stogumber	9. 5	12.49	3.49	6.34
Crowcombe Heathfield	9.12	12.56	3.56	6.41
Bishops Lydeard	9.22	1. 5	4. 5	6.50
Taunton (arrival)	9.35	1.18	4.18	7. 3

This line will open a direct Route to LYNTON, PORLOCK, MINEHEAD, etc., and well regulated coaches will run from Williton in connection with the Expresses and Third Class Trains.

by order of the Directors,
HENRY DYKES,
Superintendent.

Bristol, 19th March, 1862.

Left:
The West Somerset Railway was worked by the B&E from the outset and this poster advertises the opening of the line as far as Watchet on 31 March 1862. Norton Fitzwarren station was not added until 1873. The journey time of 50 minutes for the 16¾-mile trip was reduced by only 10 minutes a century later.
Courtesy: West Somerset Steam Railway Trust

BRISTOL AND EXETER RAILWAY.

Every MONDAY and THURSDAY

until further notice Passengers can be booked to

WATCHET,
BLUE ANCHOR, DUNSTER OR MINEHEAD,

AS UNDER, BY TRAIN LEAVING

Fares To and Fro :

		A.M.	P.M.		P.M.	WATCHET.	BLUE ANCHOR, DUNSTER, or MINEHEAD.
						3rd Class.	3rd Class.
TAUNTON	at	11 15,	1 50	or	5 40		2s.
NORTON FITZWARREN	"	11 20,	1 55	"	5 45	1s.	
BISHOP'S LYDEARD	"	11 27,	2 2	"	5 52		
CRO. HEATHFIELD	"	11 41,	2 16	"	6 6		1s. 6d.
STOGUMBER	"	11 48,	2 23	"	6 13	9d.	
WILLITON	"	11 57,	2 32	"	6 22		
WATCHET	"	12 5,	2 40	"	6 30	—	1s.
WASHFORD	"	12 13,	2 48	"	6 38	—	9d.
BLUE ANCHOR	"	12 22,	2 57	"	6 47	—	6d.

Returning by any Train on the day of issue only.

Passengers holding Tickets for Minehead can leave and rejoin the Train at Blue Anchor or Dunster.

CHILDREN UNDER TWELVE YEARS OF AGE HALF-PRICE.

The Tickets are not transferable, and are only available by the Trains and for the Stations named.   No Luggage Allowed.

Above:
Although undated, this B&E excursion handbill must have been issued between the opening of the Minehead extension on 16 July 1874 and the take-over by the GWR on 1 January 1876. The 50-mile round trip from Taunton to Minehead and back is advertised at the cost of two bob (10p).
West Somerset Steam Railway Trust

ideas having been put forward by colliery owners in the Bristol area who wanted to facilitate exports. In 1845, Brunel had come up with the idea of a floating pier at Portbury and an atmospheric railway to provide the link to Bristol but, like earlier schemes, this had passed into oblivion. A riverside terminus at Portbury was, however, included in the original plans for the B&PPR line, but this proposal was dropped in favour of development at Portishead.

When the branch was opened, there were intermediate stations at Clifton Bridge, Pill and Portbury. Ashton Gate platform was added in 1906 to cater for football specials for the Bristol City ground when the club attained first division status; the platform closed in 1917, by which time Bristol City's presence in the top flight had long since gone, but it was reopened later. A station serving Portbury Shipyard was opened in 1918 but was short-lived. The Portishead branch ran, for some of its length, along

Above right:
The original GWR terminus at Portishead can be seen on the right of the frame, The site of the goods yard serving the dock was later taken over for the construction of a power station. The single-road engine shed sits neglectedly between the station and the dock, and its 45ft turntable can be seen in front of the building in the centre foreground. Until 1896, the turntable was situated just in front of the shed and its re-siting coincided with the shed's official loss of its last allocated locomotive. The date of this picture is believed to be around 1920. Lens of Sutton

Right:
An alternative view of Portishead (GWR), this time from the south, was almost certainly taken on the same day as the previous one. The granary can be seen behind the loco shed and, in the distant haze, are the malting house and mill. The station did not receive its second platform until much later. Lens of Sutton

Left:
A GWR steam railmotor leaves Ashton Gate platform on an unusual working from Portishead to Bath. To the right of the station a 0-6-0ST simmers on the line which was opened to Canons Wharf in 1906. The freshness of the ballast on the harbour line and the fact that the cutting has yet to become overgrown suggests that this photograph was taken not long after the Canons Marsh spur was opened. Lens of Sutton

Below:
Milverton was the first station after Norton Fitzwarren on the Taunton-Barnstaple branch. It was typical of many stations in the area in that, despite being on a branch line, it had a reasonably-sized goods yard to serve the local community. The date of this picture is believed to be around 1920, some 40 years after the standard gauge replaced the broad gauge on the entire branch. Lens of Sutton

the southern bank of the River Avon and this necessitated the boring of three tunnels, one of which was directly underneath Brunel's Suspension Bridge. A fourth tunnel, at 665yd the longest on the line, was necessary under the village of Ham Green.

The Pier & Railway Co had, from the outset, plans to establish a dock at Portishead, but these did not come to fruition until 1879. By that time, a dock had already opened across the river at Avonmouth and, when Avonmouth Docks were extended in 1908, Portishead Dock was relegated from the second division to the third. Passenger steamers provided one regular source of traffic, with railway-owned vessels sailing to Newport, Cardiff and, during the summer, Ilfracombe. A large naval shipyard was planned for Portbury during World War 1 but, by the time it was completed, hostilities were all but over and the site soon fell into disuse. Portishead was never to inherit the maritime significance of Bristol.

In 1870, eight trains ran each way between Bristol and Portishead on weekdays and the return fare between those two points was three shillings (15p) first class or two shillings and threepence (11½p) second class; a third class single was 11½d (just under 5p). The journey time was, on average, 35 minutes and there was to be little improvement on this schedule until the 1940s although the number of daily trains was increased to provide a more frequent service. By 1922, a total of 12 trains ran each way on weekdays. A 50ft single-road engine shed was provided at Portishead when the line was

opened, but no allocation was recorded after 1896, although the shed remained intact for some years after that date.

At the other end of the county, the Devon & Somerset Railway's intention was to provide a link between Taunton and Barnstaple. The railway opened as far as Wiveliscombe on 8 June 1871 and finally reached Barnstaple on 1 November 1873. It left the main line at Norton Fitzwarren and criss-crossed the border between the two counties with the intermediate stations on the Somerset side being at Milverton, Wiveliscombe and Dulverton, the last-named of those three becoming a junction when the branch from Tiverton opened on 1 August 1884. Although the D&S was worked by the

Bristol & Exeter from the outset, it remained nominally independent until 1901, but it was not one of life's most successful companies. By that time, the arrears in interest payments to shareholders had amounted to over £500,000.

To the north and the east of Bristol, the Midland Railway opened two branches. An alternative route from Bristol to Bath was provided on 4 August 1869 by means of the branch, which left the main line at Mangotsfield and passed through stations at Warmley, Bitton, Kelston and Weston before terminating at Bath. The Midland's own station at Bath was used from the opening of the line but was not fully completed until 7 May 1870. It was known locally as Queen

Above:
This 1880s view of Bath Green Park station shows that the Midland 'branch' from Bristol via Mangotsfield has arrived to join the more charismatic occupants. Lens of Sutton

Square, but had no official claim to the suffix; the more familiar title of Green Park did not appear until after Nationalisation. A twin-road shed was provided at Bath but, when the Somerset & Dorset Railway arrived in the city in 1874, the S&D's premises provided much-needed overspill accommodation for the Midland.

The 12-mile Midland line between Bristol and Bath went on to see usage which was way above that of the average branch line. When the Somerset & Dorset was acquired jointly by the Midland and the London & South Western in 1875, the Midland's route from Bristol became a key section between the north and the south of the country. Nevertheless, local services were maintained, and, by 1922, the weekday service between Bristol St Philip's station and Bath consisted of 13 outward and 12 return trains. The journey times averaged between 40 and 50 minutes, although one run of 32 minutes was timetabled each way between Temple Meads and Bath.

The other Midland branch ran from Yate to Thornbury and was opened on 2 September 1872. It was 7½ miles in length, and had intermediate stations at Iron Acton and Tytherington and, by the late 1800s, was an important route for the transportation of stone from the quarries around Tytherington. Passenger services were never particularly frequent on this branch, and, by 1922, only three daily trains were advertised in each direction. A small engine shed was provided at Thornbury, but the responsibility for the branch's motive power was in the hands of the folks at Barrow Road.

In the Bristol area, the docks at Avonmouth and Portishead were treated to rail connections from the time they were opened. By contrast, the oldest working docks in the area, those in the centre of Bristol, had to wait for 41 years after the opening of Bristol's first railway until they were given the luxury of direct railway connections to the outside world. It was 11 March 1872 when the Bristol Harbour Railway was opened. The line was constructed jointly by the Great Western and the Bristol & Exeter Railways but Bristol Corporation was also entitled to a say in the proceedings as it held the responsibility for the quays. The railway crossed three streets on iron bridges, traversed a 346yd viaduct and negotiated the entrance lock to Bathurst Basin by means of a bascule bridge. As well as that little pile of engineering feats, there was a 282yd tunnel under St Mary Redcliffe churchyard, the boring of which required the removal of a number of bodies for burial elsewhere. Although the line was only ¾-mile long, the involved nature of its construction meant that almost four years were taken for completion.

The harbour line was extended for half a mile to a new goods depot behind Wapping Wharf in June 1876, by which time the original joint owner, the Bristol & Exeter Railway, had become part of the Great Western empire. Interestingly, the entire length of the line was laid with mixed gauge rails, despite the fact that the only standard gauge operations in Bristol were those of the old adversary, the Midland.

On 1 March 1882, a branch was opened between Hallatrow, on the Bristol-Frome line, and the mining village of Camerton and, due to some testing gradients, the maximum loading permitted for goods trains was 15 loaded trucks. On 26 August 1907, the branch was extended to Dunkerton where a major new colliery had been opened and, on 9 May 1910, a

Bristol St Philip's Station, 1918

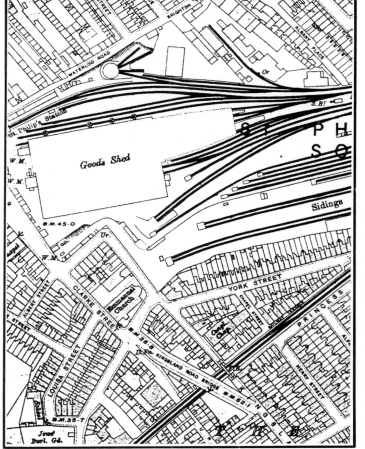

Left:
The Midland station at St Philip's in Bristol is clearly marked in this 1918 Ordnance Survey Map. The goods depot is the one opened by the Midland Railway in 1866 to supersede Avonside Wharf. The line crossing the lower right of the map leads to the old Bristol & Gloucester Railway's terminus at Cuckold's Pill and also to Avonside Wharf. Crown Copyright

Above:

The Blagdon terminus of the Wrington Vale Light Railway was the only station on the line to be built on the level. It opened with the line on 4 December 1901, but was closed to passengers as early as 14 September 1931; full closure followed on 1 November 1950 when the branch was truncated at Wrington. The station building is now a private house and the trackbed has been laid to lawn. The precise date of this photograph is not known but, judging from the relaid and reballasted track, it is believed to have been taken around 1920. Lens of Sutton

further extension was completed to Limpley Stoke to connect the branch to the line between Bath and Trowbridge. On the 11 miles between Hallatrow and Limpley Stoke, stations and halts were provided at Radford & Timsbury, Dunkerton, Combe Hay and Monkton Combe. Additional halts were opened at Dunkerton colliery and Midford in 1911, and at Paulton in 1914.

The Great Western had never anticipated a great volume of passenger traffic and so the service was provided by just one steam railmotor working a shuttle of five trains each way, but sometimes, a through service was run to Trowbridge. In 1910, the return fare between Hallatrow and Limpley Stoke cost one shilling and eleven pence (9½p) while three shillings (15p) would get one from Hallatrow to Trowbridge and back on the

occasional through workings. One odd quirk of the line was that return tickets were available only at the stations and not at any of the halts. Despite the economy standard of operations, it soon became evident that the income from the passenger services was not reaching even the modest targets set by the GWR and so passenger services were withdrawn on 23 March 1915. Although they were to be reintroduced after the grouping, the new lease of life was to be brief.

The last completely new branch, as opposed to an extension, to open in Somerset was the 6½-mile Wrington Vale Light Railway. Despite its title, it was a Great Western-promoted line, and it opened from Congresbury, on the Yatton-Witham line, to Blagdon on 4 December 1901 with intermediate stations at Wrington, Langford and Burrington. Initially, Burrington was little more than a halt as it had only a primitive shelter for the passengers and, furthermore, it was the only station on the line without separate freight facilities.

Being a light railway, the usual conditions applied to the line's construction and operation: a maximum gradient of 1 in 50, a top speed of 25mph and an axle load no greater than 14 tons. Of the line's six level crossings, only those at Wrington and Langford were required to have gates. One very unusual feature of the line, however, was that the cost of its

construction was, at £25,000, some £4,000 *less* than that projected. Just outside Blagdon, two short spurs left the line, one to a pumping station on the Yeo Reservoir, the other to the grounds of Coombe Lodge, the home of one Baron Winterstoke.

In the early years, the motive power on the line was supplied by Great Western No 1384, a 2-4-0T of 1876 vintage which had started life as Watlington & Princes Risborough Railway No 2. When that company was vested in the Great Western in 1883, the engine was given its GWR number and went on to see service in Cornwall and on the Lambourn Valley Railway before arriving in Somerset. After being replaced by '517' class 0-4-2Ts, No 1384 was transferred to the Culm Valley branch in Devon and was withdrawn in 1911. It was, however, to reappear in Somerset in later years under the guise of Weston, Clevedon & Portishead Railway No 4 *Hesperus*. GWR 0-4-0T No 101, an experimental oil-burner built at Swindon in 1902, was designed specifically for the Wrington Vale line but did not take up its intended duties. In pre-Grouping years, almost all duties on the branch were, after the departure of No 1384, handled by either 0-4-2Ts or the ubiquitous 'Metro' 2-4-0Ts.

A small shed was provided at Blagdon when the line opened but the structure burnt down in October 1912. Despite this, Blagdon remained recognised as an official allocation point and the 1921 reg-

Below:

In these Bradshaws timetables for the Wrington Vale Light Railway, both show four through trains each way on weekdays. The 1905 one also shows a service which involves changing at Congresbury but, in the 1922 timetable, this extra option no longer appears. Blagdon only featured in the public timetable for 30 years and so the inclusion of two timetables for this station is of interest.

YATTON, WRINGTON, and BLAGDON.—Great Western.

Mls									Mls								
	Yatton ....dep.	8 10	....	10 0	2 10 4	0 6 45	....	....		Blagdon ....dep.	7 35	....	9 15	1 20	3 5	5 25	....	....
1¼	Congresbury	8 15	3 19	10 4	2 14	4 6 49	....	....	1¼	Burrington	7 39	....	9 19	1 24	3 9	5 29	....	....
4¼	Wrington		8 27	10 12	2 22	4 12 6 57	....	....	2¼	Langford	7 43	....	9 23	1 29	3 13	5 35	....	....
5¼	Langford		8 34	10 19	2 35	4 25 7 4	....	....	3¼	Wrington	7 49	....	9 29	1 34	3 19	5 45	....	....
6¼	Burrington		8 40	10 25	2 35	4 25 7 10	....	....	6¼	Congresbury 28 ...	7 58	3	9 39	1 44	3 29	5 58	....	....
8	Blagdon ......arr.		8 45	10 30	2 40	4 30 7 15	....	....	8	Yatton 30, 28 ...arr.		3 10	9 45	1 50	3 35	6 7	....	....

1905 Bradshaws

YATTON, WRINGTON, and BLAGDON.—Great Western.

Miles	Down.	Week Days.				Suns.	Miles	Up.	Week Days.				Suns.
		mrn m aft aft				mrn			mrn mrn m aft				aft
	Yatton ....dep.	1015	1257	2 56	6 45	....	8 40		Blagdon .....dep.	8 40	11 30	1 37	4 55	....	7 45
1¼	Congresbury	1019	1 3	5	6 49	....	8 44	1¼	Burrington	8 47	1140	1 42	5 0	....	....
4¼	Wrington	1028	1 10	3 25	6 58	....	8 53	3¼	Langford	8 51	1155	1 46	5 6	....	7 51
5	Langford	1035	1 17	3 36	7 5	....	9 0	3¼	Wrington	8 57	1220	1 53	5 17	....	7 57
6¼	Burrington	1041	1 23	3 45	**a**	....		6¼	Congresbury (above)	9 6	1228	2 15	5 25	....	8 8
8¼	Blagdon ....arr.	1045	1 27	3 50	7 15	....	9 6	8¼	Yatton 12, 17 (above)	9 12	1245	2 7	5 34	....	8 12

a Stops at Burrington at 7 11 aft. to set down on notice being given to the Guard at Langford.

m Motor Car.   One class only.

1922 Bradshaws

ister shows '517' class 0-4-2T No 837 as the resident. The weekday passenger service between Blagdon and Yatton remained at four trains each way throughout most of the line's existence, with journey times of between 30 and 45 minutes. On peak summer Saturdays, Yatton's branch services to Wells and Clevedon sometimes caused considerable congestion and, to save adding to the mêlée, Wrington Vale trains were often stopped at Congresbury, where passengers were transferred to a train from Wells. In the early 1920s the line's regular driver was one Oliver Oliver, but the eccentric name cut no ice with the locals. The gentleman was referred to, instead, as 'Oliver Twice'.

In the centre of Bristol the harbour branch which had opened in the 1870s offered excellent access to the quays, especially from the east but, when upgrading of older quays in the docks was planned in the late 1890s, the Great Western felt that additional access to and from the south and west would be advantageous. On 4 October 1906, two new spurs into the dock area were opened and these were joined to the Portishead branch at Ashton Junction.

From Ashton, the double line crossed the New Cut by means of a twin-level swing bridge which carried a road above the railway. This steel bridge, which cost over £70,000 to construct, was one of the few of its kind in the country. Beyond the north end of the bridge, the railway divided, one line following the south bank of the New Cut and linking up with the original harbour line at Wapping Wharf, the other line crossing two entrance locks to the docks on swing bridges and continuing to a large covered goods depot at Canon's Marsh, behind which sidings ran to the quays. Canon's Marsh depot and yard had accommodation for 600 wagons, but because of the proximity to Bristol Cathedral, the Great Western had to undertake not to shunt during Sunday services.

To the north of Bristol, the fast line from Avonmouth via Filton and Badminton was opened on 9 May 1910 and, although it was intended for express traffic to and from the docks, a local service was also provided. From opening day, seven railmotors plied between Temple Meads and Avonmouth daily via the new line and, as well as a station at Henbury, special railmotor halts were constructed at Filton, Charlton and Hallen. At Avonmouth, the railmotors worked into a platform adjacent to the dock gates in Gloucester Road.

Henbury station, Avonmouth platform and the halts at Filton, Charlton and Hallen were all closed on 22 March 1915 as a wartime economy, but although Hallen halt was partially reopened in 1917 and Henbury station fully reopened in 1922, the others remained closed. Another consequence of World War 1 was the construction of several munitions factories in the Avonmouth area and these included a shell factory at Chittening. To help the transportation of staff, a temporary platform was erected at Chittening in February 1917 and this survived until October 1923, well after munitions production had ceased. Another workmen's platform had been erected at St Andrew's Road, near the Royal Edward Dock, but this became of more general use and was taken over by the Great Western on 1 March 1917. Although closed in November 1922, St Andrew's Road reopened with the status of a proper station in 1924.

Regular passenger services were restored on the Henbury line on 3 April 1922 with five trains using that route between Temple Meads and Avonmouth on weekdays. Elsewhere in the Avonmouth area, a platform was opened at Severn Beach, between Avonmouth and Pilning, on 5 June the same year. Absurd at it may sound to those who know Severn Beach today, the town was promoted vigorously as a seaside resort and the excursion trains which were operated from Bristol during the public holidays of 1922 were well and truly packed. On Whit Monday of the final year before the Grouping, the 16 special trains to Severn Beach were so popular that some passengers had to be accommodated in the guards' vans. From 10 July 1922, a scheduled public service from Bristol to Severn Beach was introduced with five trains each way on weekdays.

Although two of the branch lines in Somerset were to suffer partial cuts not long after the Grouping, the post-Grouping years were, on the whole, to be times of consolidation and growth for most of the area's branches. Despite the growth in popularity of the motor car and charabancs in the 1920s, the rural railways more than held their own, particularly those lines which headed for the seaside.

Table Two
Branch and Shunting Locomotive Sheds

Shed	Original Co	Opened	Closed	Allocation Dec 1922
Avonmouth	GWR/MR	1905	1924	1
Bath	GWR	1840(a)	1961	1
Bath	Mid	1869	1966	61
Blagdon	WVLR	1901	1924	1
Bridgwater	GWR	1893	1960	2
Chard	B&E	1866	1924	1
Clevedon	B&E	1847	1879	–
Hotwells	BPPR	1865	1875	–
Minehead	B&E	1874	1956	1
Portishead	B&PP	1867	1896	–
Radstock	GWR	1866	1929	1
Shepton Mallet	ESR	1858	1862	–
Shirehampton	BPPR	1875	1905	–
Watchet	WSR	1862	1874	–
Wells	ESR	1879(b)	1963	6
Weston-s-Mare	B&E	1861	1960	3
Yate	Mid	1872	1944	1
Yatton	GWR	1879	1960	3

Notes:
(a) First shed closed 1880. Replacement built on different site.
(b) First shed closed 1879. Replacement built on adjacent site.

3 The Legend

The Somerset & Dorset Railway was, arguably, the most charismatic of Britain's railways. In its later years it became, quite justifiably, one of the most photographed lines in the country, as few other railways were able to match the individuality or character of the line across the Mendip Hills. Admittedly, it did not offer the fastest services in the world and some of its less enlightened passengers referred to the S&D as the 'Slow and Dirty', but, to anyone with the remotest interest in railways, the line was the 'Serene and Delightful'.

The Somerset & Dorset itself was not incorporated until 1862. It was formed by the amalgamation of the Somerset Central and Dorset Central Railways, both of which were independent concerns. The initial target of the Somerset Central was the town of Street which was not only a centre of the agricultural industry but also the base of the Clark family, whose sheepskin business had diversified into shoemaking. It is a comforting thought that the fleecy footwear which protects countless sets of toes from winter chills

might well have been made by a descendant of the Somerset Central's first directors.

There was no dispute that one end of the Somerset Central should serve Street and the neighbouring town of Glastonbury, but there was considerable debate as to where the railway should go from there. The logical choice was Bridgwater, which was not only a port but also on the Bristol & Exeter Railway's main line. The fly in the ointment was that between Street and Bridgwater lay the Polden Hills and, as all good civil engineers knew, constructing a railway across hills involved a little thing called money. Instead, the projected route focused on Highbridge which, although a smaller town and a smaller port, was able to be reached, less expensively, across level ground and still provide a link with the B&E's main line.

The Bristol & Exeter's directors were exceptionally obliging. They had acquired a canal between Glastonbury and Highbridge in 1848 and they indicated their willingness to sell the canal to

the Somerset Central so that the new company could use part of its route for building. As further bonuses to the Somerset Central, the B&E was prepared to take shares instead of cash for the canal and, provided the new line was built to the broad gauge, to offer a working agreement. With the backing of a company as powerful as the B&E, the Somerset Central's Act of Incorporation on 17 June 1852 was little more than a formality.

The official unveiling of the 12¼-mile line from Highbridge Wharf to Glastonbury took place on 17 August 1854 with Bristol & Exeter 2-2-2T No 33 in charge of the ceremonial train and, 11 days later, the line was opened to the public. Initially, six trains were scheduled each way on weekdays, and the journey time, including stops at the intermediate stations at Ashcott and Shapwick, was 35 minutes. At Highbridge, the Somerset Central crossed the Bristol & Exeter main line on the level, just north of the B&E station, and this unusual feature was to remain almost until the local line closed over 100 years later.

Although Highbridge proved satisfactory as an outlet for freight, the Somerset Central considered that the nearby town of Burnham could offer improved facilities not only for freight but also for pleasure steamers. Furthermore, Burnham had potential as a holiday resort. As a result, the railway was extended for 1½ miles from Highbridge to Burnham and this new section was opened to traffic on 3 May 1858. At Burnham, the line continued beyond the station to a stone-built pier on the sea front, but the restrictions of this arrangement soon became apparent. The Bristol Channel has the second highest tidal range in the world and, while full tide provides enough of

Left:
The S&D's station at Priory Road in Wells was not the most luxurious of affairs. The fluted channel for locomotive chimneys helped to ventilate this small station, but if this scene is typical of the station's activity, there cannot have been many passengers to asphyxiate.
Lens of Sutton

Above:
This fine view shows S&D 0-4-4T No 54 leaving Wells bunker-first on a train to Glastonbury on 11 April 1914. The S&D's signalbox is on the left, and the roof of the company's good shed can be seen behind the train. The two roads in the foreground lead to the engine shed. LCGB/Ken Nunn collection

the briny to reach sea fronts throughout the channel, low tide reduces quays and approaches to extensive mud banks. The alternative was to build a non-tidal harbour at Burnham, but the estimated cost of around £250,000 proved a little daunting.

At the other end of the Somerset Central, the ceremonial opening of the 5½-mile extension between Glastonbury and Wells took place on 3 March 1859 and 12 days later public services commenced. The only intermediate station on the new section was at Polsham. With a population of nearly 5,000, Wells was by far the largest community in the area and the residents had felt that a railway into the town was long overdue. Not content when the Somerset Central arrived, several prominent locals urged the railway company to turn its other plans into reality and continue the line beyond Wells to Shepton Mallet. As things turned out, it took the East Somerset Railway to provide the link in 1862. Although the Somerset Central had looked closely at the idea of an extension,

the company's thoughts were, at the time, absorbed with the Dorset Central Railway.

The Dorset Central opened its first section between Wimborne Junction and Blandford on 1 November 1860. In itself, this event was not of earth-shattering significance but, with the Somerset Central already engaged on construction of an extension to Bruton and the Dorset Central busying itself with reaching the same place, the heady prospect of a lucrative rail link between Bristol Channel and English Channel ports seemed likely. The major obstacle was the matter of gauge. The Dorset Central was a standard gauge concern worked by the London & South Western while the Somerset Central was, by necessity of its arrangement with the Bristol & Exeter, broad gauge. Fortuitously for the Somerset Central, the B&E's lease was due to expire in 1861 and so it was considered that conversion to standard gauge throughout would be the sensible option. But things were not quite so simple.

It took a battle royal for the Somerset Central to sort out the gauge problem, and the outcome was that the company was placed under a legal obligation to provide mixed gauge rails through to Bruton. By this time, the Somerset Central and the Dorset Central had become quite matey and reciprocal running powers had been confirmed. The latter company tried to help its neighbour out by insisting that, if mixed gauge facilities had

to be provided across Somerset towards Dorset, the Bristol & Exeter should be obliged to lay a third rail between Highbridge and Bristol. It was said that it took several months for the laughter to subside at Bristol. Cole, near Bruton, was reached by both the Somerset Central and the Dorset Central almost simultaneously and, on 3 February 1862, the new lines were opened for public traffic. Between Burnham and Poole, the only section which remained uncompleted was that between Templecombe and Blandford.

Despite its loss of traffic on the Somerset Central, the Bristol & Exeter remained remarkably good-natured towards the smaller company. In the days of gauge transition, the B&E hired rolling stock to the Somerset Central to enable services to be maintained. In return, the B&E had access to the Somerset Central's line and, right up to 1868, a broad gauge B&E freight train ran daily from Bristol to Wells via Highbridge. The inevitable amalgamation of the Somerset Central and Dorset Central took effect on 1 September 1862 and the new corporate title was the Somerset & Dorset Railway. It was, however, 31 August 1863 before the outstanding 16-mile section between Templecombe and Blandford was completed to allow through running from Channel to Channel.

At Templecombe, the layout of the old Dorset Central line in relation to that of the London & South Western seemed

Right:
Evercreech Junction was where the Bath extension diverged from the original Somerset Central line to Burnham. This photograph, which is believed to have been taken around 1920, is undoubtedly a posed shot, although the engine driver does not seem to have been excused from watering duties to allow him to line up for the camera. The closure of the crossing gates purely for photographic purposes would not have inconvenienced too many motorists in those days. The locomotive at the down platform cannot be positively identified, but it could well be one of the Neilson or Vulcan-built '33' class 0-6-0s of 1878-90. Lens of Sutton

purpose-built for awkwardness and was never to be properly resolved. The original Dorset Central line passed below the L&SWR to the east of the main-line station, and a connecting loop ran into an exchange yard adjacent to the L&SWR's up line. When the Dorset Central opened to Cole on 3 February 1862, it unveiled its own twin-platform station at Templecombe, but until 1870 a number of the north-south trains used the loop to run into the L&SWR station and avoided the Dorset Central station completely. The L&SWR provided a shuttle service between the two stations and this continued until 1870, when the loop was replaced by a more permanent link. By then, fewer and fewer north-south trains used the Dorset Central station and, when the layout at Templecombe was altered in 1887, the old Dorset Central station was done away with and a short single platform was installed in its place. Right through the days of the Somerset & Dorset Railway and, later, the LMS and British Railways, the tedious practice of a reversal of north-south trains into and out of the former L&SWR station continued.

The Somerset Central had eight locomotives of its own and they all passed to the Somerset & Dorset. Built by George England and delivered in October and November 1861, they were outside-framed 2-4-0s with 5ft 0in coupled wheels and 15in x 18in cylinders. Seven were paired with four-wheeled tenders but the eighth was converted during construction to a well tank. After the incorporation of the Somerset & Dorset, the new company's first 12 locomotives were all 2-4-0s, 10 of which were tender engines. Of the other pair, one was a diminutive George England tank engine which had been built in 1862 for display at the International Exhibition at Hyde Park and, when it arrived in Somerset, it still retained the exhibition livery of Prussian Blue. The S&D crews were quick to name it 'Bluebottle', but the directors looked on things more seriously. In later

years, the same Prussian Blue was adopted as the standard S&D livery.

The stock of 20 locomotives was woefully inadequate to handle the traffic on 71 running miles of track. Frustratingly, the Somerset & Dorset's traffic figures were good and, although Burnham had proved a disappointment in the shipping stakes, the tonnage handled at Highbridge had increased handsomely. The problem was that the bank balance did not permit the purchase of any further locomotives to assist in handling the traffic which the ships generated. Things got so bad that, in June 1866, receivers were appointed.

It took four years for the Somerset & Dorset to restructure its finances to a degree that enabled discharge from receivership. The restoration of a steady financial foothold presented the directors with the quandary of whether to fight for additional traffic on the existing line or to expand. To the south, extension from Poole to the popular resort of Bournemouth was authorised and this relatively straightforward task was completed on 15 June 1874. To the north, the situation was not as clear-cut. One of the two obvious targets, Bristol, had already become well colonised by the major companies. The other likely target was the rapidly-growing traffic from the North Somerset Coalfield and, although the Bristol & North Somerset Railway had been incorporated to provide a link between the coalfield and Bristol, little

had been done to convert the B&NS's plans to reality. The S&D could expect little co-operation from the Great Western in the matter of expansion northwards but it did not go unnoticed that in 1869 the Midland Railway had arrived in Bath. Instead of picking a fight with the GWR, the S&D considered that an extension across the coalfield to Bath and a possible link with the Midland would secure its future.

The Bath extension was costly to build. The new line started quite innocuously at Evercreech Junction, on the edge of the Somerset Levels, but ahead lay the Mendip Hills and, to cross these, even extensive earthworks could not circumvent ferocious gradients of up to 1 in 50. Construction of the 26-mile line involved the building of four tunnels and seven viaducts, and the little matter of negotiating Masbury Summit, 811ft above sea level. Between Radstock and Midford, the line followed the route of the old Somerset Coal Canal, which the Somerset & Dorset had purchased for £20,000; the final approach to Bath was by means of the Midland line into Queen Square station. Remarkably, the work on the extension took just two years and the line was opened to the public on 20 July 1874 with the first train leaving Bath at 7.25am. Despite the heavy outlay on the extension, the S&D managed to rustle up the essential additional motive power. By the time the line opened, a brace of powerful 0-6-0s had been supplied by

Fowlers, and the first two of a trio of heavy-duty 0-6-0STs had been delivered from Fox Walker, the purchase of the tanks having been made possible by the part-exchange of some of the older 2-4-0s.

The new line was a major feat of engineering but the total cost of over half a million pounds proved too much for the Somerset & Dorset's ailing piggy bank. The only option was to sell out and, predictably, it was the Great Western which was waiting in the wings. It was not as if the line was of great value to the GWR as the S&D's route could offer little that Swindon didn't already have. The GWR's interest was primarily to prevent the standard gauge line which linked the Midland to the London & South Western from falling into enemy hands. Negotiations between the S&D and the GWR were slow but, when the GWR considered things to be almost sewn up,

Below:
This photograph of the S&D station at Shepton Mallet is believed to date to the 1920s. The limestone used to construct the station buildings came from one of the numerous local quarries, many of which had connections to the main S&D line. Beyond the station, the line crosses the Frome road by means of a bridge and then curves to the left over the viaduct which can just be seen in the distance behind the signal post. The fire buckets hanging beneath the steps of the signalbox are marked 'S&DJR'. Lens of Sutton

the Swindon hierarchy became rather over-confident and approached the L&SWR with a suggestion that Waterloo might want to take over the southern section of the S&D. The L&SWR attached far greater significance to the S&D than did the folks at Swindon and it swiftly arranged talks with the Midland with a view to a joint L&SWR/Midland take-over. While it had taken the GWR three months to conduct inconclusive negotiations with the S&D, a joint L&SWR/Midland deputation took just eight days to come up with terms which the S&D found acceptable. The joint lease took effect on 1 November 1875.

The new proprietors were well aware of the line's potential but upgrading was considered essential. A major accident between Radstock and Wellow on 7 August 1876 resulted in 12 fatalities, and much of the blame was attached to the haphazard methods of operation which had become the norm under the old regime. The tragedy impressed on the new lessees that the need for overall improvement was urgent. The responsibility for civil engineering and the permanent way fell to the London & South Western, while the Midland took over rolling stock matters. The Midland must have wondered what it had taken on as, when a fact-finding party was dispatched from Derby to observe the Somerset & Dorset in action, 187 of the 204 passenger services which were checked ran late

and not one of the goods trains kept to schedule. To add to the embarrassment, two locomotives broke down in service while three others failed to make it out of the sheds. A major review of the locomotive situation was deemed overdue.

In 1873, the Somerset & Dorset had appointed B.S.Fisher, late of the Taff Vale Railway, to the post of locomotive superintendent and, under the joint owners, Fisher remained in charge at Highbridge Works but his every move had to be countersigned by the Midland's Samuel Johnson. Without giving Fisher much say in the matter, Derby transferred several of its locomotives to the S&D and these consisted of both tank and tender 0-6-0s and three of Johnson's own 0-4-4Ts.

The bogie tanks were a controversial choice as they regularly caused damage to the track, which had already suffered neglect due to the Somerset & Dorset's lack of funds. Furthermore, the 0-4-4Ts had a penchant for parting company with the tracks, and this combination of deficiencies resulted in the engines being banned south of Evercreech and subjected to a speed limit of 50mph elsewhere. Both the Midland and the London & South Western drafted in 2-4-0s to help out. Johnson was not prepared to accept that his beloved 0-4-4Ts were less than perfect, despite the fact that the only other major British designer who would entertain the prospect of rear bogie

Right:

This photograph of Radstock North, the town's S&D station, dates from around 1910. The signalbox which can be seen to the left of the level crossing is actually the box at the adjacent GWR station; the GWR also crossed the road on the level, and the two level crossings side by side were, in later years, to cause much alopecia among local motorists. Lens of Sutton

Below right:

Somerset & Dorset Railway 0-4-4T No 53 was built by the Vulcan Foundry in 1884 and withdrawn as LMS No 1231 in 1930. Sadly, the date and location of this picture are unconfirmed, but it is a fair guess that the train is passing the shed yard at Highbridge in an easterly direction. R K Blencowe collection

engines on fast passenger services was William Stroudley.

Nine new 0-4-4Ts were ordered from Avonside Engine Co in 1877, and their only concession to general opinion was that they were fitted with Adams bogies rather than those of Johnson's own design. Four additional 0-4-4Ts were supplied by the Vulcan Foundry in 1884 and 1885 and delivered in Midland Red livery; like their predecessors, they were eventually superseded by more powerful engines. As a class, they spent their later years on duties between Templecombe and Highbridge, and in 1928 S&D No 32 was equipped for motor-train working on the Bridgwater and Wells branches. In this guise, it went on to survive until 1946 and, when withdrawn after spells at Bedford and Nottingham, it had clocked up over 1,600,000 miles.

By 1881 traffic on the Somerset & Dorset showed a ten-fold increase compared to 1874. The North Somerset Coalfield provided constantly-increasing mineral traffic, while the efforts of the joint proprietors secured a considerable amount of through traffic. To cope with the workload, the entire section between Midford and Templecombe was doubled between 1886 and 1894 and this involved widening the tunnel at Chilcompton and the construction of a second bore at Windsor Hill. The section between Bath and Midford remained single, largely because the prospect of widening Devonshire and Combe Down tunnels was far too daunting.

The Somerset & Dorset reached Bridgwater in 1890. On 21 July, the seven-mile single-track branch from Edington was opened by the Bridgwater Railway Company which, although a subsidiary of the joint lessors, was to retain its nominal independence until the grouping. Initially, the only intermediate station on the branch was at Cossington but a halt was to be constructed at Baw-

drip in October 1923. The station at Bridgwater was a single-platform affair and the yard housed a goods shed, an engine shed and a turntable; from the yard, a spur ran to a brickworks and a wharf on the River Parrett.

As the years progressed, the Somerset & Dorset's locomotive stock displayed

more evidence of Derby control but, paradoxically, the largest class of engines on the S&D was a batch of 28 0-6-0s, all of which were supplied by independent builders. The first six were built in 1878 by Neilson's of Glasgow and became known, not illogically, as 'Scotties'; the fact that the remaining members of the

Table One
Renaming of Somerset & Dorset Stations

Evercreech became Evercreech Junction (20 July 1874)
Wells suffixed Priory Road (October 1883)
Glastonbury suffixed and Street (July 1886)
Edington became Edington Junction (21 July 1890)
Shepton Mallett suffixed Charlton Road (16 October 1898)
Midsomer Norton became Midsomer Norton & Welton (16 October 1898)
Burnham became Burnham-on-Sea (12 July 1920)

Left:
This picture of Midford looks southwards. The viaduct beyond the station in the old shot carried the S&D over not only the road, but also the GWR branch between Hallatrow and Limpley Stoke. Although assurance has been received that this picture was taken during the 1920s, the inscription 'LMS' on the luggage trolley raises a few doubts. Lens of Sutton

Below:
The S&D station at Midsomer Norton received the suffix '& Welton' in 1898, but was to finish life as plain old Midsomer Norton South. Confusingly, in 1904 the GWR station in the town also adopted the handle of Midsomer Norton & Welton. This picture, which was taken in May 1929, shows S&D 0-6-0 No 72 piloting 4-4-0 No 44 on a train to Bath. The 0-6-0 was to survive until August 1962 as BR No 43216, while the 4-4-0, which was only 11 months old when this picture was taken, met its demise in November 1959 as BR No 40633. Photomatic

class were constructed by the Vulcan Foundry seemed to matter not one whit as these also became known as 'Scotties'. The six which were delivered in 1890, S&D Nos 56 to 61, were fitted from new with vacuum ejectors so that they could assist on passenger duties as required.

From the time of the joint agreement in 1875, the standard Midland livery of Light Green had been applied to the Somerset & Dorset locomotives and, when Head Office adopted the more-familiar Midland Red in 1883, the S&D stock was similarly treated. The individuality of the S&D was acknowledged in 1886 when the Prussian Blue livery of the old George England 2-4-0T was introduced for all locomotives and this was to be retained until 1930.

The first Derby products to be dispatched to the Somerset & Dorset were four 4-4-0s which were built in 1891 and, by 1928, a further 17 Derby-built 4-4-0s were in action on the line. Predictably, the 4-4-0s handled the faster passenger trains ('express' is a word not synonymous with the S&D) while, between 1896 and 1902, 10 standard 0-6-0s were supplied to augment the 'Scotties' on freight duties. The first five of the new 0-6-0s were built at Derby but the others, although virtually identical, were constructed by Neilsons. The Neilson 0-6-0s had originally been intended for the Midland itself and so, although sporting the letters 'S&DJR' on their tenders, they arrived in Somerset in Midland Red livery. A further five 0-6-0s which appeared in 1922 were built to a standard Derby design but constructed by Armstrong Whitworth. Similarly, seven standard '3F' 0-6-0Ts which appeared in 1928 and 1929 were the products of another outside builder, this time W. G. Bagnall.

Despite the extensive colliery shunting duties around Radstock, the Somerset & Dorset never kept more than three specialised shunters at the town at any one time. A 30-year-old Slaughter Gruning 0-4-0ST was purchased in 1882, and was joined in 1885 by a 0-4-2ST which had been assembled at Highbridge Works. On the demise of the original engine in 1895, Highbridge Works turned out a pair of 0-4-0STs and these soldiered on until 1929 when two Sentinel 0-4-0Ts were acquired. The reason why Sentinels were chosen was that their duties would include shunting under the less-than-generous clearance of Tyning Bridge, which was known locally as 'Marble Arch'. The older shunters had been constructed with the restricted height in mind and the Sentinels were one of the few types of locomotive that could squeeze under the bridge. Many years later, the departure of a Sentinel for repairs meant that the only suitable

replacement was a former Lancashire & Yorkshire 0-4-0ST. S&D nicknames were used with remarkable continuity and, when the Sentinels appeared, they were known as 'Dazzlers' despite their livery of unlined black. The nickname had originated with the earlier Radstock shunters on which an impressively-maintained Prussian Blue livery stood out clearly amidst the dust of the surrounding coalfield.

By 1911, the Somerset & Dorset locomotive department was in the charge of M.F.Ryan. The Superintendent at the time of the joint agreement, B.S.Fisher, had found the combination of increasing deafness and a penchant for taking short cuts when walking across Highbridge shunting yards to be, literally, fatal. Fisher's successor was W.H.French who, in turn, was succeeded by another ex-Midland man, Alfred Whitaker. In 1907, Head Office had offered Whitaker a choice of standard Midland 0-8-0s for the increasingly heavy freight trains on the Somerset & Dorset but the axle weights were considered too near the limits for comfort. When Ryan took over, he looked again at the idea of an eight-coupled engine and decided that, if a six ton reduction in weight on the coupled wheels could be brought about by the addition of a leading axle, such a locomotive would be ideal. Henry Fowler obliged, and the result was the S&D's most famous class of locomotives, the 2-8-0s.

Six of the 2-8-0s were delivered in 1914 and, with the use of Derby versions of Schmidt superheaters, they gave an impressive tractive effort of over 35,000lb. There was, however, one oversight. Access to the engine shed at Bath entailed crossing a bridge which could not take the heavy 2-8-0s. Until the bridge could be strengthened, the small shed at Radstock had to play host but, due to the restricted clearance in the shed, the engines had to suffer the indignity of having their cab roof vents and the

upper sections of their chimneys removed. After the initial embarrassment had been overcome, the 2-8-0s went on to perform superbly and five more examples, this time with larger boilers, were supplied by Robert Stephenson & Co in 1925. The only two real drawbacks of the 2-8-0s were their voracity for coal and their insistence on a high quality of diet. Their dislike of second-rate coal was demonstrated in 1929 when the crew of No 89 was overcome by smoke in the abysmally-ventilated Combe Down tun-

Table Two
Locomotive Classes of the Somerset & Dorset

Dimensions are for the locomotives as originally built. Letter classifications are used although they were not introduced until 1902.

Somerset Central Locomotives

Class	Wheel Arr	Builder	Driving Wheels	Cylinders (in)	Weight	Boiler Pressure	Water Capacity	Total Built
D	2-4-0	GE	7ft 0in	15x18(I)	25t 4c	115	630*	7
E	2-4-0WT	GE	5ft 0in	15x18(I)	28t 5c	115	705	1

Somerset & Dorset Locomotives

Class	Wheel Arr	Builder	Driving Wheels	Cylinders (in)	Weight	Boiler Pressure	Water Capacity	Total Built
9	2-4-0	GE	5ft 0in	16x18(I)	27t 4c	115	800*	2
11	2-4-0T	GE	4ft 0in	11x17(I)	17t 0c	n/a	520	1
12	2-4-0	GE	5ft 0in	16x18(I)	28t 5c	115	800*	4
16	2-4-0T	Bury	5ft 6in	14x18(I)	n/a	n/a	n/a	1(i)
B	2-4-0	GE	6ft 0in	16x24(I)	51t 0c	120	n/a	2(ii)
B	2-4-0	VF	5ft 0in	16x24(I))	54t 0c	120	1,575	2
G	0-6-0	JF	4ft 6in	17½x24(I)	57t 5c	140	n/a	6
K	0-6-0ST	FW	4ft 0in	17½x24(I)	45t 6c	140	1,205	9(iii)

Notes:
* Locomotives with four-wheel tenders.
(i) Built as a 2-2-0 for the South Eastern Railway in 1865.
(ii) Part of a cancelled order for 20 engines for the South Eastern Railway
(iii) One loco rebuilt as 0-6-0T and classified 'J'.

Somerset & Dorset Joint Committee Locomotives

Class	Wheel Arr	Builder	Driving Wheels	Cylinders (in)	Weight	Boiler Pressure	Water Capacity	Total Built
A	4-4-0	Derby	5ft 9in	18x24(I)	68t 18c	150	2,200	8
69	4-4-0	Derby	6ft 0in	18x26(I)	81t 6c	175	2,950	5
483	4-4-0	Derby	7ft 0½in	20½x26(I)	84t 1c	160S	2,950	5
563	4-4-0	Derby	6ft 9in	19x26(I)	95t 5c	180S	3,500	3
C	0-4-4T	AE/VF	5ft 3in	17x24(I)	43t 11c	140	876	13
C	0-4-4T	Derby	5ft 3½in	18x24(I)	50t 9c	150	876	1(iv)
G	0-6-0	N/VF	4ft 6in	17x24(I)	62t 11c	140	2,200	28
H	0-6-0	N/Derby	5ft 2½in	18x26(I)	71t 6c	150	2,950	10(v)
4	0-6-0	AW	5ft 3in	20x26(I)	88t 13c	175S	3,500	5
3F	0-6-0T	WGB	4ft 7in	18x26(I)	49t 10c	160	1,200	7
80	2-8-0	RS/Derby	4ft 7½in	21x28(o)	108t 19c	190S	3,500	11(vi)
5	0-4-0ST	SG	3ft 0in	10x14(o)	13t 15c	110	383	1
L	0-4-2ST	S&D	3ft 6in	10x14(o)	17t 3c	140	370	1
M	0-4-0ST	S&D	3ft 0in	10x14(o)	19t 8c	150	500	2
S	0-4-0T	S	3ft 2in	7x9(4)	27t 15c	275S	600	2

(iv) Replacement for one of other 0-4-4Ts which was scrapped in 1920.
(v) The five Neilson locomotives were paired with 3,250gal tenders and this increased their total weights to 76t 5c.
(vi) The five Stephenson locomotives had larger boilers and weighed 112t 15c.
S denotes locomotives built with superheaters.
Key: AE: Avonside. FW: Fox Walker. GE: George England. JF: John Fowler. N: Neilsons. RS: Stephensons. S: Sentinel. S&D: Highbridge. SG: Slaughter Gruning. VF: Vulcan Foundry. WGB: Bagnall

Table Three
Register of Somerset & Dorset Locomotives

Somerset Central Locomotives

Original No	Class	Built/ acquired	Rebuilt/ reboilered	Last S&D No	MR No	BR No	Withdrawn
1	D	1861					Sold 1874 Scr 1905
2	D	1861		25A			Scr 1882
3	D	1861					Sold 1874
4	D	1861					Sold 1874
5	D	1861					Sold 1874 Scr 1904
6	D	1861	1884	26A			Scr 1889
7	D	1861	1888	27A			Scr 1925
8	E	1861	1872/83/04	28A			Scr 1928

Somerset & Dorset Railway Locomotives

Original No	Class	Built/ acquired	Rebuilt/ reboilered	Last S&D No	MR No	BR No	Withdrawn
1	K	1874	1888/08	1	1500		Scr 1930
2	K	1874	1885/06	2	1501*		Scr 1930
3	K	1874	1893/11	3	1502		Scr 1930
4	K	1875	1890/09	4	1503*		Scr 1930
5	K	1875	1890/10	5	1504		Scr 1934
6	K	1876	1894/11	6	1505		Scr 1934
7	K	1876	1890/09	7	1506		Scr 1934
8	K(i)	1876	1889/08	8			Scr 1928
9	9	1863		29A			Sold 1878† Scr 1886
9	K	1876	1899/10	9	1507		Scr 1930
10	9	1863		10A			Sold 1878† Scr 1883
11	11	1863					Sold 1870
12	12	1864		12A			To LSWR 1878 Scr 1889
13	12	1864		13A			Sold 1878† Scr 1886
14	12	1864		14A			To LSWR 1878 Scr 1888
15	12	1864		11A			To LSWR 1878 Scr 1887
16	16	1865		19			Scr 1874
17	B	1865	1879	45			Scr 1897
18	B	1865	1879	18A			Scr 1897
19	B	1866	1880/02	15A			Scr 1914
19	G	1874	1888/08	19			Scr 1927
20	B	1866	1881/03	16A			Scr 1914
20	G	1874	1893/10	20			Scr 1928
21	G	1874	1893/11	21			Scr 1928
22	G	1874	1892/11	22			Scr 1928
23	G	1874	1892/10	23			Scr 1928
24	G	1874	1893/10	24			Scr 1928

Notes:

* Allotted numbers not carried.

† Sold to Midland Railway. S&D Nos 9/10/13 became MR Nos 1397/98/99.

(i) Reclassified 'J' when rebuilt as 0-6-0T in 1889.

Somerset & Dorset Railway Joint Committee Locomotives

Original No	Class	Built/ acquired	Rebuilt/ reboilered	Last S&D No	MR No	BR No	Withdrawn
5	5	1882	1883	45A			Scr 1895
10	C	1877	1891/07	10	1200*		Scr 1930
11	C	1877	1892/09	11	1201		Scr 1930
12	C	1877	1890/07	12	1202		Scr 1931
13	C	1877	1894/06	13	1203		Scr 1930
14	C	1877	1891/07	14A	1204*		Scr 1930
14	A	1897	1909/26	14	300*		Scr 1930
15	A	1891	1905/10	15			Scr 1928
16	A	1891	1906/10	16			Scr 1928
17	A	1891	1904/08/27	17	302		Scr 1931
18	A	1891	1904/11/28	15	301		Scr 1931
19	3F	1928		19	7150/7310(a)	47310	Scr 1962
20	3F	1929		20	7151/7311(a)	47311	Scr 1960
21	3F	1929		21	7152/7312(a)	47312	Scr 1961

THE LEGEND

Original No	Class	Built/ acquired	Rebuilt/ reboilered	Last S&D No	MR No	BR No	Withdrawn
22	3F	1929		22	7153/7313(a)	47313	Scr 1967
23	3F	1929		23	7154/7314(a)	47314	Scr 1966
24	3F	1929		24	7155/7315(a)	47315	Scr 1959
25	G	1881	1903				Scr 1928
25	3F	1929		25	7156/7316(a)	47316	Scr 1962
25A	L	1885	1896/06	25A			Scr 1929
26	G	1881	1897/08				Scr 1928
26A	M	1895		26A	1509*		Scr 1930
27	G	1881	1892/99	27			Scr 1914
28	G	1881	1891/00/08	28			Scr 1928
29	C	1877	1889/07	29A	1205		Scr 1930
30	C	1877	1893/06/28**	30A	1206		Scr 1932
31	C	1877	1891/10/28**	31A	1207		Scr 1932
32	C	1877	1893/07/28**	52	1230		Scr 1946
33	G	1878	1890	33			Scr 1914
34	G	1878	1891	34			Scr 1914
35	G	1878	1889/03	35			Scr 1922
36	G	1878	1889/98	36			Scr 1922
37	G	1878	1893/03/14	37			Scr 1922
38	G	1878	1897	38			Scr 1922
39	G	1879	1896	39			Scr 1925
40	G	1879	1890/98/08	67	2886		Scr 1930
41	G	1879	1896	41			Scr 1925
42	G	1880	1890/98	68	2887		Scr 1932
43	G	1880	1891/01	43			Scr 1914
44	G	1880	1890/08/14	69	2888		Scr 1930
44	563	1928		44	633	40633	Scr 1959
45	A	1897	1909/26	18	303		Scr 1932
45	563	1928		45	634	40634	Scr 1962
45A	M	1895		45A			Scr 1929
46	G	1884	1903	46			Scr 1925
46	563	1928		46	635	40635	Scr 1961
47	G	1884	1900	70	2889		Scr 1932
48	G	1884	1903	48			Scr 1925
49	G	1884	1903/28	71	2890		Scr 1932
50	G	1884	1901	51	2885		Scr 1931
51	G	1884	1903	51			Scr 1925
52	C	1884	1902	52			Scr 1928
53	C	1885	1902/25	53	1231		Scr 1930
54	C	1885	1907	54			Scr 1920
54	C	1921	1928**	54	1305		Scr 1931
55	C	1885	1906/25/27**	55	1232		Scr 1932
56	G	1890	1906	33			Scr 1928
57	G	1890	1906/28	34	2880		Scr 1932
57	4	1922		57	4557	44557	Scr 1962
58	G	1890	1909/29	35	2881		Scr 1932
58	4	1922		58	4558	44558	Scr 1964
59	G	1890	1907/28	36	2882		Scr 1932
59	4	1922		59	4559	44559	Scr 1963
60	G	1890	1908/27	37	2883		Scr 1932
60	4	1922		60	4560	44560	Scr 1965
61	G	1890	1908/28	38	2884		Scr 1932
61	4	1922		61	4561	44561	Scr 1962
62	H	1896	1923	62	3194	43194	Scr 1960
63	H	1896	1914/20	63	3198		Scr 1947
64	H	1896	1921	64	3201	43201	Scr 1957
65	H	1896	1921	65	3204	43204	Scr 1956
66	H	1896	1914/20	66	3211	43211	Scr 1961
67	A	1896	1907	67			Ren 1920
67	483	1921		41	324	40324	Scr 1953
68	A	1896	1908	68			Ren 1921
68	483	1921		42	325	40325	Scr 1951
69	69	1903		69			Ren 1921
69	483	1921		43	326	40326	Scr 1956
70	69	1903		70			Ren 1914

Original No	Class	Built/ acquired	Rebuilt/ reboilered	Last S&D No	MR No	BR No	Withdrawn
70	483	1914		39	322	40322	Scr 1953
71	69	1903		71			Ren 1914
71	483	1914		40	323	40323	Scr 1956
72	H	1902	1925	72	3216	43216	Scr 1962
73	H	1902	1924	73	3218	43218	Scr 1960
74	H	1902	1924	74	3228	43228	Scr 1952
75	H	1902	1924	75	3248	43248	Scr 1959
76	H	1902	1923	76	3260	43260	Scr 1949
77	69	1908	1926	77	320		Scr 1931
78	69	1908	1931	78	321		Scr 1938
80	80	1914		80	9670/13800(b)	53800	Scr 1959
81	80	1914		81	9671/13801(b)	53801	Scr 1961
82	80	1914		82	9672/13802(b)	53802	Scr 1960
83	80	1914		83	9673/13803(b)	53803	Scr 1962
84	80	1914		84	9674/13804(b)	53804	Scr 1962
85	80	1914		85	9675/13805(b)	53805	Scr 1961
86	80	1925		86	9676/13806(b)	53806	Scr 1964
87	80	1925		87	9677/13807(b)	53807	Scr 1964
88	80	1925		88	9678/13808(b)	53808	Wdn 1964 (Pres)
89	80	1925		89	9679/13809(b)	53809	Wdn 1964 (Pres)
90	80	1925		90	9680/13810(b)	53810	Scr 1963
101	S	1929		101	7190	47190	Scr 1961
102	S	1929		102	7191	47191	Scr 1959

* Allotted numbers not carried.
** Last rebuilding was as a motor unit.
(a) LMS renumbering 1936.
(b) LMS renumbering 1932.

Right:
The best-known of the S&D's locomotives were undoubtedly the 2-8-0s. Here No 86 (later BR No 53806) is photographed at Bath in March 1929 in a black livery, the Prussian Blue having been phased out for goods engines from 1924.
Photomatic

nel. The comatose duo had a rude awakening when the uncontrolled locomotive left the tracks on its approach to Bath.

The shed at Radstock which had presented a problem for the cosmetic appearances of the 2-8-0s was a twin-road stone-built structure to the east of the station. The shed at Bath was, with its four roads, the largest on the Somerset & Dorset and, with an allocation which regularly exceeded 50 locomotives, it has often been considered that such activity in and around the timber-built structure must have sent a shudder through the company's insurers. The 60ft turntable at Bath was originally situated between the entrances of the S&D and the Midland sheds and it was used by both companies. Templecombe shed was a timber-built twin-road affair with a 50ft turntable, and in the 1920s plans were discussed to make this depot the home of all of the S&D's locomotives, with the other sheds on the line being reduced to stabling points. Nothing came of the idea and the other S&D sheds in Somerset were retained. At Highbridge, the shed was adjacent to the works. It was a twin-road structure with a turntable of just under 50ft while Wells shed, again with two roads but devoid of a turntable, was slightly to the west of Priory Road station.

The idea for the 2-8-0s was, undoubtedly, a major landmark in the career of the Locomotive Superintendent, M. F. Ryan, but one of his other actions did rather less to preserve the tradition of the Somerset & Dorset. Very soon after he succeeded Alfred Whitaker, he set about running down the works at Highbridge. The premises had been opened in 1862, and had evolved in a piecemeal fashion over the years. At its peak, the workforce numbered almost 500, but apart from the assembly of the three shunters in the 1890s, the only building work carried out at the works was that of carriages and wagons. After Ryan's ratio-

nalisation, all construction of rolling stock was transferred to either Bristol or Eastleigh but the works remained open for routine repairs.

The Somerset & Dorset escaped the effects of the Grouping and, instead, became vested jointly in the Southern and the LMS on 1 July 1923. It was, unfortunately, a bad time to think about enhancing its air of independence, as the 1920s were the years when road transport started to provide serious competition to cross-country railways. Although the S&D was still a vital export route for Somerset coal, the passenger services were not the swiftest known to mankind. In the competitive pre-Grouping year of 1922, the fastest passenger service over the 71 miles from Bath to Bournemouth took almost two hours. Of the other nine

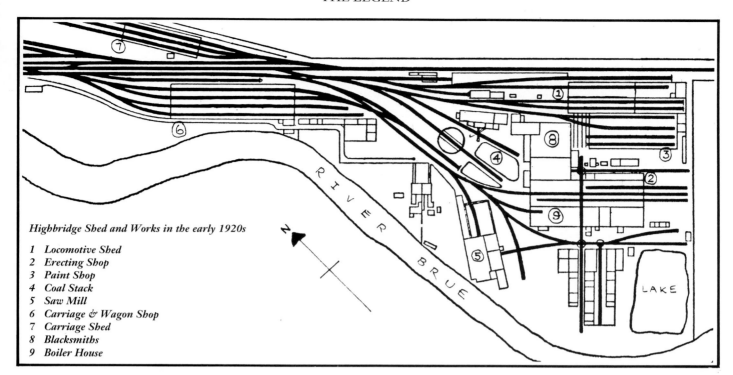

Highbridge Shed and Works in the early 1920s

1 Locomotive Shed
2 Erecting Shop
3 Paint Shop
4 Coal Stack
5 Saw Mill
6 Carriage & Wagon Shop
7 Carriage Shed
8 Blacksmiths
9 Boiler House

Right:

Highbridge works yard in May 1929 with 2-8-0 No 81 (later BR No 53801) watching its tender receive surgery. The engine shed can be seen in the middle of the frame, while in front of the water tower a trio of antique outside-framed tenders await attention. Photomatic

Below right:

Highbridge was the spiritual home of the Somerset & Dorset. In this late 1920s picture, the engine shed can be seen in the background and, judging by the number of idle locomotives, this shot must have been taken on a Sunday. On the left is 0-6-0 No 8, which started life in 1876 as an 0-6-0ST and was rebuilt as an 0-6-0T in 1898 before its final incarnation as a tender engine in 1908; it was withdrawn in 1928. Behind the 0-6-0 is 0-4-2ST No 25a, the Radstock 'Dazzler', which was built at the adjoining workshop in 1885. To the rear of the 'Dazzler' are two more 0-6-0s, the nearest of which is one of the '62' class of 1896/1902, while the rear one is a member of the '33' class of 1878-90. The 0-6-0ST on the right is one of the Fox Walker locomotives of 1874-76 showing off its longer tanks. In their original forms, the tanks of these 0-6-0STs extended only as far as the rear of the smokeboxes. Lens of Sutton

daily services, only one was scheduled at under three hours and two were timed for over four hours. Economies were needed and, on 1 January 1930, the LMS took control of the Joint Committee and, with it, the responsibility for locomotive and operational matters. The Southern retained responsibility for civil engineering. From 1924, S&D goods locomotives were painted in unlined black and, as a result of the reorganisation of 1930, the distinctive Prussian Blue livery disappeared from the passenger fleet as well.

BATH, TEMPLECOMBE, AND BOURNEMOUTH.

WEEKDAYS.

Edinburgh (Wav.) ....dep.	6U 0		9U45				10 12		9 45	
Glasgow (St. Enoch) ..	5U20		9U30 10U15						9 25	
Bradford ..	10U50		1 28		7 44		10 12		9 23	
Leeds ..	12X 5		3 6		8 15		10 47		2 55	
York ..	9I30		1 40		7 25				1 0	
Sheffield ..	1X15		4 42		9 46		11 48		3 17	
Liverpool (Central) ..	10P15			9V40	8 10		8 30		12 55	
Manchester Victoria ..	11Q45						9 33		1 15	
Central ..	12P 0			10M 0	8 55		9 55		1 50	
Mansfield ..	10b32		5 48		9 30		10 5		2 27	
Nottingham ..	11 50		7 40		10 35		12 0		3 30	
Derby ..	2X30		6 12 8 17		11 8		12 55		4 40	
Leicester ..	11A25		6 30				12 0		4 5	
Birmingham (New St.) ..	3X55		7 45 9 30	12 3	12I15		2I 5		5I35	
Worcester ..	3 50		7 52 8 38	11 30			1I30		4 48	
Cheltenham ..	5X 5		9 8 10 38	1 18		1I27	3I18		6I33	
Gloucester ..	5X27		9 25 10 54			1I42	3I33		6 46	
Bristol { Temple Mead ..dep.		6 45	9 10 10 35	1 18			3 48	5N10	7 20	
St. Philips .... ,,	5 50	7 30	9 18 11 30	1G 1 1 42			3 15	4 5 5 27	7 33	
BATH (Mid. Station) ..arr.	6 40	8 16	10 22 12 16	12G57 2 26	2 40		4 20 4 28 4 54	6 20	8 22	
BATH (Mid. Station) ..dep.	6 45	8 30	10 28 12 25	1 20 2 30	2 45 2 55	4 35	5I 0	6 30	3 30	
Midford ....arr.	6 56	8 41		1 31			5 11	6 41	3 41	
Wellow ..	7 3	8 48		1 39			5 18	6 48	3 48	
Radstock ..	7 12	8 57	10 48 12 46	1 48	3 16		5 28	6 58	3 57	
Midsomer Norton ..	7 20	9 5	12 53	1 56			5 37	7 6	4	
Chilcompton (for Downside College)	7 28	9 13	11 0	2I 4	Y		5 46	7 14	4 11	
Binegar ..	7 35	9 21		2 12			5 55	7 22	4 18	
Masbury ..	7 40	9 26	Z	2 18			6I 1	7 28		
Shepton Mallet ..	7 48	9 34	11 14 1 15	2 27	3 43	5 18	6 10	7 37	4 25	
Evercreech (New) ..	7 56	9 46	11 21 1 23	2 36			6 23	7 45	4 34	
Evercreech Junction ..	8 0	9 50	11 21 1 23	2 40	3 50	5 25	6 27	7 49	4 38	
Glastonbury & Street ..	8 32	10 34	12 43	3 12	5I 7		7I 5		10I 5	
Wells ..	8 50	11 0	1I 3	4I13	6I 3		7 44		10I28	
Bridgwater ..	10a 6	11 16	1 19	3 51	5 54		7 44			
Cole ..	8 13	10 2	11 41	2I53	4I 2		6 39	8I 1		
Wincanton ..	8 30	10 13	11 52	3I 5	4I13		6 50	8I15		
Templecombe (Upper Stn.) ..	8 37	10 20	11 59 1 46	3I12	4I20	5 42	6I57	6 22		
Barnstaple Junction ..	1I10		3I51 6I26	6I26						
Ilfracombe ..	2I20	4I10	4I46 7I20	7I20						
Henstridge ..	9 21	12I23	12I23 2 40			4I33	7 25			
Stalbridge ..	9 23	12I29	12I29 2I48			4I38	7I33	9 23		
Sturminster Newton ..	9 38	12I41	11 50 3I 0			4I45	6I19 7I43	9 33		
Shillingstone ..	9 47	12I51	11 56 3I 8			4I51	6I25 7I54	9 42		
Blandford ..	10 2	1I 5	12I 8 3 23			5I 4	6I39 8I11	9 57		
Spetisbury ..	10 9	1I12	1I12 3 30				8I19			
Bailey Gate ..	10 18	1I21	1I21 3 39				6 49 8I29	10I 9		
Wimborne ..	10C54	2G23	2G23 4G22			6G 2	7G31 9G13	10G 55		
Broadstone ..	10 27	1I30	1I30 3I48	4h 8		5I20	6I58	8I33	10I13	
Swanage ..	12I27	3I35	10I45	5J 0	5035	703S	8I20	10I14		
Weymouth ..	12I51	40 4	10I35	5J56	6031	7054	8038	9054		
Poole (Town) ..	10 36	1I38	12I30 3 56	4E14	4I34	5I28	7I 5	8I47	10I28	
Parkstone ..	10 44	1I47	12I52 4I 4	4030	4051	5I36	7019	8I54	10I35	
Branksome ..	10 49	1I53	12I58 4I 9	4036	4057	5I41	7024	9I 0	10I40	
BOURNEMOUTH (West) ..	10 54	1I 59	12I42 4I14	4g29	4I50	5I46	7I18	9I 5	10I45	
BOURNEMOUTH (West) dep.		6 55	9 30	10 25	9 35 11 45	12I10		1I15 4I 5	5I15	6 45
Branksome ..		6049	8039	10 0 4	9 39 11024			1I19 3017	5I19	6I50
Parkstone ..		6053	9 37	10 0 8	9 43 11028			1I24 4I12	5I23	6 54
Poole (Town) ..		7 7	9 44	10 37	9 50 11 58	12I24		1I32 4I18	5I29	7I 1
Weymouth ..			7020	9d20	8 35	110 5		12G 5I 2050		5015
Swanage ..			80 0	9d50	8 55	11 15		12G 0 3010	3055	4045
Broadstone ..		7 18		10d45	10 0	12I34		1I43 4I31	5I40	7I13
Wimborne ..		6G50			9G41	10G49	12G49 4G11	4G49	7G 0
Bailey Gate ..		7 29			10 11	12I45		1I58 4I40	5I53	7I25
Spetisbury ..		7 37			10 18			2I 6	6I 1	7I33
Blandford ..		7 47	10 12		10 27 12I24	12I55		2I18 4I55	6I12	7I42
Shillingstone ..		8 4	S		10 38	1I13		2I28 5I 9	6I26	7I56
Sturminster Newton ..		8 11			10 45	1I20		2I36 5I15	6I36	8I 4
Stalbridge ..		8 21			10 55	1I30		2I47 5I25	6I48	8I16
Henstridge ..		8 26			11 0			2I52	6 55	8I21
Ilfracombe ..							12I15	1I30	3I 5
Barnstaple Junction ..						7 56	1I 8	2I25	4I 3
Templecombe (Upper Stn.) ..		7 15	9 15		11 40	2I 0		4I10 5I40	6I10 7I40	9I 3
Wincanton ..		7 23	9 25		11 48	2I 9		4I19	6I19 7I49	9I11
Cole ..		7 31	9 35		11 56			4I25	6I28 7I57	9I19
Bridgwater ..		6 35		9 30	11 45			3I10	5I10 6I30	
Wells ..		7 0		9 55	12I 5			2I55	4I40 6I40	
Glastonbury & Street ..		7 50		10 14	12I26			3I56	5I13 7I11	
Evercreech Junction ..		7 50	9I50	10 49	12I 4 1I 2	2I24		4I33	6I38 8I 8	9I28
Evercreech (New) ..		8 10	10 13		12I13	2I31		4I45	6I45 8I15	9I34
Shepton Mallet ..		8 10	10 13	11 4	12I26 1I17	2I44		5I 1 6I 7	6I59 8I28	9I47
Masbury ..		8 22	10 25					5I12	8I35	
Binegar ..		8 28	10 31		12I39			2I57 5I17	7I11 8I45	
Chilcompton (for Downside College)		8 35	10 37		12I44			3I 3 5I22	7I17 8I51	
Midsomer Norton ..		8 43	10 43		12I50			3I 9 5I25 6I25	7I23 8I57	10I 5
Radstock ..		8 51	10 51		12I55			3I17 5I36 6I33	7I33 9I 5	10I13
Wellow ..		3 58	10 58					3I25 5I43	9I13	
Midford ..		9 3	11 3					3I30 5I48	9I15	
BATH (Mid. Station) ..arr.		9 15	11 15	11 40	12I24	1I15 1I52	3I43	6I 0 6I50 7I50	9I10 10I30
BATH (Mid. Station) ..dep.		9 50	11 48 12 0 12I30 12 40	1I23 2I 0	3I58	6I12 7I 5 8I45 10I 0	
Bristol { St. Philips ..arr.		10 46	12I46	2I 6 2I46	5812	7I 4 7I56 9I35	
Temple Mead ,,		10 37	1I12	3I30	4I52	7I30	10I48	
Gloucester ..arr.		11 15	12I43 1I20	2I57	5I28	8I 0 8I15	
Cheltenham ..		11I31	1I 2 1I35	3I13	5I39	8I10 8 40	
Worcester ..		12I26	3I 5 3I 5	5 41	6I42	9K 3	
Birmingham (New St.) ..		12I37	2I13 2I45	4 21	6I58	8I 0 8 55	
Leicester ..		2I46	4I49	5 57	8I16	1F35 1F35	
Derby ..		1I36	3I21 3I55	6I 7	8I24	11I 1 11I 1	
Nottingham ..		2I58	4I10 4 39	7I 1	8I49	11I33 11 33	
Mansfield ..		3I51	4I56 5I52	7I18	10I15	6T50	
Manchester { Central ..		4I25	4L50	8I45	10I25	5 15 5 15	
Victoria ..			6I15			6 27 6 27	
Liverpool (Central) ..		5I 0	5V24	9I30		7H 0 7H 0	
Sheffield ..		2I32	4I30 5I 0	6I46	9I17	1 47 1 47	
York ..		4I 0	6I10 7I31	7I31	12 17	3 13 3 13	
Leeds ..		4I 2	5I59 5I58	7I40	10I51	1e48 1e48	
Bradford ..		5I 1	6I35 6I35	8I27	10I55	2W45 2W45	
Glasgow (St. Enoch) ..		9I25				7I30	
Edinburgh (Wav.) ..		9I 2				7 12	

A Via Derby. Season Tickets are not available by this service unless so routed.

B Passengers for Bristol (St. Philips) leave Bath at 4.22 p.m.

C Saturdays only.

D Change at Poole.

E 12.7 p.m. on Saturdays.

F Via Derby. Arrives on Sundays at 12.10 a.m. (via Hinckley). Season Tickets are not available by this service unless so routed.

G Via Broadstone.

H Arrives 9.49 a.m. on Sundays.

I Exchange Station (L. & N.W.), via Thornhill.

J Arrives Swanage at 9.35, & Weymouth 9.31 p.m. until June 17th.

K 9.15 on Saturdays.

L Manchester (London Road) via Birmingham and L. & N. W. Line.

M Manchester (London Road) via L. & N. W. Line and Birmingham.

N 4.57 p.m. on Saturdays.

P On Sunday nights leaves Liverpool (Central) at 9.10 and Manchester (Central) at 10.40.

Q Sunday nights excepted.

R Mondays excepted.

S Stops at Sturminster Newton when required to take up Passengers for Bath and beyond.

T 11.11 a.m. on Sundays.

U Saturday nights excepted.

V Liverpool (Lime Street) via L. & N.W. Line & Birmingham.

W 2.23 a.m. on Sundays.

X On Sunday nights leaves Bradford at 9.25, Leeds 10.0, Sheffield 11.18, and on Monday mornings Derby at 12.40, Birmingham 2.15, Cheltenham 4.27, and Gloucester at 4.48.

Y Sets down Passengers on application being made to the Stationmaster, or at the Booking Office at Bath.

Z Sets down on Wednesdays and Saturdays only.

a 9.14 a.m. on Wednesdays.

b Leaves at 7.38 on Sunday nights.

d From May 1st to June 17th leaves Weymouth at 9.15, and Swanage at 8.55 a.m.

e Via Nottingham. Season Tickets are not available by this service unless so routed.

g Poole 4.21, and Bournemouth 4.34 p.m. commencing June 19th.

h Applies from June 15th only.

j 9.5 a.m. on Sundays.

4 The Independents

Not all railway companies were of the stature of the Great Western, the Midland or even the Bristol & Exeter and Somerset & Dorset. Most of Britain's railways started life as small autonomous concerns with aspirations of grandeur but, over the years, amalgamations and take-overs brought an end to the independence of the majority. The localised independents rarely had long lives. If a small company succeeded, a larger concern was usually waiting to take it over or, if a minnow failed, its bones could be bought by a predator at a knock-down price. The odds were stacked against small independents but, nevertheless, it was rare for one to pass completely into oblivion.

The West Somerset Mineral Railway

One of the few that was destined for an early demise was the West Somerset Mineral Railway which operated on and off for 53 years devoid of either a corporate or a permanent physical link with any other railway. The line was promoted by the Brendon Hills Iron Ore Co, which had been founded in 1853 by a syndicate of ironmasters based at Ebbw Vale in South Wales. Mining had been carried out intermittently on the Brendon Hills since Roman times and, with the technology of the mid-1800s which benefited industry in direct inverse proportion to the landscape, larger scale exploitation was planned and a railway was the logical method of transporting the ore.

The standard gauge line was opened between Watchet and Roadwater, complete with an intermediate station at Washford, in April 1857. The stations were not exactly the railway equivalent of the Savoy, but their very existences were

Right:
The ferocity of the rope-worked incline between Comberow and the top of Brendon Hill can be clearly seen in this picture which was taken circa 1895. Although now abandoned for some 80 years, the route of the incline can still be traced amidst the undergrowth without the need for a machete. Victor Bonham-Carter collection

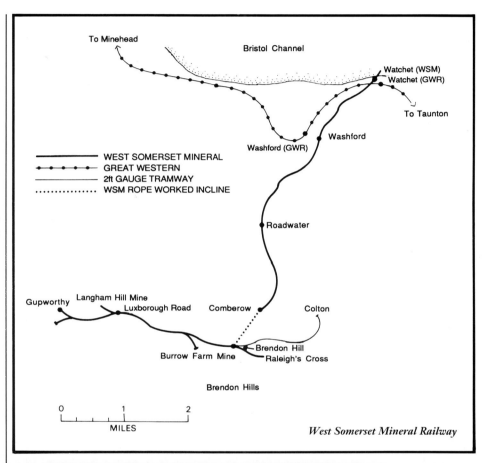

West Somerset Mineral Railway

	Fares.			From Taunton, &c., see above.	1.2.3	1.2.3	1.2.2	1.2.3	Sats. only.	1.2.3	Up.	1.2.3	1.2.2	1.2.2	1.2.3	Sats. only.	1.2.2	
Miles	1 cl. s.d.	2 cl. s.d.	3 cl. s.d.		mrn	mrn	aft	aft		aft		mrn	mrn	aft	aft		aft	
	0 4	0 3	0 2	Watchet ..dep	7 15	10 0	1 0	3 50		6 50	Combe Row d	8 5	11 0	2 0	5 10		7 30	....
	0 8	0 6	0 4	Washford......	7 25	10 10	1 10	4 0		7 0	Roadwater ..	8 15	1110	2 10	5 25		7 40	....
	1 0	0 9	0 6	Roadwater	7 35	10 20	1 20	4 10		7 10	Washford	8 25	1120	2 20	5 40		7 50	....
				Combe Row arr	7 45	1030	1 30	4 20		7 20	Watchet..arr	8 35	1130	2 30	5 50		8 0	....

Above:
Even the West Somerset Mineral Railway's passenger services found their way into Bradshaws. This 1874 timetable shows that, for a shilling (5p), one could spend 30 minutes travelling over the six miles between Watchet and Comberow.

surprising because the only passengers anticipated at first were the miners. This was emphasised on opening day, when it was considered that the customary pomp and ceremony would be wasted on a train of iron ore. At Watchet the much neglected harbour, complete with its fair quota of Bristol Channel silt, was entrusted to a board of commissioners on which the iron ore company was, conveniently, well represented. The new administration ordered the dredging of quays and approaches and the reconstruction of the West Pier for the anticipated traffic from the mines.

The railway was extended to Comberow, completing the 7½-mile run from Watchet, by the end of 1857, but its major obstacle lay ahead. The mines themselves were stretched out along the ridge at the top of Brendon Hill, some 800ft above sea level, and the connection between Comberow and the summit of Brendon Hill was made by the little matter of a ¾-mile incline on a one-in-four gradient. Although the rope-worked

incline was ready for action by May 1858, it was operated by a stationary engine until the impressive engine house was completed in March 1860. At the top of the incline, two branches extended from Brendon Hill; one ran four miles westwards to Gupworthy, the other eastwards for just half a mile to Raleigh's Cross mine.

As a carrier of iron ore, the railway served its purpose well and, in a fit of expansionism, its directors decided to offer a full passenger service between Comberow and Watchet. After the necessary upgrading of the line, a proper send-off was given to the inaugural passenger train on 1 September 1865. Four daily trains each way were scheduled and the time allowed was a sedate 40 minutes. The following year, a total of 13,000 passengers were carried and by 1872 that

Below:
When electrification rendered many of the Metropolitan Railway's steam locomotives redundant, several found new homes. Few, however, would have found such a contrast in habitat as No 37, which was bought by the West Somerset Mineral Syndicate for the reopening of the WSMR in 1907. Built by Beyer Peacock in 1881, it retained its Metropolitan number and condensing apparatus. In this picture it is seen at Roadwater on 3 July 1907, the day before the ceremonial reopening of the line. Bert Hole

figure increased to 19,000. On the section at the top of the incline, basic stations had been provided at Brendon Hill, Gupworthy and Luxborough Road since the opening of the line but no official passenger service had operated between them; the 'goods only' status of this upper section was not altered by the opening of the lower section to passengers. The formidable incline was, however, available for passenger movement, albeit highly unofficially. Mindful of both the legalities and the safety aspect, the company emphasised that these journeys were not only free of charge, but most definitely at the passengers' own risk.

In the mid-1870s, the import of cheap Spanish ore began to have a serious effect on the demand for home produced ore, and in May 1879, the Brendon Hills mines closed. Mining was, however, resumed a few months later but this new lease of life lasted only until 1883. Despite the lack of iron ore traffic after that date, passenger services were, surprisingly, retained with two daily trains each way which were scheduled to take 30 minutes on each run. Against the odds, the West Somerset Mineral Railway continued its passenger service between Comberow and Watchet until eventual closure on 7 November 1898. The surviving rolling stock was evacuated either to Ebbw Vale or to a Newport

Right:
*The West Somerset Mineral Railway's old
station at Washford was photographed on
3 September 1913, three years after closure.
This view was taken from the site of the level
crossing at the end of the station.*
LCGB/Ken Nunn collection

scrapyard via a temporary link with the Great Western at Kentsford, near Watchet. The two remaining locomotives were a Sharp Stewart 0-6-0ST named *Pontypool*, which had been delivered new in 1866 to work the lower section, and a primitive Neilson 0-4-0ST which was used on the upper section. A surprising total of eight engines, all 0-6-0STs or 0-4-0STs, had seen service on the WSMR between 1857 and 1898, but some were in action only as short-term replacements when the regular engines were away for surgery. Although there were two engine sheds, one at Whitehall near Watchet on the lower section, the other at Brendon Hill on the upper section, neither was equipped for anything more than basic maintenance.

This could well have been the end of the story for the line, but a new company, the West Somerset Mineral Syndicate, was formed in 1907 to reopen some of the mines and the still-intact railway was revived. On 4 July 1907, the ceremonial reopening train left Watchet for Comberow. It was hauled by a Beyer Peacock 4-4-0T which must have appreciated the Somerset air after 26 years of working through and under London in its former guise as Metropolitan Railway No 37. Four second-hand coaches had been acquired by the new company for passenger services and, much to the amusement of the miners, boasted three classes! The section of the line from the top of Brendon Hill incline to the Colton mines was laid with 2ft gauge tracks and worked by a pair of 0-4-0Ts but, like its predecessor, the new syndicate did not offer passenger services on this section. Unfortunately, the reprieve for the railway was brief; the mines stopped working

in 1910, and the plant and machinery were subsequently sold.

The rails, however, were left in situ and, in 1911, the lower line was pressed into action once more. This time, it was not for passenger services or ore trains but as a demonstration track for the Australian engineer, A. R. Angus, who wished to show off his new method of automatic train control. Between 1911 and 1914, various ATC trials took place with GWR 2-4-0s Nos 212 and 213, which had gained access to the WSMR over the reinstated 'temporary' link with the Minehead line at Kentsford. When Mr Angus had finished playing with the line and removed his paraphernalia, the West Somerset Mineral Railway was left to rust in peace. The rails were lifted in 1917 and dispatched to munitions factories, and on 2 August 1923 the Brendon Hills Iron Ore Co was formally wound up.

Railways to Avonmouth

The WSMR's unwanted distinction of disappearing from the railway maps in the days when complete closures were

rare was shared by the Avonmouth Light Railway, some seven miles to the west of Bristol. The ALR was opened in a piecemeal fashion between the years of 1908 and 1918. It ran from a junction with the joint GWR/MR line, just to the east of Avonmouth Dock station, and took a circuitous route to a point near St Andrew's Road. This journey was just one mile in length. The promoters' intention was to provide freight facilities for the industries which were emerging around the new dock at Avonmouth, but adequate traffic failed to materialise and so the ultimate dream, a link with the GWR's line to the Severn Tunnel, was never laid. Seldom used, the line was taken over jointly by the GWR and MR in 1927 but was reported to be abandoned just seven years later.

Avonmouth was the target of another small independent company. The steamer piers at Avonmouth offered deeper-water facilities than the old docks in the centre of Bristol and, with an eye on the potential of the piers and the possibility of their replacement by a new dock, the Bristol Port Railway & Pier was formed in 1862. The company proposed

Table One
Locomotives of the West Somerset Mineral Railway and its Successors

Name	Wheel Arr	Builder	Wks No	Driving wheel	Cylinders	Built	Acquired	Wdn
	0-4-0ST	Neilson	370	3ft 6in	11x18(o)	1856	1856	1897
	0-4-0ST	Neilson		3ft 6in	11x18(o)	1857	1857	1857
Rowcliffe	0-6-0ST	S/Stewart	995	4ft 6in	16x24(i)	1857	1857	1883
	0-4-0ST	Neilson		3ft 6in	11x18(o)	1861	1865	1883
Pontypool	0-6-0ST	S/Stewart	1677	4ft 7in	17x24(i)	1866	1866	1899
Esperanza	0-6-0ST	S/Stewart	2262	4ft 7in	17x24(i)	1872	1894	1894
Whitfield	0-6-0ST	S/Stewart	1011	4ft 7in	16x24(i)	1857	1895	1895
	0-4-0ST	Neilson		3ft 6in	11x18(o)		1896	1900
	4-4-0T	B/Peacock	1881	5ft 10in	17x24(o)	1879	1907	1910

Left:
Watchet (WSMR) station, which had closed along with the rest of the WSMR in 1910, presents a sad and sorry sight on 11 August 1935. Although the station itself has been cleared, the goods shed still stands on the right of the picture, and the continuation of the line through the gates to the harbour is clearly seen. Even today, it is not at all difficult to spot the former WSMR buildings on this site.
R W Kidner collection

Below:
The site of the Bristol Port Railway terminus at Hotwells (née Clifton) is still readily distinguishable in this picture, which was taken from the Clifton Suspension bridge in September 1990. The entrance to No 1 tunnel is visible beyond the station. The station closed in September 1921 to enable work to be started on the A4 Portway and trains subsequently terminated at Hotwells Extension platform which is at the other end of the tunnel and out of view. That platform succumbed in July 1922 when the section between Sneyd Park Junction and Hotwells was closed. Author

a line starting at Hotwells, a suburb about two miles to the west of Bristol city centre, and continuing along the north bank of the River Avon to Avonmouth. As the railway was intended to cater for local needs, the directors considered that a link to any other railway was as useful as a lifeboat station in Birmingham.

The line was completed early in 1865, but the hierarchy of the company was painfully aware that a sparseness of cash had necessitated a cut-back on frills. Rather than face embarrassment on the line's unveiling to the public, a low-key approach was adopted and the designated official opening day of 6 March 1865 was a very well kept secret. As a result, the BPR operated what must be one of the emptiest inaugural trains in railway history. The company's steamer pier at Avonmouth was opened in June and, despite the recurring problem of silting, it was kept busy by scheduled and excursion passenger traffic and freight.

The station at the Bristol end of the line, despite being in Hotwells, was named Clifton as it was felt that the upmarket image of that suburb would encourage passengers; the fact that Clifton was separated from the station by the sheer 250ft cliffs of the Avon Gorge mattered not one whit. Clifton station had one platform, a run-round loop and a carriage siding and the yard boasted a single-road engine shed which was home to two locomotives. The locomotives were the property of the contractors, Waring Bros., and were both 0-4-2Ts which had started life, one in 1853 and the other in 1854, as St Helen's Railway tender engines.

Beyond the station, the line ran through two short tunnels and followed

Mls	Fares.			Down.	gov	gov	aft	aft	aft	aft	aft		gov	aft	aft	aft	aft	aft	Up.	gov	non	aft	aft	aft	aft	aft		gov	aft	aft
—	1 cl.	2 cl.	3 cl.	Clifton ....dep	6 30	9 30	12 30	2 30	3 30	4 30	6 0	7 30	3 0	4 0	5 0	7 30	Avonmouth dep	9 0	12 0	2 0	3 0	4 0	5 0	7 0	2 39	30	6 30	7 0
2	0 6	0 4	0 3	Sea Mills	6 40	9 40	12 40	2 40	3 40	4 40	6 10	7 40	3 10	4 10	5 10	7 40	Shirehampton	9 7	12 7	2 7	3 7	4 7	5 17	7 7	2 37	37	6 37	7 7
3½	0 10	0 7	0 4	Shirehampton	6 48	9 48	12 48	2 48	3 48	4 48	6 18	7 48	3 18	4 18	5 18	7 48	Sea Mills	9 15	12 15	2 15	3 15	4 15	5 25	7 15	2 45	45	6 45	7 15
5½	1 0	0 9	0 6	Avonmouth arr	6 55	9 55	12 55	2 55	3 55	4 55	6 25	....	3 25	4 25	6 25	....	Clifton ....arr	9 25	12 25	2 25	3 25	4 25	5 35	7 25	2 55	55	6 55	7 25

Sea., Hew Dalrymple, Bristol.] BRISTOL PORT and PIER.

the bank of the river to Sea Mills station. The next station was Shirehampton where, in 1875, an engine shed was built to replace the one at Clifton which had burnt down two years earlier. Shirehampton shed was to prove similarly combustible in 1900; its replacement was opened at Avonmouth Dock station in 1905 leaving Sea Mills as the only station on the line not to have had the status symbol of an engine shed!

Despite the traffic generated by Avonmouth Pier, the Bristol Port Railway upheld the tradition of small Victorian railway companies in 1870 by going into receivership. It had suffered by not having a connection to the outside world,

and work on a proposed link to the GWR, although authorised in 1867, had been unable to be started. The BPR was rescued by the Great Western and the Midland, with whom a joint agreement was signed on 3 August 1870, and the

first thought of the new committee was to proceed with work on the link to the great beyond. Formally titled the Clifton Extension Railway, the four-mile link line was constructed to join the BPR at Sneyd Park to the GWR at Ashley Hill and also the Midland at Eastville. It was to be standard gauge throughout and the first section, between Ashley Hill and Clifton Down, was opened to passengers on 1 October 1875. An intermediate station was provided at Montpelier and was joined, in 1897, by another at Redland. Despite Cliftonians now having their own station in their exclusive enclave, another 15 years were to elapse before the original BPR terminus, Clifton, was to be renamed, more accurately, Hotwells. Between Clifton Down and Sneyd Park, the standard of the work on a tunnel and the layout at the junction with the original BPR line did not find favour with the Board of Trade inspectors and, although freight services commenced on that section on 24 February 1877, it was 1 September 1885 before the first passenger service operated over the entire length of the CER.

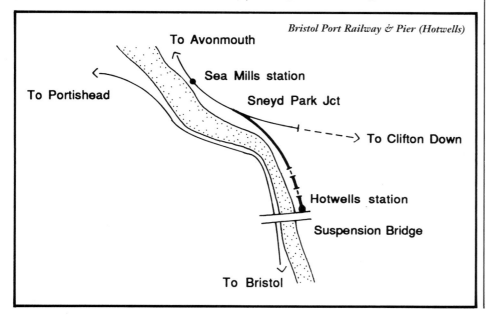

Bristol Port Railway & Pier (Hotwells)

To Avonmouth

Sea Mills station

Sneyd Park Jct

To Portishead

To Clifton Down

Hotwells station

Suspension Bridge

To Bristol

The formal take-over of the old Bristol Port Railway by the joint companies did not come about until 1 September 1890. From that date, the arrangement was that the Midland looked after the permanent way while the Great Western supplied the rolling stock. The GWR wasted no time in disposing of the two former contractor's locomotives; tank engines were the usual replacements and '517' class 0-4-2Ts and 'Metro' 2-4-0Ts are known to have been allocated to both Shirehampton and Avonmouth sheds. On the innovative side, railmotors were introduced on the Clifton Down line in 1911, but were withdrawn from the service two years later.

A new non-tidal dock had opened at Avonmouth in 1877, the same year as the first through freight trains had used the Clifton Extension Railway and, in 1903, work started on the adjacent Royal Edward Dock. The original Bristol Port Railway station at Avonmouth occupied a space which was designated for the new development and this necessitated truncating passenger services at Avonmouth Dock station which had been opened as joint GWR/MR premises in 1877.

Until the Great Western opened its Avonmouth & Severn Tunnel Railway in 1900, the Clifton Extension Railway and, earlier, the Bristol Port Railway had each enjoyed monopolies of the dock traffic in their respective days. The arrival of the newcomer provided a better escape route from the docks and, with the opening of the even faster Filton route in 1910, the CER was relegated to the second division. Traffic on the section of the original BPR line into Hotwells declined, although it had a burst of popularity towards the end of World War 1 when it was used extensively by workmen. This even necessitated the construction, in 1917, of Hotwells Extension platform northwest of the tunnels in order to accommodate the trains of eight bogie coaches which were needed to cope with the demand.

By 1920 road transport had begun to provide serious competition for the railways, and new road access to Avonmouth Docks was considered necessary. The obvious route for a trunk road was through the Avon Gorge over land which was occupied by the Bristol Port Railway and, not surprisingly, the railway had to give way. Bristol Corporation bought the railway land in 1920 and opened its road, now the A4 Portway, two years later. The last train left Hotwells on 1 July 1922 and, ironically, this was from the five-year-old Extension platform. The site of the original station had, by that time, been largely covered by the new road.

There was, however, another railway which continued operating in Hotwells until 1934. This was the Clifton Rocks Railway which operated on a 1 in 2.2 incline through a 500ft tunnel carved out of the Avon Gorge. Building started in 1891, and the railway was intended not as a tourist attraction, but as an everyday means of transport. Those upmarket residents of Clifton had resisted attempts by the Bristol Tramway Co to operate services into the suburb for fear of opening it to the working classes and the Rocks Railway would provide Cliftonians with 'suitable' access to the outside world. The railway was worked on a gravity system with water for ballast but was in decline even before 1922, when the laying of the main road through the Avon Gorge left the doors of its lower station just inches from passing traffic. The road which spelt the end for the Bristol Port Railway's original line was also a nail in the coffin for the dying Rocks Railway.

The Weston, Clevedon & Portishead

No tale of independent and light railways would be complete without a special guest appearance of Colonel Holman Frederick Stephens. The Colonel, who controlled his empire from Tonbridge in Kent, was the doyen of light railway promoters and managers, but even his expertise could not save the Weston, Clevedon & Portishead Light Railway; he was appointed to the ailing company in 1911 and, despite his military-style leadership which had been the saviour of other light railways, the WC&PR was to remain in receivership for the rest of its existence.

The Weston, Clevedon & Portishead was the brainchild of local businessmen who felt that they could capitalise on Brunel's policy of serving towns with branches, rather than diverting a broad gauge main line itself. When plans for the company were first mooted in 1870,

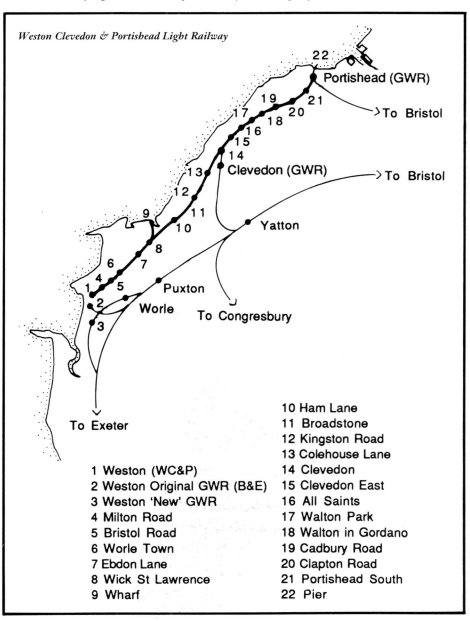

Weston Clevedon & Portishead Light Railway

1 Weston (WC&P)
2 Weston Original GWR (B&E)
3 Weston 'New' GWR
4 Milton Road
5 Bristol Road
6 Worle Town
7 Ebdon Lane
8 Wick St Lawrence
9 Wharf
10 Ham Lane
11 Broadstone
12 Kingston Road
13 Colehouse Lane
14 Clevedon
15 Clevedon East
16 All Saints
17 Walton Park
18 Walton in Gordano
19 Cadbury Road
20 Clapton Road
21 Portishead South
22 Pier

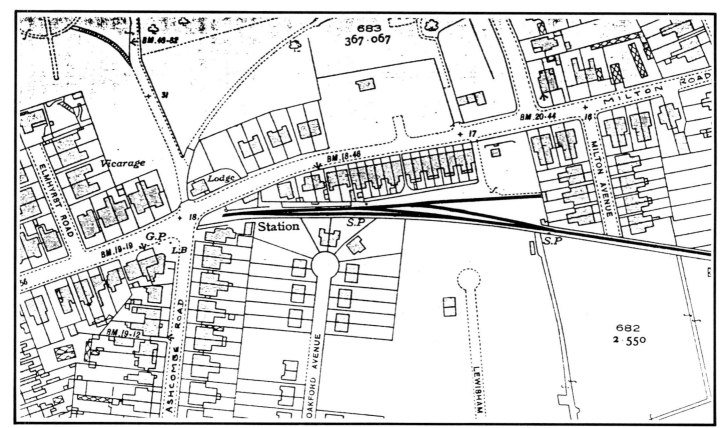

Above:
Weston-super-Mare (WC&P) Station, 1936.
The layout of Ashcombe Road station and yard
can be clearly seen just four years before closure.
Crown Copyright

all three towns in the proposed company's title were accessible only by branches from the Bristol & Exeter main line and, with the growing popularity of those towns as holiday resorts, travel between them involved long-winded journeys.

The WC&PR gained assent as a tramway company in 1885, by which time Weston had been treated to a through station by the Great Western. After financial problems in which the 'downs' outnumbered the 'ups', and also running battles with highly dissatisfied Board of Trade inspectors, the 8¼-mile stretch between Weston and Clevedon was finally covered by a test train on 18 August 1897. A ceremonial train was run on 7 October, but safety work on the line had not, at that stage, been finished and it was 1 December before the first revenue earning train completed the course. Eventually, the service became standardised at six trains each way during the winter months but this doubled during the summer. The scheduled journey time was usually 45 minutes and the fare was one shilling (5p).

At Weston, the station was at Ashcombe Road, less than a mile from the

Above:
Ashcombe Road was the terminus of the
WC&PR at Weston-super-Mare. In this view
0-6-0ST No 5 waits to leave with its train for
Clevedon on 22 May 1929. The locomotive was
bought new from Manning Wardle in 1919 but,
although it lasted until the WC&PR was
acquired by the GWR, the powers at Swindon
wasted no time in selling it. H C Casserley

Great Western station and, to the east of the Weston, Clevedon & Portishead station, a tramway provided a connection of sorts with the GWR until 1899. Between Weston and Clevedon, there were stations at Worle, Wick St Lawrence and

Kingston Lane and halts at Milton Road, Ebdon Lane, Ham Lane and Colehouse Lane. Further halts at Bristol Road and Broadstone were to be opened in 1912 and 1927 respectively while, in 1918, a spur was to be built from Wick St Lawrence to a wharf on the River Yeo. Clevedon was the head office but, although its station had only one platform, the yard boasted a two-road engine shed and a three-road carriage shed. Behind the sheds, a tightly-curved loop was laid to provide a link with the GWR but, in practice, this was rarely used. The GWR insisted that any movement on the loop was most definitely at the

Below:
The WC&PR station at Clevedon is seen from the direction of Portishead on 25 June 1938. The 'No thoroughfare' sign on the left is at the entrance to the sheds. Parts of the station site are still just about distinguishable today, but it takes a dedicated railway archaeologist to sort out what is what. H C Casserley

Left:
The WC&PR sheds at Clevedon were near the end of their existence when photographed on 15 June 1938. The carriage shed is on the right of the frame and the engine shed is left of centre; behind the water tower is the station. The locomotive standing near the water tower is one of the ex-LB&SC 'Terriers'. H C Casserley

Right:
The WC&PR station at Portishead was photographed soon after opening in 1907. To the left of the picture, the line trundles to Clevedon while, to the right, the nearest track continues to join the GWR at Portishead Dock. The best traditions of Light Railway engineering are evident in the apparent frailty of the track.
Lens of Sutton

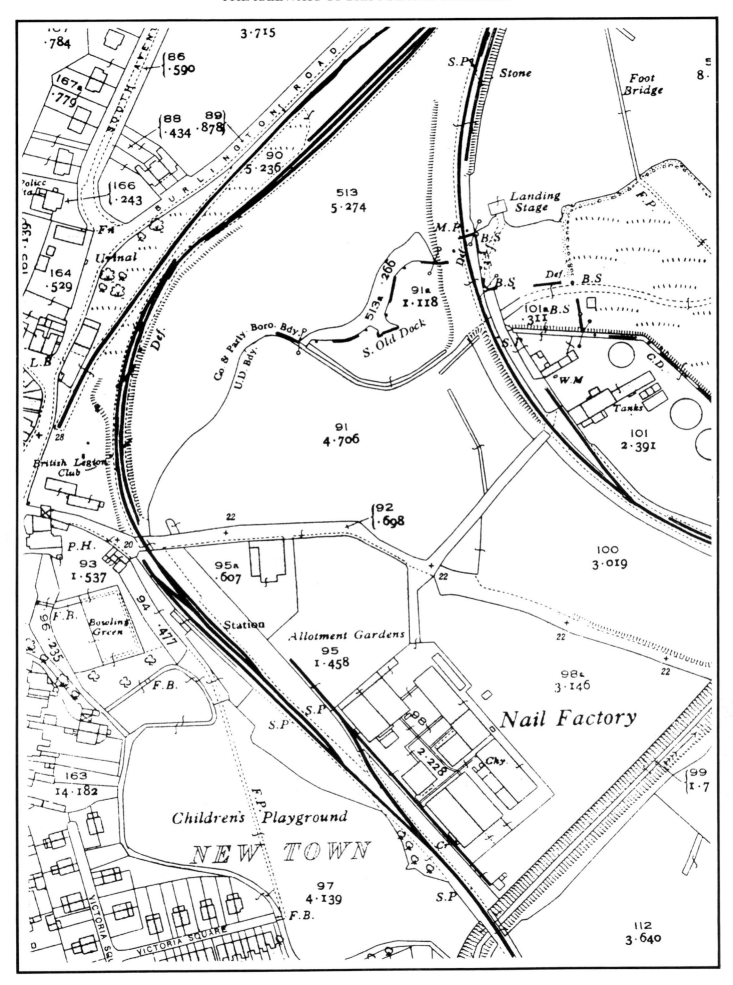

Left:
Portishead (WC&P) Station, 1931. The station can be seen just above the nail factory. The loop continuing northwards from the station is marked 'defunct'; it linked up with the GWR station which is just off the upper edge of the map. The line in the right-hand side of the map is the GWR line. Crown Copyright

WC&PR's own risk and it has been suggested that the problem with the curvature was why some of the WC&PR 0-6-0Ts came to have their rear coupling rods removed to enable them to operate, nominally, as 0-4-2Ts.

At the time of the opening of the first section, work on the extension between Clevedon and Portishead had still not started. Even in those days when the word 'environment' usually had to be looked up in the dictionary, the residents of the Gordano Valley were strongly opposed to the horrors of a railway carving up their landscape, and it took a long time for the Weston, Clevedon & Portishead to overcome the objections. The extension was not opened to traffic until 7 August 1907, by which time the company had enjoyed the status of Light Railway, instead of Tramway, for eight years almost to the day.

The new section had an intermediate station at Walton Park and halts at Clevedon East, Walton-in-Gordano, Cadbury Road, Clapton Road and Portishead South; All Saints' halt was to be added in 1927. Between Cadbury Road and Clapton Road halts, interchange sidings with the 2ft gauge tramway lines into Black Rock Quarry were established in 1919 and, at Walton Park, a siding led to Conygar Quarry, At Portishead, the line continued past the single-platform station to connect with the GWR branch from Bristol; the original intention of the connection was to take passengers to a steamer pier but there is no record of the WC&PR ever having graduated to the running of boat trains. At Clevedon, the line crossed a road junction in the town centre and, as a safety precaution, it was stipulated that the maximum speed over the road was to be 4mph and that all trains should be led by a railway official carrying a red flag. This practice quite

Below:
This timetable for the WC&PR shows the services for the summer of 1922. Seven of the line's halts are listed underneath as request stops.

Bottom:
The WC&PR obtained an 1876 Sharp Stewart 2-4-0T in 1911. It had started life with the Watlington & Princes Risborough Railway and, along with its owners, had passed into the GWR fold in 1883 where it became No 1384. It worked on the Wrington Vale Light Railway and the Culm Valley line in Devon before being sold to the Bute Works Supply Co in 1911, and it was from that company that the WC&PR acquired it. Colonel Stephens was a classical mythology buff and he selected the name **Hesperus** ***for the locomotive when it arrived in Somerset. Here, it is seen at Clevedon on 22 May 1929.*** H C Casserley

PORTISHEAD, CLEVEDON, and WESTON-SUPER-MARE.—Weston, Clevedon, and Portishead.
Gen. Man. and Eng., H. F. Stephens, Tonbridge, Kent.

Miles	Down. Week Days only.	mrn	mrn	mrn	mrn	aft	aft		m	aft	aft		
	Portishead .... dep.	....	8 45	....	1040	....	1 20	....	3 52	....	8 45	....	....
½	Portishead S. (Portb'y Rd.)	....	8 48	....	1043	....	1 23	....	3 55	....	8 48	....	....
2¼	Cadbury R. (W'ton-in-Gor-	....	8 55	....	1050	....	1 30	....	c	....	8 55	....	....
4	Walton-in-Gordano..[dano)	....	8 59	....	1054	....	1 34	....	c	....	8 59	....	....
5	Clevedon (All Saints')	....	9 5	....	11 0	....	1 40	....	4 12	....	9 5	....	....
5¼	Clevedon East	....	9 7	m	11 3	m	1 42	....	4 14	....	9 6	....	....
6	**Clevedon 41**	8 5	9 19	9 33	1115	1235	1 55	....	4 30	6 35	9 20	....	....
8	Kingston Road	8 11	....	c	1120	c	2 0	....	c	6 40	9 27	....	....
10¼	**Wick St. Lawrence**	8 22	....	9 44	1127	1246	2 8	....	4 41	6 47	9 35	....	....
12¼	Worle Town	8 30	....	9 51	1134	1253	2 14	....	4 49	6 54	9 46	....	....
12¾	Bristol Road .... [12	8 33	....	9 54	1137	1256	2 17	....	4 52	6 57	9 49	....	....
14¼	**Weston-super-Mare**.‡arr.	8 45	....	10 5	1145	1 5	2 25	....	5 5	7 5	10 0	....	....

Miles	Up. Week Days only.	mrn	mrn	mrn	aft	aft	aft	aft	aft	aft		
	Ashcombe Road Sta., **Weston-super-Mare**..dep.	9 0	1015	11 55	1 15	2 35	....	5 20	7 25	1015	....	....
1½	Bristol Road	9 6	1021	12 0	1 20	2 40	....	5 25	7 30	1020	....	....
2	Worle Town	9 9	1024	12 3	1 23	2 43	....	5 28	7 33	1023	....	....
4	Wick St. Lawrence........	9 17	1031	12 11	1 30	2 50	....	c	7 40	1030	....	....
6¼	Kingston Road..........	9 24	c	12 16	c	2 57	m	5 40	7 47	1035	....	....
8¼	**Clevedon 35**	9 35	1050	12 30	1 45	3 7	3 15	5 50	8 0	1045	....	....
9	Clevedon East..........	9 38	m	12 33	m	....	3 18	m	8 3	....	....	....
9¼	Clevedon (All Saints')	9 40	....	12 35	....	....	3 20	....	8 4	....	....	....
10¼	Walton-in-Gordano..[dano	9 45	....	12 41	....	....	c	....	8 9	....	....	....
11¾	Cadbury R. (W'ton-in-Gor-	9 49	....	12 45	....	....	c	....	8 13	....	....	....
13¾	Portishead S. (Portb'y Rd.)	9 54	....	12 49	....	....	3 35	....	8 20	....	....	....
14¼	**Portishead *49** ...... arr.	10 2	....	12 55	....	....	3 45	....	8 30	....	....	....

c Stops when required. m Motor Car, one class only. * ¼ mile to G. W. Station. ‡ Ashcombe Rd. Station.
*** All trains call at Clapton Road, Walton Park, Colehouse Lane, Broadstone, Ham Lane, Ebdon Lane, and Milton Road when required.

probably had a certain appeal for Colonel Stephens.

The extension emptied the corporate coffers, and in 1910, the company went into receivership. The arrival of Colonel Stephens the following year saw the advent of every cost-cutting exercise known in the Light Railway book of words but his entrance coincided with a period when road transport was on the increase and it was a losing battle. By 1922, there were just four through trains daily and the fastest took one hour — hardly the stuff to encourage car drivers or charabanc passengers to defect to the railway. At the Grouping, the Great Western shunned the WC&PR and, as if to emphasise its humble status, the line was ignored by the Ministry of Transport when government control of the country's railways was introduced at the outbreak of war in 1939. The sole creditor applied for winding up and, at 6.15pm on 18 May 1940, the last train left Weston for Clevedon.

The Great Western bought the assets the following month, not with a view to reopening, but simply for using the track for storage of coal trains which had been abandoned at South Wales ports when war had broken out. Of the rolling stock acquired, the GWR expressed its opinion of its inheritance by sending everything except two locomotives to the scrapyard. These were both Stroudley 'Terrier' 0-6-0Ts which had been built for the London, Brighton & South Coast Railway in 1875 and 1877 and had been bought second-hand by the Weston, Clevedon & Portishead. The GWR took them into stock as Nos 5 and 6, the former retaining the name *Portishead*, and both were to survive to see the formation of British Railways in 1948. Both 'Terriers' had arrived at Clevedon in Southern green, which helped the WC&PR coffers as, by the mid-1920s, green had replaced dark crimson as the light railway's standard livery. The exact shade of green worn by the WC&PR's locomotives and rolling stock tended, however, to vary as paint was considered to be too expensive for application either evenly or regularly. A total of 15 different locomotives, excluding rail tractors, had seen service on the WC&PR, and all but two were second-hand acquisitions. Between them, they offered a lesson in British railway history, with the Furness Railway and the Jersey Railway among their original owning companies.

The coaching stock offered little more in the way of standardisation than did the locomotives. Purchases from the London & South Western, the Great Eastern, the Taff Vale and the Metropolitan Railways

all appeared at one time or another, but the height of luxury was provided by six coaches which had been built for a South American railway. These carriages presented rather a bizarre sight on an English country railway as they had, at each end, open observation platforms

guarded by wrought iron railings. This feature was, however, well suited to the WC&PR as the company's intermediate 'stations' were often little more than roadside halts devoid of raised platforms, and so the steps from the coaches' observation platforms proved very useful for access. Three of these coaches were still in service in 1940 to claim the distinction of being present at both the grand opening and the unheralded demise of one of the country's typical light railways.

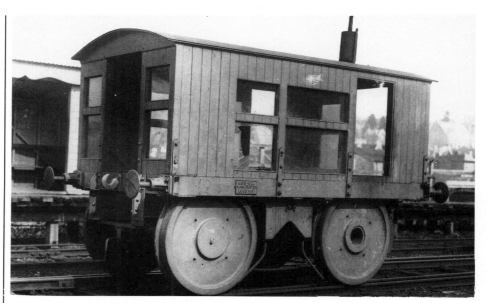

Above right:
When it realised that it would never secure the services of Nigel Gresley as its CME, the WC&PR continued its policy of gathering its motive power from whatever sources were available. It bought its first Muir-Hill Fordson rail tractor in 1925, but that one came to a sticky end in an accident the following year. Its replacement carried works No A137, and was a standard petrol-driven water-cooled vehicle weighing around four tons. It was intended for use on the Wick St Lawrence wharf branch, and so its arrival at Clevedon for this photograph in 1927 represented a major excursion for the beast. Photomatic

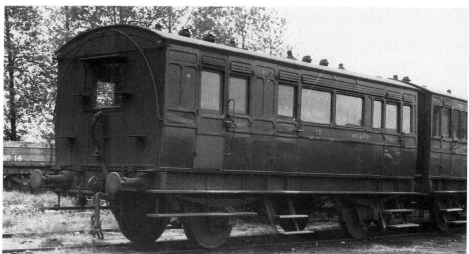

Right:
The WC&PR's coaching stock was not in the Pullman league. Three ex-L&SWR coaches were bought from the Southern in 1924 and were usually used together. The coach in the picture, No 15, accommodated first and second-class sections and also the guard's compartment. The low steps were a feature of all of the WC&PR's coaches as its stations and halts were, in the main, on street level. This picture was taken at Clevedon on 25 June 1938. H C Casserley

Table Two
Steam Locomotives of the Weston, Clevedon & Portishead Light Railway

Listed in order of acquisition

No	Name	Wheel Arr	Builder	Driving Wheels	Cylinders	Built	Acquired	Withdrawn
1	Clevedon	0-6-0T*	Walker Bros	4ft 0in	14x18(i)	1897	1897	1898
1	Clevedon	2-2-2WT	S/Stewart	5ft 6in	14x20(i)	1857	1898	1901
2	Weston	2-2-2WT	S/Stewart	5ft 6in	15x18(i)	1866	1899	1904
	Portishead	0-6-0T	Stephenson	3ft 6in	14x18(i)	1887	1899	1906
1	Clevedon	2-4-0T	Dubs	4ft 0in	10x19(o)	1879	1906	1940
2	Portishead	0-6-0ST	M/Wardle	3ft 0in	12x17(i)	1890	1907	1926
	Walton Park	0-6-0ST	H/Clarke	3ft 7in	14x20(o)	1908	1908	1917
4	Hesperus	2-4-0T	S/Stewart	4ft 0in	12x18(i)	1876	1911	1937
5		0-6-0ST	M/Wardle	3ft0in	12x18(i)	1919	1919	1940
2	Portishead	0-6-0T	LBSC	4ft 0in	14x20(i)	1877	1926	1954
3	Weston	0-6-0ST	M/Wardle	2ft 10^{1}/2in	13x18(i)	1881	1930	1940
4		0-6-0T	LBSC	4ft 0in	12x24(i)	1875	1937	1948

* Ran as a 2-4-0.

Other Locomotives of the Weston, Clevedon & Portishead Light Railway

Builder	Wks No	Type	Built	Acquired	Wdn
Drewry	1252	30hp Petrol railcar	1921	1921	1940
Drewry	1650	50hp Petrol railcar	1928	1934	1940 (Purch from SR)
Muir-Hill		Fordson rail tractor	1925	1925	1926 (Accident damage)
Muir-Hill	A137	Fordson rail tractor	1926	1926	1940

5 The Legacies

The Grouping of Britain's railways took effect on 1 January 1923 and the newly formed 'Big Four' inherited the legacies of countless smaller companies. By the close of play in 1922, five different railway companies were operating in Bristol and Somerset, but the Grouping made little immediate difference to any of them. The Great Western carried on almost unaffected, the Midland continued to be administered from Derby under its new owners, the London Midland & Scottish Railway, and the London & South Western became part of the Southern Railway. The Somerset & Dorset Railway was vested jointly to the LMS and SR, but retained its own identity right down to its locomotive livery, while the only surviving independent, the Weston, Clevedon & Portishead Railway, continued its perpetual struggle in receivership.

After 1923, the Great Western introduced standardised departure times for its main line expresses, those leaving Paddington for Bristol being scheduled to leave at 15 minutes past the hour, while West of England trains, many of which were routed through Bristol, left at 30 minutes past. This provided the citizens of Bath and Bristol with an excellent choice of fast trains. The GWR's cut-off route through mid-Somerset was used by the high-profile boat trains between Paddington and Plymouth and, with the introduction of the celebrated 'King' class 4-6-0s in June 1927, times of under four hours to Plymouth were recorded regularly. Between Paddington and Taunton, the 'Kings' were allowed 500 tons behind the tender and this compared with the 455 tons of the 'Castles' and the 420 tons of the 'Stars'. When the 'Kings' were in the planning stage in the winter of 1926, only four bridges on the Taunton cut-off route remained to be strengthened to accept the 22½-ton axle weight of the new locomotives, and the necessary work on these bridges was completed early in 1927.

Not content with its new flagships, the Great Western made repeated efforts to improve the performance of the locomotives even more and, when tests were required, the fast line through Stoke Gifford and Badminton was often used as the testing ground. By 1927, the GWR's roster of non-stop services was impressive. Among them, Bristol had four non-stop two-hour services from Paddington, two

Below:
This picture of the Royal Edward Passenger terminus at Avonmouth Dock was taken in September 1922, just three months before the Grouping. The size of the station reflects its importance as a Trans-Atlantic terminal, and the 'Ocean Mails' coach nearest the camera confirms the station's status. The Grouping affected the comings and goings at this station very little as it was already in joint use by the GWR and the Midland, while haulage in the dock area was entrusted to the port authority shunters. Port of Bristol Authority

Right:
This photograph of Templecombe (Southern) station was taken very early in the post-Grouping era, well before the rebuilding of the station in the 'Southern Odeon' style in 1938.
Lens of Sutton

Below:
'H15' class 4-6-0 No 330 looks remarkably macho while passing the level crossing at Hewish, near Yeovil, on 2 August 1928. The first 10 locomotives of this class appeared in 1913, and were the first to be designed by Urie for the L&SWR, but No 330 was one of the batch which were rebuilt in 1924 from Drummond 4-cylinder 4-6-0s of 1905.
H C Casserley

via Bath and two via Badminton while a total of 11 trains ran non-stop to Taunton on the cut-off line.

The Southern's answer to the Great Western's 'Kings' was a batch of 16 'Lord Nelson' class 4-6-0s, most of which were drafted on to West of England services through southern Somerset. To the north of Bristol, the GWR and the LMS competed on the Birmingham route but the first 30 miles from Bristol involved both companies running on the former Midland Railway line. It was not until 1924 that the LMS started using the famous 4-4-0 Compounds on this line and, until the strengthening of Stonehouse viaduct in 1927, the heaviest GWR locomotives permitted were the 'County' class 4-4-0s. One problem on the line northwards from Bristol was the bank between Barrow Road and Fishponds, and even the Compounds were restricted to 300 tons unaided. When the '5XP' 'Patriot' 4-6-0s started work on the line in 1931, they were allowed 380 tons, which compared with the 345 tons permitted for the 'Black 5s' when they emerged in 1934. Despite the loading restrictions, it was known that a 'Black 5' once managed 420 tons up the bank without assistance.

Until the arrival of 4-6-0s in the 1930s, Barrow Road's stock of locomotives was hardly the most modern on the LMS. A number of the Johnson singles remained

Left:
Southern Railway 'S11' class 4-4-0 No 399 receives attention under the sheer-legs at Yeovil Town shed on 21 May 1935. Designed by Drummond and built in 1903, the 10 members of the class were superheated by Urie in 1920-22. During World War 2 they were all loaned to the LMS for work on the Somerset & Dorset line. H. C. Casserley

at the shed until after the Grouping and one of the very last Kirtley single-framed 2-4-0s, the 61-year old No 92 (later LMS No 20092), was still allocated to Barrow Road in 1933. At Charfield, just to the north of Bristol on the Gloucester line, an accident on 13 October 1928 claimed 15 lives when, after a collision, the derailed wooden coaches of a passenger train were set alight as vapour escaping from the gas carriage lights ignited.

During the 1920s, several new stations and halts appeared in Bristol and Somerset and most of these intended to compete with the increasing popularity of road transport. On 26 September 1926, Long Ashton Halt was opened on the line to Weston-super-Mare and North Filton Platform, which was intended to serve the nearby aircraft works, materialised on the site of the defunct Filton Halt. On 23 December in the same year, a halt was opened on the Portishead branch to serve the hospital at Ham Green. May 1927 saw the opening of stations at Whitchurch and Farrington Gurney, both on the Radstock branch, and at Horfield, four miles north of Temple Meads.

In 1928, halts were opened at Pilning (Low Level), Cross Hands and New Passage, all on the northern approach to Severn Beach. That town was promoted as a holiday resort and in the 1930s excursions from Birmingham brought hordes of Midlanders to sample what was, they were led to believe, the true smell of the ocean. At Nightingale Valley, below the Clifton Suspension Bridge on the Portishead line, a platform was opened in June 1928, but the anticipated traffic to the beauty spot failed to materialise and the halt was closed in September 1929. Creech St Michael halt, between Taunton and Durston, opened in

November 1928 and Oldfield Park station, on the Great Western line west of Bath, opened the following March.

In southern Somerset, halts at Donyatt and Ilton were opened on the Chard branch in 1928 and on 1 March 1929 Chard Joint station was renamed, more simply, Chard. Although each of the two sections of the Chard branch was officially under the control of a different region, the line was worked as a single unit from Taunton. Logical though this may have sounded, through workings on the branch had to connect with main line trains at both Taunton and Chard Junction and this meant that branch trains often had to kill time somewhere along the route. Chard was the obvious place for the break, but waits of up to one hour at the town's station took a lot of explaining to the uninitiated traveller. Through working of the branch started very soon after the Grouping, and by 1924 Chard's engine shed was considered superfluous and was subsequently closed. The GWR did not operate a Sunday passenger service on the branch, but in the late 1930s the Southern decided to offer a passenger service between Chard Junction and Chard on Sundays and so a locomotive and coaches had to be brought from Yeovil for the day. At Yeovil itself, a halt was opened at Hendford adjacent to the Bristol & Exeter Railway's original terminus in the town in May 1932.

During the 1920s, one noteworthy renaming involved Keynsham station, which was retitled Keynsham & Somerdale on 1 February 1925. During the previous year, Messrs J. & S. Fry had opened their new chocolate factory near Keynsham and the winning suggestion of an in-house competition to find a name for the new site had been Somerdale. With a large number of employees at the

Above:
Former Midland '2P' 4-4-0 No 521 poses outside Barrow Road shed in Bristol in April 1932. The 4-4-0s provided the mainstay of motive power for the Midland for decades, and even when 4-6-0s started to appear in LMS days, the four-coupled locomotives far outnumbered their larger counterparts at Barrow Road. The engine in the picture was designed by Samuel Johnson and built by Sharp Stewart in 1899 as Midland No 2439; it received its new identity under the 1907 renumbering scheme. It was renewed by Richard Deeley in 1913, and went on to become No 40521 after Nationalisation. Withdrawal came in March 1956. Photomatic

new factory, the Great Western laid on works specials between Stapleton Road station and Keynsham, but these trains terminated at the GWR station as they did not have access to the lines within the Somerdale site.

Against these stories of station openings and additional traffic, the first post-Grouping line closure took place in 1925. Between Hallatrow and Dunkerton, the railmotor service had been reintroduced on 9 July 1923 in response to public requests, but the reprise was brief and the service was discontinued as early as 21 September 1925. The railmotor was used mainly by staff at Dunkerton colliery, but, when winding ceased in May 1925, the major source of traffic vanished. The section of the branch from Hallatrow to Camerton was closed and lifted soon afterwards but the coal traffic from Camerton continued and this justified the retention of the section between there and Limpley Stoke.

The General Strike of 1926 had less of an effect on the Bristol and Somerset areas than in many other parts of the country, and one of the few places to see

Right:
A pair of ex-S&D 0-4-4Ts show off their new LMS liveries at Highbridge shed in July 1930. No 1202 was former S&D No 12, and No 1305 had carried S&D No 54. The latter engine had been built for the Midland Railway in 1884, but it was transferred to the S&D in January 1920; although it was renumbered and given the letters 'SDJR' by the lads at Highbridge, it retained its crimson lake livery. Come 1930, it resumed its former number, but this did little to guarantee a long life. Like its fellow in the picture, it was withdrawn in 1931. Photomatic

extensive disruption was the North Somerset coalfield, through which both the Great Western and the Somerset & Dorset operated. The strike was, however, to throw up localised oddities and one volunteer guard on the Taunton-Minehead branch turned out to be a former station master at Paddington. The strike came, coincidentally, at the time when Radstock, at the centre of the mining area, was being established as a transfer centre for rail-to-road transhipment; Frome and Badminton were also developed as road distribution centres in the mid-1920s. The major modernisation of freight facilities in the area had taken place in 1923 when the goods depot at Bristol Temple Meads had been extensively rebuilt at a cost of over £550,000.

The major administrative change to the railways of the area took place on 1 January 1930. From that date, the Somerset & Dorset Railway lost its last chunk of individuality when, as a result of economies by both of the joint operators, the locomotives were absorbed into LMS stock and the rolling stock into the care of the Southern. The distinctive Prussian Blue livery disappeared and the locomotives were treated to uninspiring LMS Black and the coaches to Southern Green. A total of 81 locomotives remained in stock at the time of the reorganisation but, perhaps surprisingly, only six were condemned by the LMS without carrying either their new numbers or livery. The Bridgwater branch had remained the property of the nominal subsidiary, the Bridgwater Railway, after its opening and, although the company had been formally absorbed by the Southern at the Grouping, it had made no discernible difference to the everyday working of the branch.

It has often been suggested that the reason why the Somerset & Dorset escaped from the Grouping in 1923 was simply because the authorities did not know where it should be allocated. Geographically, a large part of the S&D system was situated in what was, unmistakably, Great Western territory but, in view of the furore surrounding the joint agree-

ment half a century earlier, any moves to wrest the railway from the LMS and the Southern would not have been the epitome of tact and diplomacy. In the event, the joint operators' agreed reorganisation of 1930 did for the S&D what the Ministry of Transport had been scared to attempt seven years previously. Apart from the new division of responsibilities, other early economies included the cessation of former Somerset & Dorset shipping services in 1933 and, in the same year, the abolition of the position of station master at Templecombe (Lower).

After bridge strengthening work between Mangotsfield and Bath in 1933, the LMS was able to start considering the replacement of some older Somerset & Dorset locomotives which had been transferred to that section. In 1935, ex-London, Tilbury & Southend Railway 4-4-2T No 2103 was put through its paces only to display a prodigious appetite for coal but, in October of that year, a greater degree of success was found with standard LMS Stanier 2-6-2Ts Nos 179/180/181 which had been transferred to Bath. By this time, the Bristol line had been treated to an additional station at Oldland Common. It was 2 May 1938 before the first 'Black 5', No 5432 appeared on the former S&D section but, in keeping with the habits of its class, it paved the way for an eventual mass influx of the characterless creatures.

The only closure in the area during the 1930s involved the former Wrington Vale Light Railway. The decline in passenger traffic was illustrated by comparing Langford station's issue of less than 1,000 tickets in 1930 with the 7,000-plus issued in 1903. Economies failed to arrest the decline and passenger services were withdrawn on 14 September 1931. It

seems that the line's PR officer must have gone at an early stage as, when the announcement about the passenger trains was made, nobody explained that the line was to remain open for goods. Although most of the line's freight customers made hasty alternative arrangements, part of the branch was kept open for goods traffic for over 30 more years. In the last years of the branch, four trains operated each way on weekdays and, occasionally, the Clevedon branch railmotor was used although this was not a popular unit with the crews. The railmotor had an exceptional appetite for water and, after leaving Yatton, there was no source of water until Blagdon was reached. Three years after the official closure to passengers, the first of several special trains ran from Bristol to Burrington to convey a party of church-goers to the Rock of Ages where, allegedly, the well-known hymn of that name was written.

The early 1930s were times of mass unemployment throughout the country and so the government offered substantial subsidies towards schemes which would help to create jobs. All of the major railway companies took advantage of the subsidies, and government help enabled the considerable enlargement of Temple Meads station, which was completed in December 1935. Further works which were made possible by financial backing included the rebuilding of the engine sheds at Bath Road and the quadrupling of the lines from Temple Meads as far as Ashton to the south and Filton to the north.

The most extensive Government-backed changes in the area were at Taunton. The 7½-mile section between Cogload and Norton Fitzwarren played host to two very busy main lines and four

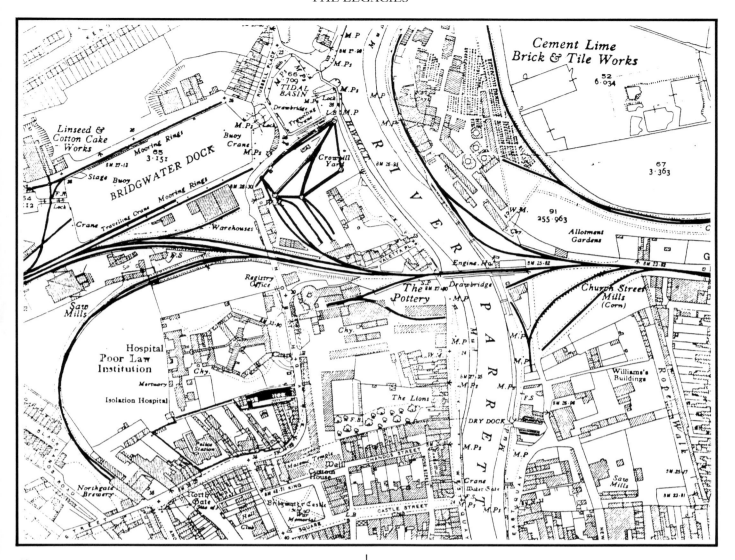

Above:
The GWR's lines in the vicinity of Bridgwater Dock are shown in this 25in/mile Ordnance Survey map of 1930. Almost every industrial concern in the area was rail-connected and the siding to the brewery, pottery, Cotton Cake works and corn mills can be seen. The unlinked spur which passed the Brick & Tile Works in the northeast of the map is the S&D's dock branch. Crown Copyright

Below:
This view shows Congresbury station in the early 1930s. Taken from the overbridge carrying the A370 Bristol-Weston road, the single-track branches to Wrington (left) and Wells (right) can be seen diverging in the distance. Despite the comparatively extensive pointwork, the goods yard housed just two sidings, one to the goods shed behind the station building and the other (hidden by the trees to the left of the station) to a weighbridge. H C Casserley

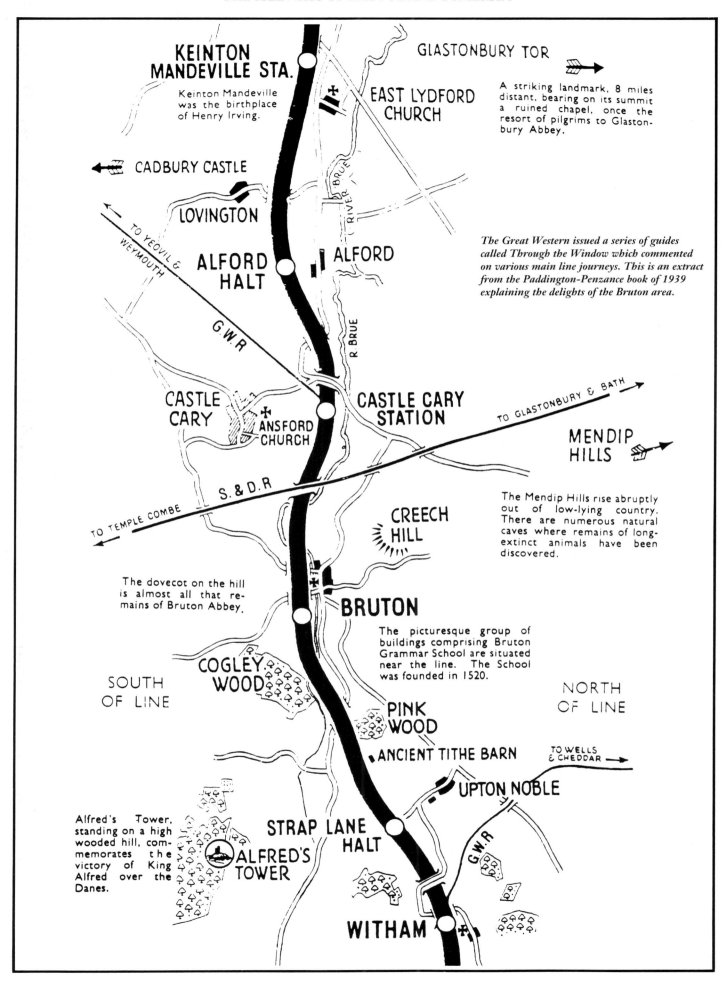

KEINTON MANDEVILLE STA.

Keinton Mandeville was the birthplace of Henry Irving.

GLASTONBURY TOR

A striking landmark, 8 miles distant, bearing on its summit a ruined chapel, once the resort of pilgrims to Glastonbury Abbey.

EAST LYDFORD CHURCH

← CADBURY CASTLE

LOVINGTON

ALFORD

RIVER BRUE

TO YEOVIL & WEYMOUTH

ALFORD HALT

R. BRUE

G.W.R

The Great Western issued a series of guides called Through the Window which commented on various main line journeys. This is an extract from the Paddington-Penzance book of 1939 explaining the delights of the Bruton area.

CASTLE CARY

✝ ANSFORD CHURCH

CASTLE CARY STATION

TO GLASTONBURY & BATH →

MENDIP HILLS

S. & D.R

TO TEMPLE COMBE

The Mendip Hills rise abruptly out of low-lying country. There are numerous natural caves where remains of long-extinct animals have been discovered.

CREECH HILL

The dovecot on the hill is almost all that remains of Bruton Abbey.

BRUTON

The picturesque group of buildings comprising Bruton Grammar School are situated near the line. The School was founded in 1520.

COGLEY WOOD

SOUTH OF LINE

NORTH OF LINE

PINK WOOD

ANCIENT TITHE BARN

TO WELLS & CHEDDAR →

UPTON NOBLE

Alfred's Tower, standing on a high wooded hill, commemorates the victory of King Alfred over the Danes.

ALFRED'S TOWER

STRAP LANE HALT

G.W.R

WITHAM

Above:
This splendid photograph was taken inside Barrow Road shed in Bristol on 27 May 1935 and shows that a modern 35mm SLR camera is by no means essential for first class photography. The locomotives are, from left to right: Deeley 4-4-0 No 1030, Johnson 0-6-0 No 3173 and Johnson 0-4-4T No 1228. The 4-4-0 was still allocated to Barrow Road at the time of Nationalisation, but was retired after less than four years of State ownership. H C Casserley

branches, most of which were worked to capacity during the holiday season, and the availability of subsidies enabled the long overdue quadrupling of the whole section. At the same time, Taunton station was rebuilt with four main-line platforms, three of 1,200ft and the other of 1,400ft, to replace the two original platforms. On the fast line to Taunton, cut-offs were constructed at Westbury and Frome, the latter being two miles long while the branches from Taunton to Barnstaple and Minehead were treated to several additional passing loops.

A few years later, Taunton was the starting point for what could have been the start of a total revolution in the running of the Great Western. In the three years up to 1937, the cost of coal had increased by more than one-third and, although the GWR had had considerable success with its innovatory alternative of diesel railcars, including an experimental through service between Taunton and Weymouth, a project was launched in

February 1938 for conversion of all lines west of Taunton for electric traction. The electrical consultants engaged by the GWR were Messrs Merz & McLellan and their report, which was published in May 1939, concluded that the overhead system would be preferable to the third-rail system for the nature of the lines but, while the scheme would cost over £4,000,000, the savings to the GWR would only be around £100,000 per annum. The project was, therefore, abandoned.

The idea of electrification had manifested itself less than two and a half years after the Great Western's Centenary celebrations in 1935. Among the events which marked the Centenary was the introduction of The Bristolian on 9 September 1935. Amidst the obligatory pomp and ceremony, a train of six ocean

liner coaches hauled by No 6000 *King George V* left Paddington at 10am and arrived at Bristol two hours later. The return left Bristol at 4.30pm and completed the journey in 1¾ hours.

Four years after the inaugural 'Bristolian', the outbreak of World War 2 played havoc with the scheduling of train services. In October 1939, the time allowed between Bristol and Paddington

Below:
LMS '3F' 0-6-0 No 3178 is shown alongside Barrow Road shed in Bristol in 1932. This Johnson-designed locomotive of 1887 started life as Midland Railway No 1786, and was still allocated to Barrow Road at the time of Nationalisation, by which time it had become British Railways No 43178. It survived until March 1960 and was outlived by only four of its 60 classmates. Photomatic

Above:
This photograph showing Yeovil Junction looking to the east was taken in the 1920s, and an unidentified Southern tank engine departs with a two-coach shuttle service to Yeovil Town. The signalbox stands in the junction of the Yeovil Town line (left) and the Waterloo line (right). Lens of Sutton

was two hours and 35 minutes but, with the disruptions, the average time taken was only just short of three hours. Although all of the railways were affected to one degree or another by the requirements of war traffic, the through route offered by the old Somerset & Dorset became, arguably, the most military-orientated line in Somerset. The familiar workhorses, the Stanier 2-8-0s, hauled much of the additional traffic as 'Black 5s', used on the line before the war, were required for mixed traffic duties elsewhere on the LMS. In 1935, a new 60ft turntable had been installed at Bath and, while it accommodated the 'Black 5s' and 2-8-0s, it was found inadequate in post-war years when the 67ft 6in Bulleid Pacifics started working through to Bath. In 1943, the first Horwich-built 'Crab' 2-6-0 appeared in Somerset but, despite its usefulness, few members of the class notched up many regular appearances on the S&D.

During the war, the Southern was quick to provide additional motive power on the Somerset & Dorset line and 'S11' class 4-4-0s Nos 395-404, 'T9' 4-4-0 No 304 and veteran 'T1' 0-4-4Ts Nos 1-6 were all transferred. Throughout the war, LNER 'B12' 4-6-0 No 8549 and a train of ambulance coaches were stationed at Templecombe and kept per-

manently prepared for immediate use. At Glastonbury, where the Somerset Central had started it all in 1854, the engineer's department was pressed into use as a transit camp for American troops. Elsewhere in Somerset, War Department funds enabled the construction of a loop at Yeovil in October 1943 to enable through running from Pen Mill station to Yeovil Junction while, at Pen Mill shed, the regular Evershot banker, a 0-6-0T, was joined by bigger locomotives for assistance on the heavy military trains. On at least one occasion, four engines, two hauling and two pushing, were required to get a train loaded with Army vehicles up the bank. During the war Taunton saw a daily through working of a Southern-hauled train en route from Exeter to Yeovil, in order to familiarise Southern crews with the alternative route over Great Western tracks.

To the north of Bristol, the very rare occurrence of a wartime line closure was seen. From 19 June 1944, passenger services on the branch between Yate and Thornbury were withdrawn, but the line was to remain open for freight for another 22 years. Locomotives working on the branch were stabled at the small shed at Thornbury but were serviced by Barrow Road shed and, although '3F' and '4F' 0-6-0s were the usual peace-time engines, the war years saw Southern 'K10' 4-4-0 No 135 on regular duties to Thornbury. The engine was one of three Drummond 'K10s' transferred to Barrow Road during the war and a further Southern engine, an 'F1' class 4-4-0, also spent some time helping out at Bristol.

Many railway installations in Bristol and Somerset suffered bomb damage

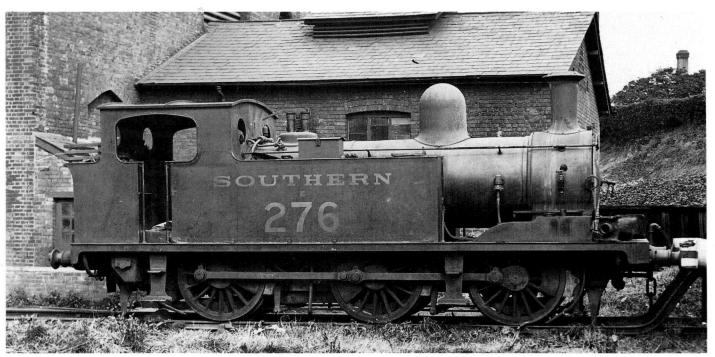

Above:
Southern Railway 'T9' class 4-4-0 No 283 stands at Yeovil Junction on a Exeter-Yeovil Town working on 25 May 1935. The 'T9s' were introduced in 1899 as the L&SWR's standard express locomotives, and the class eventually comprised 66 examples. They were superheated soon after the Grouping and a number survived until the early 1960s. H C Casserley

during the war but, mercifully, there was comparatively little that could count as wholesale destruction. The old Somerset & Dorset offices at Green Park Buildings in Bath were destroyed in April 1942, and the Southern Railway's station at Templecombe was hit four months later. The irony about Templecombe station was that it had been extensively rebuilt only four years previously, the work having

included an extension of the main platforms to accommodate 14-coach trains, a third platform to provide proper facilities for passengers arriving on the old S&D loop and a stylish new signalbox in the Southern 'Odeon' style.

The worst railway accident in the area during the war years was not caused directly by enemy action, although it was later realised that the stress of the war had contributed significantly to the 'human error' factor. A derailment occurred at Norton Fitzwarren on the night of 4 November 1940, very nearly 50 years to the day after another major accident at almost the same spot, and resulted in 27 deaths and 56 cases of serious injury.

When peace was restored, the country's railway system was in a state of total

disruption and, when the electorate voted in a Labour Government, the Nationalisation of Britain's railways soon became a subject of major discussion. On 1 January 1948 British Railways was born and, under the division of administration, the Great Western, the Southern and the London Midland & Scottish Railways became the Western, Southern and London Midland Regions respectively.

Below:
During the war, the services on the Clevedon branch still numbered around 20 trains each way on weekdays. The GWR timetable for May 1943 shows the journey time was all of one minute faster than in 1922. The very last pre-Nationalisation timetable of October 1947 has been included for comparison.

YATTON AND CLEVEDON. (Week Days only. Third class only.)

		a.m.	a.m.	a.m.	a.m.	a.m.	a.m.	a.m.	noon	p.m.	p.m.	p.m.	p.m.	p.m.	p.m.	p.m.	p.m.	p.m.	p.m.	p.m.	p.m.	p.m.	p.m.		p.m.
Yatton	dep.	6 55	7 34	8 18	8 37	9 0	9 35	10 50	12 0	12 57	1 27	2 12	2 55	3 58	4 33	5 13	5 38	6 8	6 35	7 0	8 10	8 40	9 18	...	10 25
Clevedon	arr.	7 2	7 41	8 25	8 44	9 7	9 42	10 57	12 7	1 4	1 34	2 19	3 2	4 5	4 40	5 20	5 45	6 15	6 42	7 7	8 17	8 47	9 25	...	10 32

		a.m.	a.m.	a.m.	a.m.	a.m.	a.m.	a.m.	a.m.	a.m.	p.m.	p.m.	p.m.	p.m.	p.m.	p.m.	p.m.	p.m.	p.m.	p.m.	p.m.	p.m.	p.m.		p.m.	p.m.
Clevedon	dep.	6 38	7 20	8 0	8 28	8 47	9 10	10 20	11 10	12 23	12 30	13 7	1 40	2 23	3 40	4 18	4 50	5 25	5 50	6 17	6 45	7 35	8 22	8 55	...	10 0	10 38
Yatton	arr.	6 45	7 27	8 7	8 35	8 54	9 17	10 27	11 17	12 30	12 37	13 14	1 47	2 30	3 49	4 25	4 57	5 32	5 57	6 24	6 52	7 42	8 29	9 2	...	10 7	10 45

3 May 1943 Timetable

66 YATTON AND CLEVEDON. (Week Days only. Third class only.)

		a.m.		a.m.	a.m.		a.m.	a.m.		a.m.		a.m.	a.m.		a.m.		a.m.			p.m.	p.m.		p.m.	p.m.	
Yatton	dep.	6 54	...	7 25	7 45	...	8 18	8 37	...	9 0	...	9 30	9 58	...	10 48	...	11 28	...	...	12 5	12 55	...	1 7	1 50	...
Clevedon	arr.	7 1	...	7 32	7 52	.	8 25	8 44	...	9 7	.	9 37	10 5	.	10 55	...	11 35	.	.	12 12	12 42	.	1 14	1 57	...

		p.m.	p.m.		p.m.		p.m.	p.m.		p.m.	p.m.		p.m.		p.m.		p.m.		p.m.	p.m.		p.m.		p.m.	
Yatton	dep.	2 5	2 55	...	3 30	...	4 7	4 50	...	5 13	5 38	...	6 8	6 37	...	7 5	...	...	8 8	8 40	...	9 18	...	10 17	...
Clevedon	arr.	2 12	3 2	.	3 37	.	4 14	4 57	.	5 20	5 45	.	6 15	6 44	.	7 12	.	.	8 15	8 47	.	9 25		10 24	.

		a.m.		a.m.	a.m.		a.m.		a.m.	a.m.		a.m.	a.m.		a.m.		a.m.		a.m.	a.m.		a.m.	p.m.		
Clevedon	dep.	6 35	...	7 5	7 35	...	8 0	...	8 28	8 47	...	9 10	9 40	...	10 30	...	11 0	11 40	...	12 20	12 45	...	12 50	1 50	...
Yatton	arr.	6 42	.	7 12	7 42	.	8 7	.	8 35	8 54	...	9 17	9 47	.	10 37	.	11 7	11 47	.	12 27	12 52	.	12 57	1 57	.

		p.m.		p.m.	p.m.		p.m.		p.m.		p.m.	p.m.		p.m.		p.m.		p.m.		p.m.	p.m.		p.m.	p.m.	
Clevedon	dep.	2 25	...	3 10	3 48	...	4 25	...	5 0	...	5 25	5 55	...	6 17	...	6 47	...	7 35	...	8 27	...	8 55	...	9 45	10 33	...
Yatton	arr.	2 32	.	3 17	3 55	.	4 32	.	5 7	.	5 32	6 2	.	6 24	.	6 54	.	7 42	.	8 34	.	9 2	.	9 52	10 40	.

3 October 1947 Timetable

6 The Decline

In the motive power stakes, one of the most innovatory changes in the early years of British Railways had, in fact, originated with the Great Western. On 3 February 1950, the Western Region took delivery of a gas turbine locomotive which had been ordered by the GWR from Messrs Brown-Boveri of Switzerland in 1946.

The engine was numbered 18000, and was initially used on expresses from Paddington to Bristol and Plymouth, although in its later years, its regular turn came to be the 9.15am Paddington to Bristol and the 4.15pm return. A second gas turbine locomotive, No 18100, was delivered from Metropolitan Vickers on 16 December 1951 and, like its older brother, was used most frequently on West of England expresses. Unfortunately both locomotives were found to consume nearly as much fuel when idling as when running and, therefore, neither was considered to have any advantages over the more conventional diesel-electric locomotives which had started to appear elsewhere. No 18100 was transferred to the London Midland Region in January 1958 and was converted for electric traction, while No 18000 was retired in December 1960. The Southern Region was not to be outdone, and in 1952 its new 135-ton diesel-electric locomotives, Nos 10201 and 10202, were sent to fly the flag on Waterloo-Exeter services

through southern Somerset. In 1954, the more-powerful variant, No 10203, was put to regular use at the head of the 'Atlantic Coast Express', the loading of which was often close on 400 tons.

By contrast, the railway staff at Bath did not hold with all this modern technology. Traditionalists to the last, much of the shunting at Bath's Western Region station continued to be done by horse until 1950, although from that year 'Dobbin' had the honour of hearing his home referred to as Bath Spa instead of the single-word title that had sufficed for over a century. Not to be outdone, the former Midland station formally adopted the sub-title of Green Park on 18 June the following year.

In April 1950, boundary changes resulted in London Midland Region lines south of Birmingham being transferred to the Western Region, and this affected not only the main line northwards from Bristol, but also the line from Mangotsfield to Bath. Between late-1946 and early-1949, Stanier 0-4-4Ts Nos 1900/02/03/04 (later BR Nos 41900/02/03/04) had been resident at

Below:
Those double demons, Nationalisation and dieselisation, seem a world away, although this picture was taken on 24 August 1956. Former GWR clerestory coach No 9902 saw out its days as a camping coach at Cheddar. H C Casserley

Bath, and had often appeared on local services to Bristol but, after demonstrating their dislike for gradients of any sort, they were relegated to station pilot duties. The Western Region's replacements for the 0-4-4Ts on the Mangotsfield-Bath line were the versatile 2-6-2Ts. One economy on this line had taken place under London Midland Region auspices on 1 January 1949 when the station at Kelston had been closed, and on 21 September 1953 the Western Region followed suit with the closure of St Philip's station in Bristol to passengers and the centralisation of all local services at Temple Meads. Three months before the Western Region assumed control of the ex-Midland line to Bath, it had taken over responsibility for the section of the former-Somerset & Dorset north of Cole. Prior to this, the ex-S&D engine sheds had been included in the former LMS '22' group but, with the transfer, they passed to the Southern Region's '71' group.

The early 1950s saw the first spate of closures but none was to have such a colourful post-closure story as that of the Camerton branch. The original section of the branch from Hallatrow to Dunkerton had been one of the first post-Grouping casualties and, after the closure of Camerton colliery in 1950, one goods train each month was adequate to cope with the remaining traffic. Unsurpris-

Above:
An AEC works excursion enters Bristol Temple Meads on its return journey from Weston in June 1953. The two railcars are Nos 33 and 36, and they are separated by a decidedly non-dedicated additional carriage. Behind the train can be seen the yard of Bath Road shed.
Photomatic

Right:
Grubby-looking 'County' class 4-6-0 No 1005 County of Devon *simmers outside Bath Road shed in September 1954. If the angle of the lighting is examined critically, experts will be able to tell that the picture was shot around 4.20pm. No 1005 was a Bristol-based locomotive for almost all of its life and was retired from St Philips Marsh shed in June 1963, still not having reached its 18th birthday.* Photomatic

Right:
A former S&D 2-8-0 poses in its BR clothing as No 53810 in the yard of Bath Green Park shed in August 1957. Built in August 1925, it originally carried S&D No 90, and for its first two years of LMS ownership wore No 9680 before becoming No 13810. It was eventually withdrawn in December 1963. Photomatic

ingly, this state of affairs was not destined to last and the last public goods train, which comprised just three vans, left Monkton Combe on 14 February 1951 behind 'Dean Goods' 0-6-0 No 2444.

The tracks were left in situ, and in 1953, Ealing Studios used the section between Midford and Limpley Stoke for the filming of 'The Titfield Thunderbolt' which starred Stanley Holloway and John Gregson. The locomotive graced with the screen name of *Thunderbolt* was the Liverpool & Manchester Railway 0-4-2 *Lion* which, although built in 1838, worked under its own steam for the film cameras. It was joined by the comparatively youthful ex-GWR 0-4-2Ts Nos 1401 and 1456. Monkton Combe station became 'Titfield', while main-line scenes for the film were shot at 'Mallingford', a thinly-disguised Bristol Temple Meads. Two other films had previously featured the Camerton branch, 'The Ghost Train' and 'Kate Plus Ten' which were filmed in 1935 and 1937 respectively, but the line's celebrity status did not win it a reprieve, and the remaining track was lifted on 15 February 1958.

Of the closures of the 1950s, the only other ex-Great Western lines to be affected were the branches from Congresbury to Blagdon, and from Bristol to Frome. The Blagdon branch was that of the old Wrington Vale Light Railway and it had lost its passenger services in 1931. On 1 November 1950, the line was truncated at Wrington but a daily freight train continued on the remaining section until complete closure on 15 July 1963. The old station at Blagdon now provides a good example of how to convert a disused station into a home.

On the Frome branch, the usual number of weekday trains in each direction since Nationalisation had been eight but, by the late 1950s, passenger receipts had dwindled. A reduction of services in 1958

Above:
The pathway once carried the Hallatrow branch under the A36 at Limpley Stoke. This picture was taken in August 1990, 38 years after the branch closed and almost as long since 'The Titfield Thunderbolt' was filmed on the line.
Author

Left:
In the days before the Severn Bridge carried the M4 motorway across the estuary, the alternative to a round trip via Gloucester was to put one's car on a train at Pilning (High Level) station. Here, on 14 July 1958, a car train arrives from foreign soil after its journey through the Severn tunnel. In recent years it has often been remarked that with the constant lane closures on the Severn road bridge, the reintroduction of the car trains might not be such a bad idea.
H C Casserley

Left:
Hallatrow station was once the junction of two branch lines. The 'main' branch was the Bristol-Frome line via Radstock, and the other one was the line to Camerton and Limpley Stoke. The section between Hallatrow and Camerton was lifted as long ago as the early 1920s, but the station still served the Frome branch until its closure to passengers on 2 November 1959. Basic freight facilities were retained at Hallatrow until 15 June 1964, and this picture shows how the station building had fared against the elements up to August 1984.
Author

Right:
The '1366' class of 0-6-0PTs were built in 1934 primarily for shunting at Swindon wagon works. Three eventually found their way to Weymouth and worked the boat trains through the streets for decades, but No 1366 spent many years working on the dock branches at Bridgwater where its short wheelbase was found to be ideal. It remained at Bridgwater until its withdrawal in January 1961; this photograph shows it in action on 25 September 1956.
H C Casserley

failed to restore the line to viability and so passenger services were withdrawn from 31 October 1959. The last train left Frome for Bristol at 9.25pm behind ex-LMS '2MT' 2-6-2T No 41203, and the five carriages were so heavily loaded that banking assistance from 0-6-0PT No 9612 was required to get the train from Frome to Mells Road. The branch was, however, kept open for freight for another nine years.

The other closures of the 1950s affected the old Somerset & Dorset. The former-Somerset Central branch from Glastonbury to Wells succumbed to the axe on 29 October 1951 with Johnson 0-4-4T No 58086 in charge of proceedings on the last day. Even the most hardened railway enthusiast could not have disputed the reason for closure as, in the last years of the branch, the average number of daily passengers was just six. On the same day, scheduled passenger services were withdrawn from the extension beyond Highbridge to Burnham-on-Sea, but excursion traffic continued to operate to Burnham until 8 September 1962, and the occasional freight train appeared until complete closure on 20 May 1963. The

ex-S&D Bridgwater branch lost its passenger services on 1 December 1952, but retained a daily freight working until 1 October 1954 by which time Edington Junction had been renamed, less confusingly for passengers, Edington Burtle. With the total closure of the Bridgwater branch, a spur was constructed to link the remains of the ex-S&D sidings around Bridgwater Docks to the ex-GWR dock lines. In complete contrast to these closures of former S&D property, the original timber-built engine shed at Templecombe was replaced by a smart brick-built shed in 1951.

Ivatt '4MT' 2-6-0s had started to appear on the former-Somerset & Dorset main line as early as 1948 when Nos 43012/13/17/36 had been allocated to Bath and these paved the way for the introduction of standard British Railways

Below:
The services on the Frome branch during the summer of 1955 were more prolific than in the pre-Nationalisation year of 1947, but things were not to last. The branch lost its passenger services on 31 October 1959.

'4MT' 2-6-0s in 1955. Other 2-6-0s, the Southern's Maunsell 'U' and 'U1' Nos 31621 and 31906, had been tried on the line in 1954. By the mid-1950s, the ex-S&D 2-8-0s were often used on passenger services and, although some of the class had spent over 40 years fighting the Mendip Hills, they were still plenty fit enough for the task. Another local veteran was Johnson 0-4-4T No 58072, which had been built in 1893 for the Midland Railway but had spent most of its working days in Somerset. Without having had a major rebuild throughout its long life, it was transferred from sedate duties on the Highbridge branch in 1955 to assist on more-demanding general duties at Bath.

The poor old Somerset & Dorset system was subjected to another change of administration on 1 February 1958 when the Western Region assumed control of everything north of Henstridge. The ex-S&D offices at Bath became redundant and were closed, less than four years after the centenary of the company, and

Table 74												BRISTOL, RADSTOCK WEST and FROME											
Miles		Week Days									Sundays			Miles		Week Days						Sundays	
		am	am	pm	pm	pm	pm	pm	pm P	pm U	am	pm	pm			am	am	am	pm	pm	pm	pm U	pm	noon	pm	pm
—	Bristol (Temple Meads) .. dep	6 47	1017	1 30	2 53	5 20	6 15	7 45	9 48	1035	10 04	508	5	—	Frome .. .. dep	6 26	7 37	1050	..	1 10	4 55	5 56	5 9 25	..	12 06	1 59	9 35
2	Brislington	6 55	1025	1 38	3 05	5 27	6 22	7 51	..	..	10 74	578	11	5½	Mells Road	6 38	7 49	11	..	1 22	4 17	..	6 20 9 37	..	1212	6 26	9 47
4½	Whitchurch Halt	7 3	1032	1 45	3 7	5 34	6 29	7 58	10 2	1049	1014	5 48	18	8½	Radstock West A	6 45	7 56	11 8	..	1 30	4 24	6 11	6 27 9 44	..	1219	6 33	9 55
6½	Pensford	7 10	1039	1 53	3 16	5 41	6 36	8 5	1010	1056	1021	5 118	25	9½	Midsomer Norton & Welton	6 49	8 0	1112	..	1 34	4 28	..	6 32 9 48	..	1223	6 37	9 59
10	Clutton	7 21	1043	2 3	3 25	5 50	6 45	8 14	1019	11 5	1030	5 208	34	11½	Hallatrow	6 57	8 11	20	..	1 42	4 35	..	6 42 9 56	..	1227	6 41	10 3
11½	Hallatrow	7 29	1052	2 7	3 29	5 54	6 52	8 18	1023	11 9	1034	5 248	38	12½	Farrington Gurney Halt	..	8 14	..	..	1 44	4 40	..	6 46 10 0	..	1235	6 45	10 7
12½	Farrington Gurney Halt	7 34	1056	2 11	3 35	5 58	6 56	8 22	1027	1113	1038	5 288	42	14½	Clutton	7 1	8 18	12	1124	..	1 46	4 40	..	6 46 10 0	..	1235	6 49	1011
14½	Midsomer Norton & Welton	7 39	11 02	2 17	3 37	6 0	7 0	8 26	1031	1117	1042	5 328	46	17½	Pensford	7 12	8 20	1132	..	1 54	4 86	3 26	5 8 10 9	..	1243	6 57	1018
16	Radstock West A	7 46	11 52	2 18	4 16	1 07	4 8	30	1035	1121	1046	5 368	50	20	Whitchurch Halt	..	7 19	8 27	..	..	2 1	4 55	..	7 8 1016	..	1250	7 4	1026
19	Mells Road	7 55	1112	2 32	4 93	4 96	2 07	1 28	38	1043	1129	1054	5 448	53	22½	Brislington	7 24	8 31	Ss	..	2 6	5 0	..	7 15 1021	..	1255	7 10	1031
24½	Frome .. .. .. arr	8 7	1124	2 40	4 06	3 17	2 28	49	1053	1139	11 45	549	9	24½	Bristol (Temple Meads) arr	7 30	8 38	1148	..	2 12	5 66	5 27	5 30 1031	..	1 67	7 21	1038

A	Adjoins Radstock North Station	Ss	Stops on Saturdays only at 11 42 am to set down	V	Third class only on Mondays to Fridays. First and Third class on Saturdays	For OTHER TRAINS between Bristol (Temple Meads) and Frome, see Table 62
P	Except Wednesdays and Saturdays	U	Wednesdays and Saturdays only			

Table One
Shed Reclassifications

The familiar system of shed codes was introduced by British Railways in 1950 and followed the system which had been instigated by the LMS before Nationalisation. Some sheds in Bristol and Somerset were subjected to recoding as a result of divisional boundary changes. The full list of post-1948 sheds and sub-sheds with their changes of codes is as follows:

1950:
Midland Region
22A Bristol (Barrow Road).
Southern Region
71G Bath (S&D); sub-shed: Radstock.
71H Templecombe.
71J Highbridge.
72C Yeovil Town.
Western Region
82A Bristol (Bath Road); sub-sheds: Bath, Weston, Wells, Yatton.
82B Bristol (St Philip's Marsh).
82D Westbury (Wiltshire); sub-shed: Frome.
82E Yeovil (Pen Mill)
83B Taunton; sub-sheds: Bridgwater, Minehead.

1958:
Southern Region
72C Yeovil Town.
Western Region
82A Bristol (Bath Road).
82B Bristol (St Philip's Marsh); sub-sheds: Bath, Weston, Wells, Yatton.
82D Westbury (Wiltshire); sub-shed: Frome.
82E Bristol (Barrow Road).
82F Bath (S&D); sub-sheds: Highbridge, Radstock.
82G Templecombe
83B Taunton; sub-shed: Bridgwater.

1963:
Western Region
82A Bristol (Bath Road); sub-shed: Marsh Junction.
82B Bristol (St Philip's Marsh); sub-shed: Wells.
82E Bristol (Barrow Road).
82F Bath (S&D); sub-sheds: Highbridge, Radstock.
83B Taunton.
83C Yeovil Town.
83G Templecombe.

Right:
Diesel traction started to displace steam in 1958 Swindon-built 'Warship' class B B No D810 Cockade leaves Taunton with the down 'Cornish Riviera Express' on 2 December 1961, and passes locally-based 'Hall' No 4932 Hatherton Hall and its train of empty stock.
Harold Ball

the locomotive sheds in Somerset were transferred to the Western's '82' group. Many observers remarked that the 1958 boundary changes gave the Western the opportunity to avenge the events of 1875 when the S&D had sided with the Midland and the London & South Western instead of the Great Western. Flexing its muscles, the Western Region ordered that the use of former S&D headcodes should be stopped immediately, but after a diplomatic period of obedience S&D crews unofficially reintroduced the headcodes.

With indecent haste, the Western rerouted two of the trains which had been a regular feature of the ex-Somerset & Dorset line since the days when the bow and arrow had been a secret weapon: the beer trains from Burton to Bournemouth and the fertiliser trains from Avonmouth to Blandford Forum. Should anybody have had any doubts

Below:
In maroon livery with full yellow ends, 'Western' Class C C No D1056 Western Sultan is seen at the head of a westbound freight passing Bedminster Park in Bristol on 9 March 1968. These locomotives were introduced for express passenger work but soon saw use on less exalted duties. David Wharton

about the Western's plans for the line, Sunday trains to Bournemouth were soon withdrawn, despite many being so full that only standing room was available and, in September 1962, the famous 'Pines Express' was rerouted via Didcot and Basingstoke. The last 'Pines' over the old S&D was hauled by '9F' 2-10-0 No 92220 *Evening Star*. The 2-10-0s had been introduced on the line in March 1960 when No 92204, and later Nos 92203/05/06 had been allocated to Bath but, after the running down of the line had commenced, these gigantic machines with a tractive effort just short of 40,000lb and the ability to haul 410 tons unaided, were often to be seen in charge of three-coach stopping trains.

The projected change in the face of British Railways motive power became evident in Bristol and Somerset in 1958. In that year the first examples of two types of diesel-hydraulics, both classified as 'Warships', appeared and they were put to use on express trains on the Bristol and Plymouth routes. By June 1959, they had taken over the 'Bristolian' and, with an average speed of 71mph on a 100 minute run, produced the fastest scheduled service in Britain. The last steam hauled 'Bristolian' operated on 12 June 1959 with 'Castle' class No 5085 *Evesham Abbey* in charge. In 1961, the first of 74 'Western' class diesels, No D1000 *Western Enterprise*, appeared and, eventually, this more-powerful class replaced the 'Warships' on many express services from Bristol.

Dieselisation of local services first manifested itself in November 1958 when three multiple-units were delivered to the Bristol division and were used, initially, on the Severn Beach branch. In April 1959, the Portishead branch saw its first DMU, and two months later some of the services from Bristol to South Wales were taken over by similar units. The Midland Region took delivery of its first 'Peak' class main-line diesels in 1959 and these were soon put to use on services between Bristol and the North; it took another four years for the 'Peaks' to pluck up courage to negotiate the line from Mangotsfield to Bath.

The mechanically-suspect 'Blue Pullmans' started work on the Bristol-Paddington service in 1960 and, whether out of prestige or necessity, were the only trains in the country to carry a resident engineer. The eight-car units comprised two classes but their schedules showed no improvement on the 100 minute runs achieved by the 'Warships'. The Pullmans lasted until 1973 and, two years later, their modern counterparts, the 125mph High Speed Trains, appeared on trial runs. The HSTs started work on scheduled services on 4 October 1976 and soon reduced the time between Temple Meads and Paddington to under 90 minutes. They were used to best effect on the route from Bristol Parkway, the station which had been opened as an experiment on 1 May 1972. Parkway

Below:
Almost-new Hymek No D7000 shows up sombre-looking 'Warship' No D810 Cockade *on 9 August 1961. The location is Bath Road shed, which closed to steam in 1960 for rebuilding as a diesel depot; it was officially reopened in 1962.* Brian Haresnape

Right:
Type 3 Hymek No D7047 and Type 4 'Warship' No D806 Cambrian *leave Bristol Temple Meads on Sunday 2 June 1963 with the 4.30pm to Paddington.* J S Whiteley

became a success as a commuter station, and it was later rebuilt as a permanent structure; the car park was extended to accommodate over 1,000 vehicles. The fastest trains between Parkway and Paddington are now timed at only 65 minutes.

The spread of dieselisation rendered Bristol's steam sheds redundant. Bath Road depot was the first to go and, when it closed on 12 September 1960, the remaining locomotives were divided between St Philip's Marsh and the ex-Midland shed at Barrow Road. Bath Road was rebuilt as a diesel depot and was reopened in 1962, a DMU depot having been opened at Marsh Junction three years previously. The steam shed at St Philip's Marsh closed on 13 June 1964 and, although the surviving allocation was transferred to Barrow Road, that shed itself succumbed on 16 November 1965 and the locomotives were removed four days later. Despite being officially closed, Barrow Road was required to service visiting steam engines as the Bristol-

Below:
It's 3 August 1959 and the school holidays provide the opportunity for three lads to sample the intricacies of Swindon engineering. The odd layout at Yeovil Pen Mill meant that three platform faces served two tracks and this extravagance would certainly have been dealt with at once had the GWR ever appointed Colonel Stephens to its staff. Lens of Sutton

Birmingham route was not fully dieselised until August 1966. The shed's most impressive servicing duties had been seen in the 1950s when a Toton-based Beyer-Garratt had been the usual form of traction on a daily service to Westerleigh, and the locomotive had been given overnight accommodation at Barrow Road.

In the south of Somerset, the Southern Region was less impatient to convert to diesel or electric traction. The electrification in the south-east of England had been extended in the late 1950s displacing many of Maunsell's excellent 'Schools' class 4-4-0s from their traditional duties and, as a result, a number of

the class had been transferred to duties on the West of England route through Yeovil and Chard. At Yeovil, the practice of starting some trains at the Town station instead of the Junction continued and a brace of Maunsell's 'U' class 2-6-0s were usually allocated to Yeovil Town shed for services which originated locally. In the late 1950s and early 1960s, the shuttle between the two Southern stations was normally in the care of one of the resident 0-4-4Ts, 'M7s' Nos 30129/31 or 'O2' No 30182.

Yeovil Junction had seen its share of named expresses, even if they had not stopped there. The 'Atlantic Coast Express' had been the first named train

on the London & South Western when introduced in July 1926, and it continued hurtling through southern Somerset until September 1964. The 'Devon Belle' had appeared in the timetables on 20 June 1947, and, until 1954, an observation car was always attached to the rear of the train so that passengers could scrutinise the delights of Yeovil and Chard at 60mph.

The Western Region shed at Yeovil Pen Mill closed in January 1959 and the remaining eight locomotives, six 0-6-0PTs and two 2-6-2Ts, were transferred to the Southern Region's shed, Yeovil Town, which survived until 12 June 1965. Even in its last years, Town shed continued to act as an overnight resting place for locomotives on their way from Devon and Cornwall to Eastleigh Works. When Wadebridge's veteran Beattie well tanks became due for overhauls at Eastleigh, enthusiasts in Yeovil knew that the local shed would offer first class bed & breakfast for the celebrated little engines.

The branch between Yeovil and Taunton closed to passengers on 13 June 1964 with the last train being hauled by Standard 2-6-2T No 82001 but Hendford goods station, the original home of the Bristol & Exeter Railway in Yeovil, remained open and shunting was usually

Right:
The Midland shed at Bath (Green Park) was photographed in April 1959. A pair of ex-LMS 0-6-0s stand in the foreground but a BR Standard 2-6-2T in the entrance of the shed betrays the changes in the face of local motive power. Photomatic

taken care of by 0-4-2T No 1442. That locomotive became one of the last two working examples of this delightful class, and eventually passed into preservation. The last regular steam workings through the Yeovil area were by Westbury-Weymouth trains, which were often hauled by 'Hall' class 4-6-0s. Yeovil Town station finally closed its doors to passengers on 2 October 1966.

Back on the former Somerset & Dorset line, even the most hardened optimist had to admit that, when the Western Region's attitude to the line was fuelled by the infamous Beeching report, the future of the cross-country route did not look at all rosy. The General Election of October 1964 resulted in a Labour Government replacing the Tory regime and the Minister of Transport, Tom Fraser,

Above:
Bath Road shed at the southern end of Bristol Temple Meads was, and still is, a frustrating place for gricers. The locomotives on view are just a little too far away for positive identification, and the illegal alternative of a leap over the rear wall will invariably be met by the shed foreman. In steam days, Barrow Road was no easier for the uninvited guest, but there was always St Philip's Marsh. Author

announced the cessation of major railway closures. In Somerset, it was assumed that Mr Fraser and his civil servants had a reasonable grasp of geography and, as the line between Mangotsfield and Bournemouth was all of 104 miles, it fell into the category of a major route and would, therefore, have the threat of closure lifted. Giving plenty of substance to

Above:
British Railways Standard '4MT' 2-6-0 No 76027 pulls out of Bath (Green Park) some time in 1965 at the head of a Bournemouth train. Many a Sainsbury's shopper has since had the privilege of parking his or her car on the very spot on which the locomotive is pictured.
Photomatic

Right:
Much to the delight of the starlings and pigeons, the overall roof at Bristol Temple Meads was completely renovated during 1990/91. An Inter-City 125 arrives on 26 August 1991 with a train-load of passengers who will no doubt appreciate the light and airy atmosphere under the new roof. Author

the notion that a politician's words and a politician's deeds are two distinctly different things, Fraser announced that the entire S&D system would close in September 1965.

Of all the anti-closure lobbies of the early 1960s, that for the old Somerset & Dorset was one of the most vociferous. Many of the communities en route had poor road connections and the pupils at several major schools in the area had only the railway as their means of transport. A reprieve was granted but only until 3 January 1966, the date which, cynically, was scheduled as the final day of steam services on the Western Region. At the last moment, one of the bus operators which had been licensed to provide the replacement service withdrew and an emergency service was reintroduced on the line. It was, fittingly, steam hauled despite the conversion to diesel elsewhere on the Western Region. The now inevitable final closure took effect on 7 March 1966 and, over the last weekend, over 2,000 people travelled on the line in specially chartered trains. The last train on Sunday 6 March ran from Bath to Bournemouth and, in the best traditions of the S&D was double-headed. The locomotives were Bulleid Pacifics Nos 34013 *Oke-hampton* and 34057 *Biggin Hill*.

Two small sections of the Somerset & Dorset survived for a while. At Radstock, a spur was constructed to link part of the

original line to the Western Region branch, which still retained its freight facilities despite the withdrawal of its passenger services in 1959. The reason for the link was that collieries joined to the ex-S&D line around Radstock were still working and British Railways had a contract with the National Coal Board for the transportation of Somerset coal to the power station at Portishead. The link enabled coal wagons to be transferred from the short surviving section of the ex-S&D line to the former Great Western line, over which they would continue to Portishead. This worked well until July 1968 but, that month, the area was hit by storms so severe that local people started worrying when they saw animals walking in pairs. At Pensford the railway

was damaged beyond economical repair and so a hasty reopening of the Radstock-Frome section, which had been closed on 15 August 1966, was required for the coal traffic.

The other ex-Somerset & Dorset section which survived the 1966 massacre was between the dairy at Bason Bridge and Highbridge. In May 1965, a spur had been laid between the once grand seven-platform S&D station at Highbridge and the Western Region's main line, and this link became the escape route for the milk trains which were to continue until 2 October 1972. One further section which lingered on was, admittedly, not true S&D but still warrants a mention. This was the ex-Midland line from Mangotsfield to Bath which was kept open for coal trains to Bath gas works, adjacent to the engine shed, until 28 May 1971. Nowadays, the entire ex-Midland

Below:
This Western Region timetable for the summer of 1955 is included to illustrate the level of branch line service in the pre-Beeching era. Although the times of the trains have been changed since 1948, the frequency of the services has not altered significantly. The branch closed to passengers on 7 September 1963.

| Table 79 | YATTON, CHEDDAR, WELLS and WITHAM |

[A detailed Western Region railway timetable for Table 79 showing train services between Yatton, Cheddar, Wells and Witham, with weekday and Sunday columns. The mileages and station names are listed down the left side: Bristol (T. Meads), Yatton, Congresbury, Sandford and Banwell, Winscombe (Somerset), Axbridge, Cheddar, Draycott, Lodge Hill, Wookey, Wells, Shepton Mallet D, Cranmore, Wanstrow, Witham. The lower half shows the reverse direction from Witham back to Bristol.]

Notes at foot of timetable:
B Arr 3 54 pm
D High Street Station; about 1 mile to Charlton Road Station
E Except Saturdays
S Saturdays only
V Third class only, Mondays to Fridays. First and Third class on Saturdays
T First and Third class. Dep 2 15 pm on Saturdays

line from Barrow Road right through to Bath is a popular cycle track.

In Bath the legacy of the Somerset & Dorset can still be seen. The disused Green Park station was given the status of a listed building in November 1971 and, 10 years later, Sainsbury's purchased the site for use as a covered car park for its supermarket. By then, the structure was in a poor state and it took £1,500,000 and 11 months solid work to complete a thorough restoration. On 1 December 1982, the superbly-restored building was reopened by HRH Princess Margaret who became, almost certainly, the first member of the Royal family to officiate at the opening of a supermarket.

Another major restoration scheme of the early 1980s involved the original Brunel terminus at Temple Meads in

Above right:
Decay and neglect have taken hold at Chard Central as unkempt 0-6-0PT No 3736 stands with a three-coach train. This picture was taken on 11 July 1962, two months before the station closed to passenger traffic. The locomotive itself survived until March 1963, when it was withdrawn from Taunton shed. H C Casserley

Right:
The former Bristol & Exeter station at Wells was photographed on 16 July 1958, with BR Standard 2-6-2T No 82041 waiting to depart for Witham. H C Casserley

Right:
Cheddar was the epitome of a GWR country station. Here, 0-6-0PT No 3731 of St Philip's Marsh shed percolates while waiting to depart with a train to Yatton on 24 August 1956. The branch closed to passengers on 7 September 1963. H C Casserley

Bristol. In its later years, prior to its closure on 12 September 1965, that part of the station had been given over, most irreverently, to London Midland Region trains but, in 1981, the Brunel Trust started work on what turned out to be an excellent restoration. More recently, the Hannaford overall shed at Frome station has also been well restored.

Returning to the 1960s, that decade saw the death of most of the remaining branch lines in Somerset. On 10 September 1962, passenger services between Taunton and Chard were withdrawn, not only on the ex-Great Western section but also on the former Southern section through to Chard Junction. In the early years of British Railways, the old Joint station at Chard had been renamed once again, this time as Chard Central, but the locals were unimpressed. Despite the new name, the station remained firmly in place on the outskirts of the town. In 1950 boundary changes had resulted in the transfer of the Chard branch to the Southern Region but, although Ilton Halt acquired green station nameboards and Southern-style signals appeared near Hatch, the branch continued to be operated from Taunton. The continued use of 2-6-2Ts and 0-6-0PTs made it very difficult for the observer to believe that the branch had come under Waterloo control.

On the Yatton-Witham branch, the last passenger train ran on 7 September 1963 behind 0-6-0 No 3218 of Wells

Above:
Ex-GWR Collett 0-6-0 No 3215 passes Axbridge station on 8 July 1959 with a Yatton-bound freight train. The signalbox on the extreme left of the frame was built in 1907 to replace the original Bristol & Exeter box, and in 1924 the goods yard was reorganised. As for the locomotive in the picture, it was allocated to St Philip's Marsh for almost all of its life, but spent its final days at Templecombe before retirement in January 1963. H C Casserley

Left:
The site of the old station at Portishead was acquired by the Electricity Board, which footed the £250,000 bill for the construction of the new station, seen here on 15 July 1956. It opened on 4 January 1954, and closed to passengers on 7 September 1964. Such is foresight.
H C Casserley

Right:

On 12 July 1984, the line from Ashton to Wapping Wharf in Bristol Docks saw a most unusual working. A special train of Venice-Simplon Orient Express Pullman stock brought a party of VIPs from London for the opening of the World Wine Fair in Bristol, and it deposited the thirsty entourage adjacent to Bristol Industrial Museum where they were greeted by a military band. Only a handful of passenger trains have ever used the Ashton/Cumberland Road route into Bristol, and these have all been special workings which have been subjected to a strict 10mph speed restriction. The train was hauled by Class 37 diesel No 37206 and, attached to its rear was classmate No 37229. The purpose of the second locomotive was to provide the power for the empty stock journey to Malago sidings as there was no room to run round the train at Wapping Wharf. When the Cumberland Basin double-deck bridge was opened in 1906, its use by a rake of Pullmans can hardly have been foreseen. Author

shed but Standard 2-6-2Ts had been the more usual passenger locomotives on the line in its later years. The 0-6-0s tended to be kept for freight duties but, as they were restricted to 12 loaded coal wagons on the haul between Wells and Shepton Mallet, it was common practice for a heavy train to be taken up the 1 in 37 bank at Wanstrow in two parts. The section between Witham and Cranmore continued to see regular usage until September 1985 for traffic to the bitumen tanker yard adjacent to Cranmore station. At Wells, three different railway companies had once served the city, each with their own station and engine shed, but with the closure of the remaining shed in November 1963 and the withdrawal of the last freight facilities in July 1964, the city's public transport was left in the hands of Bristol Omnibus Co.

The branch to Portishead lost its passenger services on 7 September 1964, just 10 years after £250,000 had been spent on a modern station and a large goods yard on a new site in the town. The bill for construction of the new station was paid by the Electricity Board which wanted the site of the original premises for an extension of the town's power station. When unveiled on 4 January 1954, the new station was illuminated by fluorescent lighting but it seemed that the Electricity Board was keen to recoup some of its outlay. The lighting bills for the station were so high that the station master was instructed to remove every alternate tube. Ashton Gate platform, near the Bristol end of the branch, had two temporary reprieves, the first between 1970 and 1977 for football trains when Bristol City hit the heady heights of the First Division again, and the second for a week in May 1984 when the

attraction at the football ground was the well-known evangelist, Billy Graham.

In its last years, the Portishead branch saw a bewildering variety of motive power. Despite the introduction of DMUs in 1959, the standard '3MT' 2-6-2Ts were often seen on passenger workings but freight duties saw the use of 0-6-0PTs, 'Halls', 'Granges', the occasional 'Castle' and 2-8-0s of both Great Western and LMS origin. On the diesel front, locomotives ranged from the lightweight North British 'D63xx' class through to 'Warships', 'Westerns' and even 'Peaks'. The branch remained open for freight traffic to Portishead for a further 20 years and, at the time of writing, the entire length of the line still remains in situ. The freight branch to Bristol docks, which left the Portishead branch

at Ashton, was officially closed on 11 January 1964 but the Wapping Wharf section played host to special services after that date. One occasion was in July 1984 when a contingent of VIPs arrived in diesel-hauled Pullman coaches for the opening of the World Wine Fair, and, in

Below:
This photograph of Milverton station on the Taunton-Barnstaple branch was taken in the early 1950s and can be compared to the picture in Chapter 2. Precious little has altered and even the benches on the platform on the right are the same. The only readily-identifiable difference is the removal of the connection beyond the platforms. The locomotive on the mixed freight train cannot be positively identified but, judging from the size of its dome, is very probably an ageing 'Dean Goods' 0-6-0. Lens of Sutton

May the following year, the Severn Valley Railway's ex-LMS 2-6-0 No 46443 appeared on the old dock line in charge of a 'GWR 150' special.

The avoiding line through Filton and Henbury to Avonmouth Docks had its passenger services withdrawn on 23 November 1964 but remained open for freight and was singled in 1966; the last Avonmouth boat train to use the line ran as recently as 26 August 1964. On 3 October 1966 the branch from Yatton to Clevedon had its passenger services withdrawn but, despite its lightweight construction, it had had its moment of glory when it had accommodated 2-8-0T No 7250 on a Bank Holiday special in August 1957. The shed from which the branch was serviced, Yatton, had closed in August 1960.

Of the two branches westwards from Taunton, one was closed in 1966 and the other in 1971, although both lines had lost their freight facilities in 1964. Passenger services between Taunton and Barnstaple were withdrawn on 3 October 1966 but services on the Minehead branch were not discontinued until 2 January 1971. Little over five years after the closure of the Minehead branch, the privately-owned West Somerset Railway reopened Minehead station, which had been greatly extended in 1934, for steam services. At Watchet, much of the former railway land was acquired by the dock authorities but, ironically, when the shipping trade increased there was no railway left to assist in the transport of goods. The last freight spur at Watchet was to the paper mill but this was removed in 1967. When Taunton's branch services were in an advanced state of decline, the town's engine shed was rendered superfluous and it was closed in October 1964, the small sub-shed at Minehead having been closed as far back as November 1956.

During the peak years of the 1950s, over 170 trains had passed through Taunton on summer Saturdays and, even apart from main line services, an interesting selection of motive power appeared in the town. A stud of the large 2-6-2Ts was allocated to Taunton for banking duties at Wellington while, at the other end of the scale, former Cardiff Railway 0-4-0ST No 1338 had been on Taunton's books since 1943 although it was, in fact, based at the sub-shed in Bridgwater for dock shunting. Commercial shipping at Bridgwater had been on the decline for some years and the services of No 1338 were finally considered unnecessary in June 1960; it was transferred to Swansea and, the following month, Bridgwater shed was closed.

Left:

Ex-GWR 0-4-2T No 1463 waits patiently in the bay platform of Yatton station in April 1959 in the seemingly forlorn hope that somebody will, sooner or later, want to go to Clevedon. Many of these delightful little tank locomotives lasted into the 1960s and No 1463 itself survived until April 1961, by which time it had been transferred from the Bristol Division to Gloucester. The last scheduled steam working on the Clevedon branch was on Sunday 7 August, and the locomotive in charge of proceedings was No 1463 itself. Photomatic

Below:

The former-GWR branch terminus at Clevedon was photographed during a lull on 24 August 1956. During the mid-1950s there were approximately 20 trains each way over the branch on weekdays, and so a lull in proceedings was nowhere near as common or as lengthy as on many other branch lines. Clevedon was originally a broad gauge station and the platform length was greatly extended simultaneously with gauge conversion.
H C Casserley

Above:

British Railways' printing department was fully occupied with the production of closure notices during the early 1960s, but few were more worthy of the addition of black ribbons than this one. Photomatic

Left:
Sentinel 0-4-OTG No 47190 started life as Somerset & Dorset No 101 in 1929. Seen here at Barrow Road shed in August 1951, it remained in the Radstock, Bath and Bristol areas for all of its useful life until retirement in March 1961. Photomatic

Right:
A Paddington-Bristol HST arrives at Bath Spa on 26 August 1991. The gentle curve and wide trackbed of the approach are legacies from Brunel's broad gauge engineering, and nowadays seem tailor-made for high-speed express running. Author

Below:
Network Southeast might have a strong market identity, but it has little idea about geography. Here, in the heart of the 'south-east' at Yeovil Junction, a Class 50 arrives 15 minutes late on the 14.22 Exeter-Waterloo on 2 July 1991. Despite the best efforts of Herr Beeching and his stormtroopers, the delightful old LSWR footbridge survives at the west end of the station. Author

Interestingly, from February 1955 No 1338 had held the distinction of being the only ex-Cardiff Railway locomotive still on British Railways duties, and it was to continue in service until September 1963.

The former Midland shed at Barrow Road in Bristol had also had its share of small 'foreign' shunters. The branch to Avonside Wharf, which had been the original home of the Bristol & Gloucestershire Railway in 1835, presented limitations as to the size of engines. Ageing Johnson '1F' 0-6-0Ts had been used in the 1930s and had later been replaced by

Sentinels but, in 1952, ex-Lancashire & Yorkshire Railway 'Pugs', the diminutive 0-4-0STs, were found to be ideal. Nos 51202/12 were used regularly on the branch until their retirement in 1957 and were replaced by sister engines Nos 51217/18. This pair was succeeded, in 1961, by lightweight 0-6-0 diesel shunters Nos D2134/35.

On the Southern Region's main line, the stations at Sutton Bingham and Chard Junction were closed to passengers in 1962 and 1966 respectively. Milborne Port station had been relegated to a halt in 1961 and closed on 7 March 1966, the same day as Templecombe station. In 1967 the entire section between Wilton, near Salisbury, and Pinhoe, near Exeter, was reduced to single track although several passing loops were retained. The once grand main line which had taken generations of holidaymakers to the West Country was reduced to the status of a secondary route, and even some of the motive power was, 'foreign'. The Western Region's 'Warship' class diesels became regulars on the route which, only a few years previously, had still accommodated a steam-hauled named express. The last 'Atlantic Coast Express' had run as recently as 4 September 1964.

Against the trends, Templecombe station reopened in 1983 after extensive talks between Somerset County Council and a Station Working Group and part of the agreement was that the reopening would be for a trial period of three years, during which receipts should reach £31,000 per annum. The first year's target sum was achieved in just six months. The usable length of the present platform is less than before but eight-coach trains can be accommodated. The Art Deco signalbox, which now houses 16 levers compared to the original 60, doubles up as the ticket office, and a sign on the platform proudly declares that Templecombe has won a 'Best Kept Station' award. It is not hard to see why.

Now, in the early 1990s, the railway system in Bristol and Somerset shows similar characteristics to systems elsewhere in Britain. Services on the main lines, in this case those from Paddington to Bristol and via Badminton to South Wales, are aimed at the business traveller and, although British Rail is often the butt of tired jokes by second-rate comedians, the passengers who regularly use the express routes around Bristol are more likely to praise the speed and reliability of the services than to offer criticism. The legacy of Brunel's broad gauge trackbeds seems tailor-made for today's InterCity 125s. On cross-country services, the introduction of Sprinter diesel units in 1988 presented the public with clean, comfortable and relatively speedy transportation.

Table Two
Closure Dates of Stations on Lines which remain open

The reference numbers can be used to locate the stations on the map.

1	Alford Halt	10 September 1962
2	Athelney	15 June 1964
3	Bathampton	3 October 1966
4	Bathford	4 January 1965
5	Bleadon & Uphill	5 October 1964
6	Brean Road Halt	2 May 1955
7	Brent Knoll	4 June 1971
8	Chard Junction	7 March 1966
9	Charfield	4 January 1965
10	Charlton Mackrell	10 September 1962
11	Chipping Sodbury	3 April 1961
12	Coalpit Heath	3 April 1961
13	Creech St Michael	5 October 1964
14	Dunball	5 October 1964
15	Durston	5 October 1964
16	Flax Bourton	2 December 1963
17	Hampton Row Halt	29 April 1917
18	Horfield	23 November 1964
19	Keinton Mandeville	10 September 1962
20	Langport East	10 September .1962
21	Limpley Stoke	3 October 1966
22	Long Ashton	6 September 1941
23	Long Sutton & Pitney	10 September 1962
24	Lyng	15 June 1964
25	Milborne Port	7 March 1966
26	Norton Fitzwarren	30 October .1961
27	Puxton & Worle	6 April 1964
28	St Annes Park	5 January 1970
29	Saltford	5 January 1970
30	Somerton	10 September 1962
31	Strap Lane Halt	5 June 1950
32	Sutton Bingham	31 December 1962
33	Templecombe	7 March 1966(*)
34	Twerton	2 April 1917
35	Wellington	5 October 1964
36	Weston Junction	1 March 1884
37	Weston Milton Halt	4 June 1951(*)
38	Wickwar	4 January 1965
39	Winterbourne	3 April 1961
40	Witham	3 October 1966
41	Yate	4 January 1965(*)

Note: (*) denotes station subsequently reopened.

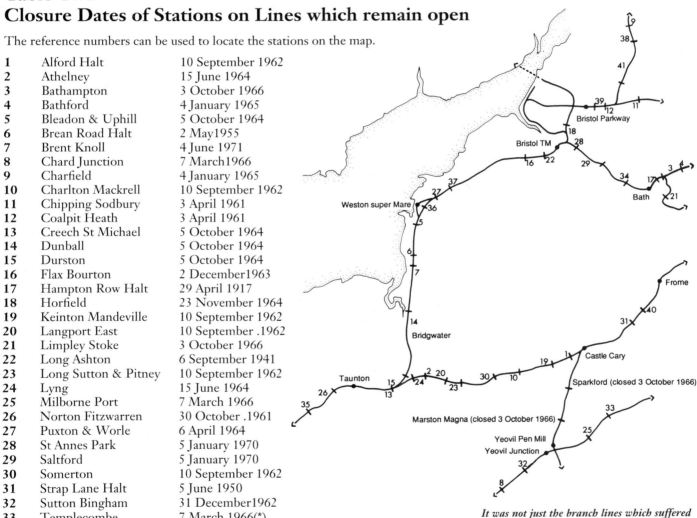

It was not just the branch lines which suffered during the cuts of the 1960s. Many intermediate stations were closed on lines which remained open to through services. The numbers on the plan refer to the list opposite.

7 The Industrials

Neither the city of Bristol nor the county of Somerset is associated with heavy industry but, between them, they have acted as hosts to well over 100 privately-owned, locomotive-operated industrial railways. In the best traditions of railway history, several of the earliest industrial lines in the area evolved from the tramways which were laid to serve the numerous mines of the North Somerset coalfield.

These days, Somerset is more synonymous with cricket, cider and cheese, but back in the 1600s, the time-consuming occupation in the northern part of the county was not the discussion of leather and willow but the extraction of coal. It was the opening of Old Pit at Radstock in 1763 which signalled the real expansion of the mining industry and, although that pit closed in 1854, the coalfield went on to produce, at its peak, 1,750,000 million tons annually. The last North Somerset pit closed as recently as 1973 and, to the end, it kept the flag flying by having its own internal railway. Many of the area's pits converted to steam traction on either their internal lines or their links to the outside world but, sadly, some of the earliest pits ceased working before the advantages of railways were fully appreciated. Had some of the old trendsetters lasted into the railway age, colliery branches with such romantic local names as 'Duck's Nest', 'Atkin's Gout' and even 'Ruth's Arse' would have gone down in the annals of industrial railway history.

Below:
The Radstock 'Dazzler', alias S&D 0-4-2ST No 25A, is shown in fully lined Prussian Blue livery while standing in front of Writhlington Colliery, just to the east of Radstock (S&D) station. The lettering on the two wagons on the colliery road shows the 'grouping' of the mines in the area. Two of those inscribed, Writhlington and Kilmersdon, were the last two pits in the North Somerset coalfield to close.
Lens of Sutton

Before the arrival of the railways, the Somerset Coal Canal was the area's main means of transportation for its most valuable export, and most of the main collieries were connected to the canal by tramways. Horse-power was of course the early method of traction but the Somerset mine owners were an adventurous lot, and as early as August 1827, a steam locomotive was built and tested at Clandown Colliery. This was two years before the emergence of the famous locomotive, Stephenson's *Rocket*, but the forerunner did not reach the dizzy heights achieved by its successor. Weighing a smidgin over 2¼ tons, the Clandown engine could haul nine tubs of 27cwt apiece at a speed of 3¾ miles per hour on the level but its drawback was that it was somewhat heavier than the horses and consequently performed an impressive demolition job on the tracks. Instead of finding a place in history, the locomotive was withdrawn for use as a stationary haulage engine.

The first serious competition to the Somerset Coal Canal materialised on 14 November 1854 in the shape of the Wilts, Somerset & Weymouth Railway's broad gauge branch from Frome to Radstock. This signalled the start of a flurry of promotions to get railways into the mining area, and the first company to challenge the WS&W's sole occupation was the Bristol & North Somerset Railway. Plans for the B&NS were passed in 1863 but it was 1873 before the company managed to open its line. The following year, the Somerset & Dorset Railway opened its financially suicidal Bath extension across the coalfield and this altered the transport map of North Somerset beyond redemption. The S&D's course north of Radstock was on the route of the Somerset Coal Canal's tramway, and the railway company had had to purchase the canal company in order to acquire the land. Considering that the canal was, by that time, in its death throes as a result of railway competition, its proprietors were most grateful for the windfall.

The Wilts, Somerset & Weymouth branch was inherited by the Great Western which, sensibly, converted it to standard gauge in order to facilitate through running over the Bristol & North Somerset. The expense of conversion proved well worth it as by the mid-1880s the GWR was carrying 250,000 tons of Somerset coal per annum as opposed to the Somerset & Dorset's 40,000 tons. This difference was largely explained by the GWR's superior tactics in laying outlet lines directly into collieries, and also its acquisition of the branch from Hallatrow to Camerton, which the absorbed B&NS had managed to open in 1882 to serve the colliery in the village. The 'direct line'

sales pitch had been taken up by Wellsway colliery in 1875 and Welton Hill in 1878 but, emulating its neighbour, the Somerset & Dorset succeeded in signing up Clandown colliery and the neighbouring Middle Pit for a similar service in 1882. Clandown closed in 1929 and Middle Pit followed suit four years later, leaving Radstock gas works as the only regular user of the line, although the disused sidings at Middle Pit saw a brief burst of activity for storage purposes during World War 2.

In the locomotive stakes, 55 years elapsed after Clandown colliery's experiments with locomotive haulage before the next steam tramway engine appeared in North Somerset. Built by Hunslet in 1882 to the 2ft 8½in gauge, it was an inside cylindered 0-4-0ST with 1ft 8in wheels and was named *Enterprise*; the owner was the Lower Writhlington colliery which used it for shunting between the colliery and the foot of Foxcote incline. In 1886, Lower Writhlington was treated to a siding from the Somerset & Dorset line but this did not make Foxcote incline redundant as locomotive haulage over the narrow gauge line continued until 1940. Impressed by Writhlington's locomotive, the colliery at Foxcote followed the leader and converted to locomotive power in 1890 while, across the hill, Kilmersdon colliery's standard gauge rope-assisted system saw its first steam locomotive in 1896. Below Kilmersdon, Ludlows' pit had, at different stages of its existence, connections to both the S&D and the GWR but, apart from a brief flirtation with locomotives, the only mechanical shunting to appear at Ludlows' was done by the road tractors which replaced the horses in 1947.

At Norton Hill colliery, a siding was laid by the Somerset & Dorset in 1900 in preparation for the opening of a new shaft, and steam traction was used from the beginning right up until the pit's closure in 1966. Slightly to the north of Radstock, the former Bristol & North Somerset Railway's branch from Hallatrow had been built with sidings to serve Dunkerton and Camerton collieries and, although Dunkerton was to close in 1925, Camerton was to keep going until 1950.

Right:
Bristol-built Peckett 0-4-0ST Kilmersdon (works No 1788) was built in 1929, and became the last NCB locomotive to see service in the North Somerset coalfield. The NCB presented the locomotive to the S&D Museum Trust and at the time of writing, its restoration is nearly complete and it will soon be delivered to the Trust's home at Washford. This picture shows the locomotive working at Kilmersdon colliery on 20 March 1972. D K Jones collection

Dunkerton was in its heyday the biggest colliery in Somerset, but suffered from cheapskate management. It had its own standard gauge locomotive, a Peckett 0-4-0ST imaginatively named *Dunkerton*, between 1910 and 1925. On the colliery's demise, the engine was transferred to Camerton, but was considered superfluous and was disposed of almost immediately.

West of Midsomer Norton, three collieries operated at Farrington Gurney. Farrington colliery had opened in the 1730s, but had a history of closures and reopenings; its final revitalisation in the 1880s was the result of new management. The colliery was connected to the Bristol & North Somerset Railway in 1882 and maintained its own locomotive for transfer work; three different engines, all 0-4-0STs, are known to have been used on the standard gauge sidings at different times until closure in 1921. To the east of Farrington colliery, Springfield and Old Mills collieries stood almost next to each other. The former, which had the luxury of standard gauge sidings joining the B&NSR, was linked to the latter by a narrow gauge tramway. Old Mills was closed in 1941 but Springfield lasted until 1966, having converted to locomotive haulage in 1940 when a Ruston & Hornsby diesel was acquired.

Northwards from Farrington Gurney, the village of Clutton had four pits at different times and two of these had standard gauge connections to the Bristol & North Somerset Railway. Greyfield colliery, which was opened in the early 1830s, had utilised a double track tramroad until the laying of the B&NSR sidings in 1876. A succession of steam locomotives was used from 1885 until the pit's demise in 1911, and these were all 0-4-0STs. The nearby Fry's Bottom Colliery, which opened in the late 1830s was linked to Clutton station yard in 1873 by a ¾-mile branch, but the pit was closed in 1895 without having had any locomotives of its own.

Further northwards again, Bromley colliery near Pensford had delusions of grandeur in the transportation league. Despite its very modest output, it lent its voice to the 1905 proposal of the Blagdon Light Railway which was planned to connect Blagdon, at the end of the former Wrington Vale Light Railway, to the colliery. The proposal was dropped but, when a colliery was opened at Pensford in 1909, Bromley was linked to Pensford by a 2ft gauge tramway which provided access to exchange sidings with the Great Western's branch. Bromley colliery's tramway was treated to locomotive haulage in 1911 with the delivery of an Avonside 0-4-0ST, but it was found to be

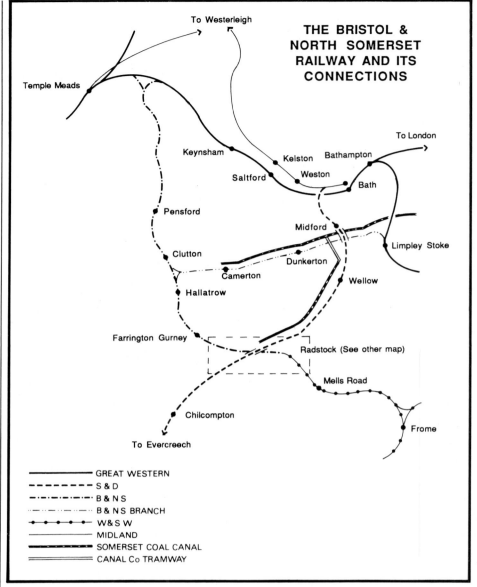

THE BRISTOL & NORTH SOMERSET RAILWAY AND ITS CONNECTIONS

underpowered and was sold in 1913. Rope haulage was reintroduced as a more reliable alternative.

By the time the National Coal Board came into existence on 1 January 1947, all but 12 of the North Somerset pits had closed, and many of the survivors were in decline. The NCB proclaimed that the area's pits were too labour-intensive and it spoke of problems in maintaining staffing levels. As a wonderful piece of public relations, it did, however, instigate a recruitment drive in the 1950s — in Italy! Predictably, the remaining pits closed one by one and after 1966 only Lower Writhlington and Kilmersdon were left. These two were subsequently joined underground and worked as a single unit, with the main customer being the power station at Portishead, near Bristol. The last coal was raised in September 1973 and the last train carrying the dark stuff left Lower Writhlington on 16 November; early the following year, dismantling and removal of equipment was completed and the shafts were capped. One of the last pieces of equipment to go was a Peckett 0-4-0ST which had been delivered new to Kilmersdon in 1929 and, apart from two short spells on loan to Norton Hill colliery, had lived at Kilmersdon all of its life and had seen off the former Great Western and Somerset & Dorset lines. Appropriately, the engine was presented to the Somerset & Dorset Railway Museum Trust.

Only a few of the North Somerset coalfield's mines were to the south or the east of Radstock, and none of the outsiders lasted until NCB days. Moorewood colliery in the Nettlebridge Valley was sunk in the 1860s, and, in 1914, its 2ft gauge tramway was opened to take coal to standard gauge sidings off the Somerset & Dorset line near Chilcompton. The tramway was worked by a Peckett 0-6-0ST which was replaced by a Hudswell Clarke locomotive in 1917. The line was reported to be in disuse by the late 1920s.

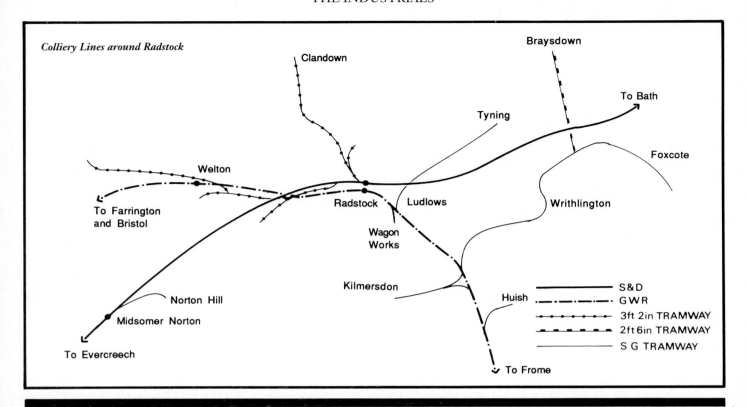

Colliery Lines around Radstock

Table One
Coal Mines with own Railway Sidings or Connections

Name	Location	Railway opened	Railway closed	Gauge
Ashton Vale	Ashton	c1890	1902	2ft 0in(*)
Braysdown	Radstock		1956	2ft 6in(*) †standard
Bromley	Nr Pensford	1909	1957	2ft 0in
Camerton	Camerton	1882	1950	standard
Clandown	Nr Radstock	1827	c1828	2ft 0in(*)
Clutton	Clutton	1912	1921	standard
Coalpit Heath	Coalpit Heath	1832	c1950	standard
Dunkerton	Dunkerton	1906	1925	standard
East Bristol	Speedwell	c1886	1958(iii)	standard
Farrington	F/Gurney	1882	1921	standard
Foxcote	Radstock	1890	c1931	2ft 8½in
Frys Bottom	Nr Clutton	1873	1895	standard
Greyfield	Nr Clutton	1873	1911	standard
Hanham	Hanham	c1886	1926	2ft 0in(*)
Harry Stoke	Harry Stoke	1953	1963	3ft 6in(*)
Kilmersdon	Radstock	1896(i)	1973	standard
Ludlows	Radstock	c1947	1954	standard
Lower Conygre	Timsbury	c1900	1906	2ft 4½in
Lower Writhlington	Radstock	1886(i)	1973	2ft 8½in+standard
Moorewood	Nr Binegar	1913	c1930	2ft 0in
New Mells	Nr Vobster	1857	1943	standard
Newbury/Mackintosh	Nr Coleford	c1910	1927	2ft 0in
Norton Hill	Mid Norton	1903	1966	standard
Old Mills	Nr F/Gurney	c1900(ii)	1966	standard
Old Wood	Rangeworthy		c1900	standard(*)
Springfield	Nr F/Gurney	c1900(ii)	1966	standard
West End	Nailsea	1877	1879	standard
Yate	Yate	c1854	c1894	2ft 0in(*) †standard

Notes:

(*) Locomotives rarely, if ever, used.

(i) Two collieries later connected underground and worked as a single unit.

(ii) Two collieries later connected underground and worked as a single unit.

(iii) Pits ceased winding by 1936. Railway retained for other uses.

Right:
A Somerset colliery shunter with an unmistakably GWR number-plate takes a little explaining. Once upon a time, the Lambourn Valley Railway in Berkshire owned a pair of Chapman & Furneaux 0-6-0Ts named Ealhswith *and* Aelfred. *They were purchased new in 1898 but, in 1904, the LVR's coffers were empty and the GWR took over the working of the line and sold the LVR engines to the Cambrian Railway. When the Grouping fairy waved her magic wand, the two 0-6-0Ts returned to the GWR fold and became Nos 820/21. The former was retired in 1930 and sold to the Mells Colliery Co near Frome the following year. It survived in Somerset until the closure of the mine in 1943, and was eventually cut up in 1945. In this picture, the well-groomed No 820 is seen at Mells colliery in the late 1930s.* F Jones

Below right:
Kerr Stuart 0-4-0ST Nidd *(works No 3112) was built in 1918 and materialised on quarry duty in East Somerset in 1948, prior to which it had seen service at Conygar quarry near Clevedon. This picture was taken at Vobster quarry near the end of the Newbury Railway in the late 1930s.* F Jones

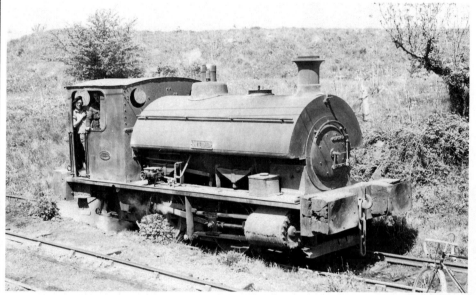

To the east of Radstock, the collieries in the Mells area had erratic existences but boasted the sophistication of their own broad gauge branch line, the Newbury Railway. Just under two miles long, the branch opened in 1857 to link Newbury colliery to the Frome/Radstock line near Mells Road station. The arrival of the branch triggered the sinking of the shafts at Mells, Breach and Mackintosh and the line was subsequently managed by the Mells Siding Committee, on which each user was represented. Horses

Table Two
Standard Gauge Colliery Locomotives inherited by the NCB on 1 January 1947

Listed in order of acquisition.

Wheel Arr	Name	Builder/No	Built	Acquired	Wdn	Location
0-4-0ST	Grazebrook	WB 1884	1908	1903	1951	Norton Hill
0-6-0ST	Lord Salisbury	P 1041	1906	1906	1965	Coalpit Heath
0-4-0ST		P 1788	1929	1929	1974	Kilmersdon
0-6-0ST		HC 1029	1913	1932	1951	Norton Hill
0-4-0D		RH 200793	1940	1940	1967	Springfield
0-4-0D		RH 242869	1946	1946	1968	Coalpit Heath

Locomotives acquired by the NCB after 1 January 1947

Wheel Arr	Name	Builder/No	Built	Acquired	Wdn	Location
0-4-0ST	Leonidas	HL 3159	1916	1951	1955	(Norton Hill)
0-4-0T		H 1684	1931	1964	1971	(Norton Hill)

Builders:
WB: Bagnall
H: Hunslet
HC: Hudswell Clark
HL: Hawthorn Leslie
P: Peckett
RH: Ruston Hornsby

Right:
One of 101 uses for a dead saddle tank is illustrated by the remains of 1903 Barclay 0-4-0ST Medway. *The locomotive was retired from active service at Hapsford, near Whatley, in 1956, but remained in use as a mobile water tank until 1965. This photograph of the once-industrious industrial locomotive was taken on 10 October 1964.* R K Hateley

provided the haulage power at first but a new Hudswell Clarke 0-6-0ST was bought in 1874, by which time the line had been converted to the standard gauge. Each of the collieries which used the line had its own internal railway to transport its coal to the Bilboa coal depot and it was Newbury colliery which, in 1910, became the first to opt for locomotive haulage on its own line. The fortunes of the collieries varied greatly and by 1927 Mells colliery was the only one of the four still operating and it struggled on through several closures and reopenings until 1943.

The 0-6-0T used at Mells Colliery had an interesting history. Built by Messrs Chapman & Furneaux in 1898, it was delivered new to the Lambourn Valley Railway where it was named *Ealhswith*. The Lambourn Valley was purchased by the Great Western in 1905, by which time *Ealhswith* had been sold to the Cambrian Railways where it was given the number 26. At the Grouping, the Cambrian became part of the Great Western; No 26 became GWR No 820 and was overhauled at Swindon in 1922 before being returned to Oswestry for branch duties. After its withdrawal in March 1931, No 820 was purchased for use at Mells colliery, where it continued to sport its GWR brass numberplates. After the colliery's final closure in 1943, the locomotive was left on site and its rusting remains were sold for scrap in February 1945.

The closure of Mells colliery did not signal the end for the old Newbury Railway. At the end of the 1800s, a sizeable quarry had opened at Vobster, just off the railway, and the line was taken over by Mendip Mountain Quarries Ltd. That company was acquired by Roads Reconstruction Ltd in 1934 and a 2ft gauge system was established in the quarry. The narrow gauge lines lasted until 1949, but the standard gauge branch to Mells Road station remained in action until 1965. Although battery-operated locomotives had been introduced at Vobster in 1927, it was a pair of Sentinel steam locomotives which remained on duty at the time of closure.

The quarry at Vobster was just one of many in Somerset which came under the wing of Messrs Roads Reconstruction.

Emborough and Windsor Hill quarries both had their own internal railways to transport stone to transfer sidings on the former Somerset & Dorset line near Binegar but the quarry company's largest workings were around the Frome area and these survive today as part of ARC (Southern) Ltd. At Whatley, a 2ft 3in gauge tramway operated in the quarry until the 1930s and was worked by a pair of Kerr Stuart 0-4-0STs. The link to the great beyond was provided by a 2ft gauge line which connected the quarry to the Frome/Radstock line at Hapsford.

In 1943, the narrow gauge connecting line was replaced by a standard gauge railway which followed the Mells River for 2½ miles through Vallis Vale and, near Hapsford, a yard housed offices, a workshop, two engine sheds and a stone processing plant. Second-hand 0-4-0STs were acquired to work the line at the start, but in 1947 the first of four new Sentinel steam locomotives was delivered. In 1963 the first diesels appeared and,

interestingly, these were Thomas Hill rebuilds which used the frames of recently-deceased Sentinels. By 1965, the centre for operations was centralised at the quarry and so Hapsford yard was left to fall into disuse; it was finally abandoned in 1974 when a new railway into the quarry was opened. This new heavy-duty line was realigned to obviate the sharp curves of the Vallis Vale route and this involved building a viaduct over Mells River and the boring of two new tunnels. Today, ARC's fleet of shunters operates around Whatley quarry but the heavy trains of roadstone are now taken directly from the quarry by ARC's own Class 59/1 diesels.

Roads Reconstruction Ltd, the fore-runner of ARC, had a plant depot at Cranmore on the site of the old Waterlip quarry, and the company stored and repaired its locomotives at this depot. East of Cranmore, Foster Yeoman operate their massive quarry at Merehead which, when modernised in 1971, was

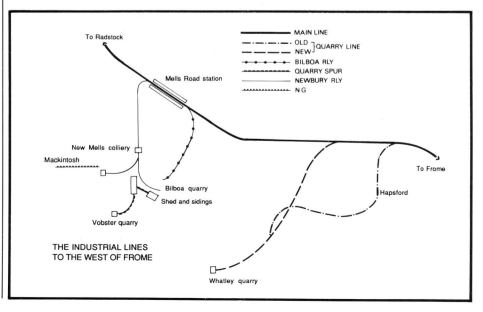

THE INDUSTRIAL LINES
TO THE WEST OF FROME

linked to the former East Somerset Railway. Internal shunting at Merehead is performed by the quarry company's own 1,100hp locomotive which was built by General Motors of Illinois, USA; the same manufacturer supplied the 126ton Class 59 diesels which take the trains from the quarry to Acton in West London. Foster Yeoman's American Class 59s were delivered in January 1986. They were the first privately owned diesels to haul freight over British Rail's main lines and they set a record by hauling 4,692tonne trains, the heaviest ever to run on BR. Foster Yeoman have another quarry at Dulcote near Wells, but although a 2ft gauge tramway was once operated by the company's own engines, road transport took over in 1955.

Elsewhere in Somerset, Roads Reconstruction Ltd had three other quarries which boasted their own railway systems. Sandford quarry, near Banwell, had its

Table Three
Steam Locomotives used by ARC and its Predecessors

Listed in order of acquisition
Standard Gauge

Wheel Arr	No/Name	Builder/No	Built	Acq	Wdn	Location(s)
0-4-0ST	Daphne	P 737	1899	1899	1923	Tytherington
0-4-0ST	Bulford	HC 1045	1914	1915	?	Sandford
0-6-0ST	386	HC 153	1874	1918	1928	Vobster
0-4-0ST	Finetta	A 1565	1911	1919	1934	Sandford & Conygar
0-6-0ST	385 Mildred	A 1763	1917	1920	1959	Vobster
0-4-0T	154	S 6090	1925	1927	1969	Whatley
0-4-0T	1700	S 6219	1927	*	1960	Sandford & Vobster
0-4-0ST	Catherine	H 282	1882	1928	?	Tytherington
0-4-0ST	758	V 798	1876	1942	1949	Sandford & Whatley
0-4-0ST	Medway	B 969	1903	1943	1956	Whatley
0-4-0T	784	S 9374	1947	1947	1965	Whatley & Vobster
0-4-0ST	292 Nidd	KS 3112	1918	1948	1955	Conygar & Vobster & Whatley
0-4-0T	789	S 9386	1948	1948	1967	Whatley
0-4-0T	794	S 9387	1948	1948	1971	Whatley
0-4-0T	1262	S 9391	1949	1949	1965	Sandford & Whatley
0-4-0T	Sentinel	S 9398	1950	1953	1965	Vobster

*Rebuilt from older petrol-mechanical locomotive.

2ft 0in Gauge

Wheel Arr	No/Name	Builder/No	Built	Acq	Wdn	Location(s)
0-4-0ST	Gamecock	P 1030	1904	1904	1927	Cranmore
0-4-2ST	41	KS 3065	1918	1920	1951	Tytherington & Whatley
0-4-2ST	157	KS 856	1904	1924	1951	Sandford
0-4-0WT	3	B 1855	1931	1941	1959	Tytherington
0-4-0T		A 2072	1933	1941	1951	Whatley
0-4-0T		A 2073	1933	1941	1951	Tytherington

Makers:
A: Avonside
B: Barclay
H: Hunslet
HC: Hudswell Clarke
KS: Kerr Stuart
P: Peckett
S: Sentinel
V: Vulcan.

Above left:
This ramshackle engine shed housed the locomotives which brought the stone from Whatley quarry to the exchange sidings on the Frome-Radstock line. The shed was situated at Hapsford, in Vallis Vale, which is now well-known locally as a beauty spot, but the old transfer line was superseded by a new line in 1974 and subsequently lifted. The shed itself had closed about a decade earlier when operations became centred on the quarry. The locomotives on view on 10 October 1654 were a Sentinel (works No 6090) and a Thomas Hill diesel.
R K Hateley

Above:
The ultimate in private-owner locomotives is seen at Merehead quarry on 25 June 1989 when Foster Yeoman's five American-built Class 59 diesels were presented to the public.
Stephen Widdowson

own 2ft gauge locomotive-operated tramway linked to standard gauge transfer sidings which were, in turn, connected to the Great Western's Yatton/Wells branch. Sandford's first standard gauge quarry locomotive, a Hudswell Clarke 0-4-0ST, appeared in 1915 and, at close of play in 1964, steam still ruled in the form of a Sentinel 0-4-0. The narrow gauge tracks at Sandford had first fallen into disuse in the early 1930s but had had a brief reprieve later that decade. Conygar quarry, near Clevedon, had standard gauge transfer sidings which provided a link to the Weston, Clevedon & Portishead line at Walton Park station. The quarry closed in 1935 and its Avonside 0-4-0ST was made redundant. Black Rock quarries, south of Portishead, were also linked to the WC&PR and a succession of seven different locomotives was used on the 2ft gauge line from 1922

until the quarry's closure in 1949, although onward movement by rail had been made impossible by the WC&PR's demise in 1940.

Outside of the Roads Reconstruction empire, Backwell, Downhead, Holcombe and Winford quarries in Somerset all had locomotive-operated tramways which used the ubiquitous 2ft gauge. Downhead's internal system closed in 1925 but the other quarries retained theirs until the postwar years; the last of the four to close was at Holcombe which remained operative until 1958. After closure of the tramway, Holcombe's nine-year old diesel shunter was found a new home in Kent.

To the north of Bristol, Grovesend, Church and West Quarries were all operating near Tytherington by the late 1800s. Church was given a standard gauge siding to the Thornbury branch in 1901 and West, which had boasted a 2ft gauge locomotive-operated system since 1898, followed suit in 1915. The sidings to both quarries were worked by a Peckett 0-4-0ST named *Daphne*. Rail traffic was discontinued in 1948, but in 1972, the expansion of Grovesend quarry justified the relaying of a section of the Thornbury branch, which had closed seven years previously. Today, quarry trains are hauled by British Rail's own locomotives. Elsewhere to the north of Bristol, Barn Hill Quarry at Chipping Sodbury and the workings at Cromhall, Wick and Wickwar all had 2ft gauge locomotive-operated tramways at varying stages of their lives. The last to remain in use was the one at Wick quarry which survived until 1959.

Still to the north of Bristol, the local penchant for digging things up extended

beyond stone: that old faithful, coal, was not exclusive to Somerset. The tale of the Bristol & Gloucestershire Railway's line to collieries at Coalpit Heath has already been told, but mining did not come to a halt in the village until 1950. The one-mile branch from Coalpit Heath to Westerleigh was part of the old B&G and it saw its last usage in 1947, after which the two remaining locomotives, a Peckett 0-6-0ST and a Ruston Hornsby diesel, were transferred to Ludlow's and Old Mills collieries in Somerset. The drift mine at Harry Stoke, close to the present-day Parkway station, survived until 1963 but, although equipped with a 3ft 6in gauge tramway, locomotives were very rarely used.

There were several pits in northeast Bristol which dated back to the mid-1800s and most were under the control of East Bristol Collieries Ltd. Speedwell and Deep Pit collieries were linked to a standard gauge branch which was laid from the Midland line near Fishponds and, although the collieries closed in 1936, the branch was retained for access to the Peckett locomotive works until 1958. Pecketts had used the services of the colliery locomotives for shunting but, with closure of the pits, one of its own 0-6-0STs named *Nancy* was bought from a Staffordshire colliery for shunting duties. By the time the good lady was retired in 1958, she was 53 years old.

Apart from the mines in and to the north of Bristol and those of the North Somerset coalfield, the only other working in the region which progressed to locomotive haulage was West End colliery at Nailsea. This was one of the larger pits in an area which was under scrutiny for potential traffic by the Bristol

Left:
An unidentified Port of Bristol Authority 0-6-0ST poses with assorted staff on the Junction Cut swing bridge at Avonmouth docks circa 1908/09. Port of Bristol Authority

In all, 31 steam locomotives were owned by the Authority at different times and all but one were outside-cylindered 0-6-0STs built by Bristol companies. The first new steam locomotives were delivered from Fox Walker in 1875, and the last were built by Pecketts in 1943. The first diesels appeared in 1952 and, by 1966, the 27-strong diesel fleet had completely ousted steam. Locomotives were sometimes transferred between Avonmouth and Portishead, although the latter saw its last locomotive haulage in the early 1970s. At Avonmouth, only seven wharves and one warehouse still had rail connections in 1980 with just three locomotives being retained to cover all duties and, predictably, all internal railway workings at Avonmouth Docks came to a halt within a few years.

As the docks grew, a variety of industries appeared in Avonmouth and several

& Exeter Railway in the 1830s, but ironically, the colliery's purchase of a brand new Fox Walker 0-6-0ST in 1877 came just two years before the pit ceased production.

Although the mining and quarrying industries were prolific users of private railways, the largest system in the Bristol area was operated by the Port of Bristol Authority. The older docks near the centre of Bristol did not get rail connections until comparatively late in the day, and shunting was performed by locomotives of the major railway companies. At Avonmouth, the original dock was opened in 1877 and, in 1908, the new Royal Edward Dock increased the size of the site several-fold. A dock at Portishead had been opened in 1879, but in 1884 it was purchased by the city council. At its peak in the 1950s, the Port of Bristol Authority administered nearly 100 miles of railway lines, over 1,500 wagons and thirty locomotives. In 1955, more than 1,750,000 tons of freight was handled by the Authority's own locomotives.

Below:
A Port of Bristol Authority 0-6-0ST hauls a train out of the Royal Edward passenger station at Avonmouth docks in September 1927. The ship is believed to be one of the Elders & Fyffes fleet, which had a long association with Avonmouth. Port of Bristol Authority

firms had their own internal railways. The National Smelting Co, now a subsidiary of Rio Tinto Zinc, opened its zinc smelter in 1924 using the premises of the Ministry of Munitions which had operated until 1921. A locomotive-worked 2ft gauge system lasted until 1971, but the main duties were done on the standard gauge sidings which linked up with the Great Western at Hallen Marsh. A total of 10 different standard gauge steam locomotives have been used on the site at different times and all but one were second-hand acquisitions. In 1959, the first diesel locomotive was purchased, and steam vanished two years later. At present, the company has two Sentinel diesels and, as these are permitted to run over British Rail lines at Hallen Marsh, the crews have to be familiar with the BR rule book. Today, incoming traffic consists mainly of coke from Margam while outgoing traffic comprises lead bullion, sulphuric acid and lead dross for both domestic and foreign customers.

The other remaining locomotive user in the Avonmouth industrial area is ICI Severnside, and the arrangement at this site is the opposite of that at the Smelting company. ICI's two centre-cab 0-6-0 diesels perform the internal shunting duties and are not allowed on to British Rail's tracks but incoming trains hauled

Above:
The locomotives being loaded onto the SS Beljeanne *at 'S' shed, Avonmouth Docks, on 13 June 1930 were built by the Vulcan Foundry for a South American railway. It was not just the products of the Bristol builders which were exported through Avonmouth, and many of the Avonside and Peckett dock shunters must have envied their cousins' trips to warmer climates.* Port of Bristol Authority

Left:
This Hudswell Clarke diesel shunter was at first numbered D3002 by the Port of Bristol Authority; later, it became No 17 and was named Camelot. *The photograph is dated July 1952 and, as the diesel had only just been delivered at that time, this shot alongside one of the older Peckett 0-6-0STs was undoubtedly for publicity purposes.* Port of Bristol Authority

Right:
Pecketts of Bristol delivered 'M5' class 0-4-0ST (works No 1267) to Bath gas works in June 1912, and it remained in use at that site until 1964. The date of this picture is unconfirmed but it is believed to be 1963. Photomatic

by BR locomotives have access to the ICI site. One of ICI's neighbours is British Gas, which until recently had its own diesel locomotive for its internal railway system.

Across the river from Avonmouth, Albright & Wilson's chemical plant at Portishead and the uncompleted World War 1 shipyard at Portbury both had their own standard gauge railway systems. In Bristol, standard gauge lines at Lysaght's Iron Works in St Philip's and also the gasworks at Canon's Marsh and at Eastville were operated by company-owned locomotives. Narrow gauge industrial lines were represented by locomotive-operated systems at St Anne's Board Mills and Cattybrook Brickworks at Almondsbury, but these were abandoned in 1967 and 1975 respectively.

In Somerset, Fisons Ltd had its own 2ft gauge tramways at its peat workings at Ashcott, Shapwick and Westhay and, between the late 1940s and abandonment

of the company's railways in 1983, a total of 21 different petrol or diesel locomotives saw service on one or other of the sites. Locomotive-operated narrow gauge systems have been used at the Portland Cement works at Dunball, Chilton Trinity tileworks at Bridgwater, Colthurst Symons brickworks at various locations around Bridgwater and also by Oakhill Brewery. Standard gauge industrial lines have operated at British Cellophane in Bridgwater, Petters (now Westlands) in

Yeovil and Unigate Foods at Chard, and even the Government has put in an occasional appearance as a railway operator in the county. Ministry of Defence depots at Norton Fitzwarren and Puriton have involved the use of the MOD's own locomotives, but the most unlikely engine to be used by order of Whitehall was, surely, the former London & South Western 2-2-0T No 738, which was bought for use at the munitions factory at Bridgwater in 1917.

Table Four
Locomotives used by South Western Gas and British Gas

Listed in order of acquisition

Wheel Arr	No/Name	Builder/No	Built	Acqd	Wdn	Location(s)
0-4-0ST		P 451	1886	1886	1939	Eastville
0-4-0ST	1 *J.W.S.Dix*	HL 2184	1891	1891	1960	Canons Marsh & Eastville
0-4-0WT		AP 4909	1901	1901	1928	Bath
0-4-0ST	2 *G.K.Stothert*	P 864	1901	1901	1939	Eastville
0-4-0ST	3 *Fenwick*	P 1221	1911	1911	1960	Canons Marsh
0-4-0ST	1	P 1267	1912	1912	1964	Bath
0-4-0ST	*Weaste*	HC 302	1888	1918	1922	Weston
0-4-0ST		P 1612	1922	1922	1947	Weston
0-4-0ST	2	A 1978	1928	1928	1964	Bath
0-4-0ST	*J. Fuller Eberle*	P 1967	1939	1939	1968	Eastville
0-4-0D		H 2914	1944	1944	1968	Weston
0-4-0D		H 3057	1946	1946	1968	Weston
0-4-0D		RH 281268	1950	1950	1971	Eastville
0-4-0D		RH 321731	1952	1952	1958	Canons Marsh
0-4-0ST		P 1611	1923	1957	1957	Eastville
0-4-0D		RH 418602	1958	1958	1971	Eastville
0-4-0D	24	RH 210479	1941	1964	1971	Bath
0-4-0D	23	RH 306089	1950	1964	1973	Bath & Eastville
0-4-0D		RH 418792	1959	1968	1970	Hallen

Makers:
AP: Aveling & Porter.
A: Avonside
H: F.Hibberd
HC: Hudswell Clarke
HL:Hawthorn Leslie
P: Peckett
RH: Ruston Hornsby

8 The Builders

Over 4,000 locomotives were built in Bristol and Somerset, of which all but five were steam powered. A number of Bristol-built steam locomotives remained active for some years after the last steam haulage on British Railways, and when the last locomotive rolled off a Bristol assembly line in August 1959, it was 132 years to the month after the first locally-built product was shown a pair of rails.

The very first locomotive to be constructed in the area was the Clandown colliery shunter, the tale of which is related in Chapter 7. Sadly, only the sparsest details of this contraption are known, but there is one point about which surviving records agree and that is its unspectacular nature. Built in 1827, it predated the next locally-built engine by 14 years.

Even in those pioneering days of the railways, there could hardly have been a greater difference between the Clandown locomotive and the next to be built locally. In July 1841, a pair of 24-ton 2-2-2s with 7ft 0in driving wheels was built to a Daniel Gooch design for the Great Western Railway by Stothert & Slaughter, a company which was situated just a few hundred yards from Temple Meads station in Bristol. The firm of Stothert & Slaughter had started life as an ironworks under the guidance of

Henry Stothert, the son of a Bath foundry owner, at Cuckold's Pill, on the banks of the Avon. The location of the works was of strategic importance as, not only was it adjacent to the Bristol & Gloucestershire Railway's terminus, but also just upstream from Bristol's docks where pig iron could be imported and the company's products shipped to customers which had yet to be connected to Britain's embryo railway network.

In 1837, Stothert had taken on Edward Slaughter as a partner, the latter having had two years' invaluable experience as an engineer on the Great Western in the railway's formative years and, despite being only 25 years old, his expertise was held in high regard. Caustic comments about Slaughter's youthfulness were usually countered by the observation that a certain Daniel Gooch had designed locomotives for a not insignificant company while still under 21. Stothert & Slaughter's first order was for 'Firefly' class broad gauge locomotives which, on delivery, were named *Arrow* and *Dart*. The GWR became a regular customer as did other broad gauge concerns. Eight 'Sun' class 2-2-2s and the solitary member of the 'Avalanche' class, an 0-6-0ST built in 1846 for banking duties at Box, were built for the GWR and, by 1849, 18 of the 28 locomotives on the Bristol & Exeter's

Above:
This broad gauge 4-4-0ST (works No 857) was built by the Avonside Engine Co in 1872 for the Bristol & Exeter Railway as B&ER No 85. It became GWR No 2048 and lasted until the end of the broad gauge in 1892. Ian Allan Library

stock list were Stothert & Slaughter products. By 1865, the South Devon Railway had 26 Bristol-built locomotives on its fleet.

The firm rapidly gained a reputation for providing good quality locomotives at fair prices at a time when Britain's railway network was expanding rapidly. Customers were not just broad gauge West Country concerns; 16 passenger locomotives were ordered by the London, Brighton & South Coast Railway in 1846 and, by the mid-1850s, the Taff Vale, Monmouthshire, West Cornwall and Brecon & Merthyr Railways were all using Stothert & Slaughter locomotives. The first engines built for export were six for the Maria Antonia Railway in Tuscany. They were constructed in 1847 and, in the following years, orders were won from railways in Scandinavia, the Middle East and Asia.

In 1856 the company's name was changed to Slaughter, Gruning & Co when Henry Gruning was recruited to replace Henry Stothert after the latter's retirement four years previously. Gruning arrived at a difficult time. Many major railway companies had, by then, opted to build their own locomotives, and this obviously reduced the potential market place. The smaller railway companies, which were so vital for the independent manufacturers, gradually became swallowed up by larger concerns and the minnows' motive power requirements were subsequently taken care of by head office. However, Slaughter Gruning did not suf-fer as badly as many of its competitors. This was due, largely, to shrewdness in the export market and, in particular, India. Between 1857 and 1881, the company supplied almost 200 locomotives to four different Indian railway companies and, with a further 79 sold to New Zealand, the firm weathered the storm. Despite the lull in the home market, Slaughter Gruning's customers during this period included the Great Eastern Railway, for which a batch of Sinclair 2-2-2s was built, the London, Chatham & Dover Railway and the North London Railway. The profit margins on those locomotives for home markets might have been slim, but the clients provided impressive names for the portfolio.

Slaughter Gruning & Co was reconstituted as the Avonside Engine Co Ltd on 11 April 1864 and, among the locomotives which emerged from the works soon afterwards were four 0-8-0Ts, a design which had been almost unheard of at that time. The first two were built in 1864 for the Vale of Neath Railway and were, at

Table One
Broad Gauge Locomotives built by Avonside and its Predecessors

Abbreviations:
B&E: Bristol & Exeter Railway
GWR: Great Western Railway
L&O: Llynfi & Ogmore Railway
SDR: South Devon Railway
T&B: Torbay & Brixham Railway
VoN: Vale of Neath Railway
WCR: West Cornwall Railway

Wheel Arr	Works No	Built	Last wdn	Customer	Total	GWR Nos/Class	Notes
2-2-2	1/2	1841	1870	GWR	2	'Firefly'	
2-2-2	3-10	1841/42	1875	GWR	8	'Sun'	
0-6-0ST		1846	1865	GWR	1	'Avalanche'	
4-2-2		1849	1889	B&E	10	2007/8/9	(i)
0-6-0		1849	1887	B&E	8	2065-72	
4-4-0ST		1853	1878	SDR	2	2105	(ii)
0-6-0		1853	1884	B&E	4	2073-76	
0-4-2		1853	1875	WCR	1		
0-6-0		1856	1888	B&E	4	2059-62	
4-4-0ST	*	1859-65	1892	SDR	16	2106-21	
0-6-0ST	392-396/523-4/558	1860-64	1892	SDR	8	2143/44/48-53	
0-6-0ST	466-469	1861	1886	VoN	4	16-19	
2-4-0	594-605/625-632	1865/66	1892	GWR	20	'Hawthorn'	(iii)
0-6-0ST	470/471	1862	1886	L&O	2	2146/47	(iv)
4-4-0ST	518	1863	1885	L&O	1	2145	(v)
4-4-0ST	661-668	1866	1892	SDR	8	2122-27/54-55	
0-6-0ST	775	1869	1905	SDR	1	2170	(vi)
2-4-0T	804	1871	1907	T&B	1	2171	(vii)
4-4-0ST	857-861	1872/73	1892	B&E	6	2048-53	
4-4-0ST	894/95/1050/51	1872/75	1893	SDR	4	2128-31	
0-6-0ST	896-899/988-993	1872-74	1932	SDR	10	2160-69	(viii)
0-4-0WT	900-902	1873	1913	SDR	3	2172-74	(ix)
0-4-0ST	913	1872	1912	WCR	1	1391	(x)
0-4-0ST	1052-56	1874/75	1929	SDR	5	2175-79	(xi)

Notes:
* Works Nos 360-68,411-12, 522,559,592-93.
(i) Seven withdrawn before absorption.
(ii) The other locomotive was withdrawn before the GWR takeover of 1876.
(iii) Seven converted to saddle tanks in 1877.
(iv) Exchanged with the SDR in 1876.
(v) Converted to a 0-6-0ST and exchanged with the SDR in 1876.
(vi) Converted to standard gauge in 1894 and renumbered 1326.
(vii) Acquired by the SDR from the T&B. Converted to SG by the GWR in 1878 and renumbered 2.
(xiii) Converted to standard gauge and survivors renumbered 1317-25. Nos 1317/24 sold to South Wales Mineral Railway and became Nos 6 and 7. At the grouping,they became GWR Nos 817/18.
(ix) Converted to standard gauge and survivors renumbered 1327/28.
(x) Scrapped in private ownership in 1948.
(xi) Converted to standard gauge and renumbered 1329-33. Four sold 1906-1910 to Powlesland & Mason and returned to the GWR as Nos 1330-1333.

the time, the most powerful tank engines in Britain. The second pair were built two years later for the Great Northern Railway, and were fitted with condensing apparatus for heavy transfer work in the yards around King's Cross. The Great Northern was not a new customer as, between 1864 and 1866, Avonside had supplied it with 15 0-4-2Ts to a Sturrock design. The same company returned in 1867 with an order for Stirling-designed 2-4-0s.

The reconstitution of Avonside and its handling of work for such names as Sturrock and Stirling coincided with the emergence of a local competitor. In 1864, Francis Fox, the Devon-born son of a banker, went into partnership with Edwin Walker, an engineer whose work had included a spell at the Leeds-based locomotive manufacturers, Hewitson & Kitson. The company of Fox Walker & Co established its works in Bristol at Deep Pit Road, St George and the premises, known as the Atlas Works, were connected to a colliery branch which joined the Midland Railway at Kingswood Junction. The Avonside Engine Co was, naturally, concerned about the arrival of another builder in the area, but the newcomer chose to exploit a different market. Avonside's policy was 'big is beautiful' and, although it turned out the occasional industrial locomotive, it equated prestige with main line engines. Its sales catalogue included details of some adventurous designs, many of which had never progressed past the planning stage. Fox Walker arrived at the time when the country was in the grip of a civil and industrial engineering boom and the new company realised that any self-respecting industrialist just had to have his own locomotives. It was this industrial locomotive market which Fox Walker proposed to attack.

From the outset, Fox Walker pursued the then unusual course of standardisation. The partners' Quaker backgrounds no doubt helped them realise that the Victorian penchant for size and elaboration was often in direct inverse proportion to both taste and effectiveness. The company was quite happy to ignore the high-profile main line market and, instead, concentrate on building small tank engines to a handful of standard patterns. The standardisation permitted reasonable scope for variety to suit the needs of individual customers and, in the company's first 14 years, 40% of its output was for the export market, in particular narrow gauge railways in Scandinavia and South America.

Although Fox Walker had arrived at a time of market buoyancy, the late 1860s and early 1870s saw another downturn in the locomotive building industry throughout the country. This was not helped by some main line railway companies which embarked on constructing engines, not only for themselves, but also private buyers. The knock-on effect of the recession was well illustrated at the Avonside Engine Co. Although that company did not count industrial users among its major customers, its output of 36 locomotives for the home market in 1866 dropped to just 24 in total from 1867 to 1871. In order to obviate the threat from railway company-owned works, the Locomotive Manufacturers' Association was formed in 1875 and, with Henry Stothert's son, John, and the former Avonside works manager, Alfred Sacre, on the committee, an injunction was obtained in 1876 to prevent the railway companies from supplying the private sector.

During those years of upheaval, both Bristol companies looked to other markets. Avonside was the more successful and, in 1871, it started building articulated locomotives under licence from the designer, Robert Fairlie. These engines were the result of lateral thinking. Many foreign railways needed locomotives for hauling heavy trains over steeply-graded lines, but frequently the tight curvature and lightweight nature of the permanent way prevented the use of conventional engines of adequate power. Fairlie's answer was to build a pair of locomotives back to back and to mount them on either 0-4-0 or 0-6-0 bogies, thereby creating an 0-4-4-0 or an 0-6-6-0. This simple but most effective idea was later used by Beyer Garratt for its massive main line beasts, but the original Fairlie engines were not subjected to the same limelight. Perhaps the best known nowadays are those used on the Festiniog Railway in Wales, although the survivors came from builders such as Sharp Stewart and Bagnalls and not the Avonside works; those which Avonside supplied to the Festiniog Railway have long since gone to the great yard in the sky. Over 100 articulated Fairlies were built in Bristol, the majority going to Central and South America.

Avonside's successful departure into the industrial field did not go unnoticed by the folks at Fox Walker. In 1875, the latter company became the main shareholder in the Handyside Steep Gradient Co Ltd, a concern which had been incorporated to market a locomotive designed by Henry Handyside in 1873. This machine required a central rail on to which it would clamp itself, thereby enabling it to attack gradients of 1 in 10. Although satisfactory in trials, some of which were conducted on the site of the construction of Avonmouth Dock, the engine did little more than the rack and pinion systems which were already in use worldwide. Mr Handyside's pride and joy passed peacefully into oblivion. As if

Table Two
Fox Walker Locomotives used by Companies which became part of the Great Western Railway

Wheel Arr	Works No	Built	Acq	Wdn	Owner	No	GWR No
0-6-0ST	170	1872	new	1912	Whitland & Cardigan	1	1385(i)
0-4-0ST	185	1873	1889	1898	Alexandra Docks	*	
0-4-0ST	200	1874	new	1917	Cardiff	17	
0-6-0ST	271	1875	new	1911	Whitland & Cardigan	2	1386 (ii)
0-6-0ST	279	1875	1885	1925	Llanelly & Mynydd Mawr	*	969
0-6-0ST	327	1876	1897	1898	Port Talbot	*	(iii)
0-6-0ST	340	1877	new	1950	Whitland & Cardigan	3	1387
0-6-0T	410	1878	new	1910	N.Pembs & Fishguard	*	1378

Notes:

*   Name carried instead of number.
(i)   Ran for a time as an 0-4-2T. Scrapped in private ownership 1952.
(ii)   Scrapped 1934 by East Kent Railway.
(iii)   Scrapped 1911 by Swansea Harbour Trust.

Left:
Fox Walker built nine heavy 0-6-0STs for the Somerset & Dorset between 1874 and 1876. S&D No 5 was built in February 1875 (works No 258) and lasted until October 1934, by which time it sported LMS No 1504.
R K Blencowe collection

to keep ahead of the competition, Avonside built its own steep gradient engine in 1875 but, unlike Fox Walker's, the Avonside version was constructed to a customer's order. It was a four-cylindered Fell locomotive for the Rimutaka Incline in New Zealand.

Between bouts of playing with the Handyside machine, Fox Walker constructed its heaviest and most powerful locomotives. They were nine 0-6-0STs which were ordered for the Somerset & Dorset Railway in preparation for the opening of its extension to Bath and, in order to reduce its expenditure, the S&D gave four ageing 2-4-0s in part-exchange. Despite the strenuous work these locomotives undertook over the Mendips, eight of them were still alive and kicking when the S&D was absorbed by the LMS in 1930. These survivors took LMS numbers 1500-07 and the last was not retired until November 1934.

Avonside, too, provided locomotives for the Somerset & Dorset. In November 1877, the first of nine 0-4-4Ts was delivered but, as the S&D's order had to be ratified by its then joint operators, the Midland, the completed engines were sent, not to Highbridge, but to Derby. The Midland played with them first to ensure their suitability for the S&D and this resulted in their eventual arrival at Highbridge in Midland Green livery. The choice of 0-4-4Ts for fast passenger work was controversial as it was considered that the rear bogie would be prone to derailment on bunker-first running. The originator of the design, the Midland's Samuel Johnson, was unmoved by the criticism at first but became suitably embarrassed when derailments started to occur. Grudgingly, the Johnson bogies were eventually replaced by those to an Adams design. The last of the Avonside S&D 0-4-4Ts survived until 1946, by which time it had become LMS No 1230.

Despite winning the battle with the main line railway companies and the success of the Fairlies, Avonside started to feel the full effects of the recession in the late 1870s. The company's drastic course of action was to announce a 12½% reduction in wages for its workers but, not altogether surprisingly, this was not too popular among the workforce of 800. Industrial action followed, and this resulted in delays to production and cancellation of orders. Fox Walker was also finding the going tough and, although the company had built over 400 locomotives with a workforce that rarely exceeded 200 men, the letters from the bank manager were becoming increasingly regular and, as a result, the partnership was wound up in December 1878.

Almost a year after Fox Walker's demise, Avonside narrowly escaped winding up orders, and this reprieve was due to a major reconstitution of the company after the problems of 1878. Ironically, the 'new' Avonside did very well in what was, generally, an unspectacular market. Orders for 20 2-6-0s and 25 0-6-0s for India, combined with 17 Fairlies for Burma and a further seven for New Zealand kept the company busy under the management of one John Platts, the miscreant who was eventually made the scapegoat for the company having come perilously close to extinction. Platts was replaced in June 1881 by Edwin Walker who, since the death of his own company, had found thumb-twiddling rather tedious. But despite healthy order books, patient shareholders and the leadership of Walker, Avonside was forced into liquidation in July 1881.

That could have been the end of private locomotive building in Bristol, but in 1881 the former Fox Walker concern was taken over by Birmingham-born Thomas Peckett and his four sons. Corporate identity was not a problem for our Thomas; he lost little sleep before deciding to name his acquisition Peckett & Sons. Avonside resurfaced in 1882 when Edwin Walker bought the remnants of

Left:
Fox Walker built 0-6-0ST works No 242 in 1874. Its last duties were at Mountain Ash colliery in South Wales, and on its retirement it was acquired by the Bristol Industrial Museum for restoration. Here, it sits patiently at the rear of the museum in August 1991 awaiting a bit of that tender loving care. Author

the company for £20,000. Much of the original works had, by that time, been acquired for other purposes, but Walker was optimistic that the reputation of the original Avonside company was strong enough to provide him with a flying start. He retained the old concern's name and, in his publicity material, emphasised that the company had been established in 1837, a statement which, although not untruthful, was challenged as unethical by his competitors. The rumpus over Walker's misleading use of Avonside's history came to an end in 1887 when the old company was officially liquidated. Part of the formalities included an order that the records of the original Avonside concern should be destroyed so that they could not be used by Walker to gain an unfair advantage. Although the edict forced Walker to be a little more honest, it has resulted in alopecia among railway historians. Trying to put together the Avonside works lists has become akin to doing a jigsaw which has missing pieces.

Fortuitously for both the Avonside and Peckett concerns, the locomotive market made a significant recovery in the 1880s. Walker abandoned the old Avonside gravitation towards large locomotives and, like Peckett's, began to concentrate on a small number of standard designs for

Table Three
Standard Gauge Locomotives built by Avonside and its Predecessors for the Great Western Railway and its Subsidiaries

Wheel Arr	Works No	Built	Last wdn	Customer	Total	Original Nos	GWR Nos	Notes
0-6-0		1846	1876	Taff Vale	4	13-16		
0-6-0		1847	1890	Monmouthshire	3	6-8	1315-17	(i)
0-4-0WT		1850	1873	Monmouthshire	2	14/15		(ii)
4-4-0		1850	1882	Monmouthshire	1	16	1303	(iii)
0-6-0		1851	1864	Taff Vale	4	22/24		(iv)
2-4-0		1852	1874	Taff Vale	2	25/26		
0-6-0		1852	1889	Monmouthshire	4	17-20	1318-21	(v)
2-4-0		1853	1888	West Cornwall	1	*	2136	(xii)
4-4-0T		1853	1890	Monmouthshire	6	21-26	1322-27	(vi)
0-6-0WT		1854	1889	Monmouthshire	6	27-32	1328-33	
0-6-0		1857	1878	Taff Vale	3	38-40		
0-6-0		1857	1882	Brecon & Merthyr	2	7/8		(vii)
0-6-0		1860	1893	Taff Vale	2	49/50		
0-6-0	475-86	1863	1925	Great Western	12	137-48	137-48	
0-8-0T	556/57	1864	1871	Vale of Neath	2	22/23	415/16	
0-6-0	†	1865	1887	West Cornwall	1	*	2156	(xii)
0-6-0ST	††	1871-3	1910	Monmouthshire	5	42-46	1345-49	
0-6-0	868-71	1871	1905	Taff Vale	4	31/2/84/5		(viii)
0-6-0ST	942/3	1873	1931	Neath & Brecon	2	5/6	2199/89	(ix)
0-4-4T	**	1873-5	1908	Monmouthshire	3	5/47/51	1308-10	
0-6-0ST	1013-16	1874	1921	Neath & Brecon	4	7-10		(x)
0-4-4T	1244	1878	1892	M&SWJ	1	4		(xi)
0-4-0ST	1386	1897	1932	Alexandra Docks	1	*	1340	
0-6-0ST	1421	1900	1914	BP&GVR	1	2		
0-6-0T	1448	1902	1929	Llanelly & MM	1	*	944	
0-6-0ST	1463/91	1903/5	1953	BP&GVR	2	4/5	2194/95	
R/motor	1474-79	1904	1920	Taff Vale	6	2-7		
0-6-0ST	1519/35	1907	1956	BP&GVR	2	6/7	2196/76	
0-4-0T	1987-92	1926	1960	GWR	6	1101-06	1101-06	

Notes.
††   Works Nos 842/928/927/974/975 respectively.
**   Works Nos 976/1057/1058.
†   Delivered in kit form and assembled by WCR.
*   Name carried instead of number.
(i)   Converted to saddle tanks 1868-73.
(ii)   Eventually converted to 0-6-0T.
(iii)   Converted to tank locomotive by 1854.
(iv)   Other two withdrawn before numbering replaced names.
(v)   MR No 20 (GWR No 1321) converted to saddle tank.
(vi)   Converted to 0-6-0T.
(vii)   Acquired from T.Savin, the contractor who worked the B&M.
(viii)   Later converted to saddle tanks.
(ix)   Later renumbered as N&B Nos 1 and 2; GWR No 2199 (ex No 1) sold into private ownership and scrapped 1955.
(x)   N&B Nos 7/8 sold to the Brecon & Merthyr and withdrawn as B&M Nos 30/31 in 1921. Nos 9/10 renumbered 3/4 and withdrawn by 1917.
(xi)   Fairlie locomotive acquired by the Swindon, Marlborough & Andover Railway in 1881; the company became part of the Midland & South Western Junction Railway in 1884.
(xii)   Sold to South Devon Railway and converted to broad gauge.

industrial tank engines. Peckett's inheritance had, of course, included designs and features which had originated with Edwin Walker in the days of Fox Walker, and many of the new Avonside drawings displayed a continuity of Walker's ideas. In the engineering world, many observers found it difficult to differentiate between the products of the two companies but, as both had excellent reputations, the word 'Bristol' was often sufficient to sell a locomotive.

By the turn of the century, both Bristol builders were working steadily with Peckett's construction averaging 25 locomotives per year and Avonside's 16. In 1904 Avonside moved from its cramped site next to the Midland Railway's goods depot to a purpose-built factory adjacent to Fishponds station and, the following year, Peckett's Atlas Works were enlarged by the addition of a modern construction shop. Avonside continued to rely on the export market, and even printed copies of its brochures in Spanish for the benefit of South American customers; Peckett's was confident enough of sales to construct engines for stock without having definite buyers for them.

Below:
The picture of the inside of the finishing shop at Peckett's Atlas Works in Bristol was taken in 1905. It shows a rake of mixed saddle tanks, which were typical of Peckett's industrial designs. Bristol Industrial Museum

Since its introduction, Peckett's 'W4' class of 0-4-0ST had proved a success and, the year after the expansion of the works, an updated version appeared and was designated 'W5'. Like their predecessors, the 'W5s' were built in batches of four at a time and, usually, their sales were secured before they had left the assembly line. Similarly, the 'M5' class 0-4-0ST which had replaced the 'M4' in 1905 and the 'R2' 0-4-0STs, which were introduced in 1910 to replace an older design, were each constructed in pairs with the company being confident of obtaining early sales.

Walker was constantly looking for new outlets for his Avonside products. The fashion for steam railmotors on both major and secondary railways throughout the country looked like a promising avenue, and the company built six power units for the Taff Vale Railway in 1904, the coach work being done by the Bristol Wagon & Carriage Co at its Lawrence Hill workshop. However, the anticipated advantages of railmotors over locomotive-hauled trains on suburban services did not fully materialise and the fad died. Avonside's representatives on the Taff Vale were all scrapped by 1920.

In 1913, a seemingly innocent little innovation emerged from the Avonside works but was to become, unwittingly, a trend-setter. It was a 0-4-0 which was powered by a Parsons petrol engine and, when the Great War broke out the following year, the War Department ordered a quantity of similar units for its

The GWR ordered six deceptively powerful 0-4-0Ts from Avonside in 1926 for shunting duties at Swansea docks; with 16in x 24in cylinders and 3ft 9½in driving wheels, these locomotives produced a commendable tractive effort of 19,150lb. Their works numbers were 1987-92 and the GWR allocated them Nos 1101-06. No 1104 is pictured at Danygraig shed minus its coupling rods, and the lettering on the tank indicates that this photograph was taken in pre-Nationalisation days. The locomotive was withdrawn in January 1960. F W Day

Top left:
The Avonside Engine Co built this 0-4-0ST (works No 1386) in 1897 for the contractors Dunn & Co, who undertook shunting duties at the Town dock in Newport. When the Alexandra Dock & Railway Co took over the shunting work at the port, it bought the contractor's locomotives, and this one, named Trojan *retained its name after the ADR was absorbed by the GWR at the Grouping. The GWR gave it No 1340, and sold it in 1934 to the Victoria colliery at Wellington. It went on to have a couple more owners and was reported awaiting cutting up at Alders paper mills at Tamworth in 1966. Fortunately* Trojan *escaped the cutter's torch, and is now preserved at the Didcot Railway Centre.* Locomotive Publishing Co

2ft 6in gauge lines at depots throughout the country. The Government was to become a major customer during the war years. Many of the dockyard engines required by the Admiralty were ordered from Avonside, as were the 0-4-0Ts which the War Department used extensively on its 1ft 6in gauge lines on the Continent. Unlike Peckett's and many of its competitors elsewhere, Avonside's production increased dramatically between 1914 and 1918, with over 120 locomotives being completed during those years.

Apart from the construction of new locomotives, companies such as Avonside and Peckett also undertook repair work. During the difficult time of the 1870s, both companies had often sold their products at little or no profit, and had counted on the repair and overhaul bills which those locomotives would eventually generate. In the mid-1920s, however, repair contracts became available by the handful as a result of the Grouping of the country's railways; the workshops of the 'Big Four' simply could not cope with the amount of repairs needed for the locomotives they absorbed from smaller compa-

nies, many of these acquisitions having suffered both overwork and mechanical neglect during the war years. But, once the honeymoon was over, there was little work, constructional or repair, which the 'Big Four' could not handle. Coupled to that, many absorbed locomotives became surplus to requirements and were offered to private buyers at knock-down prices, thus minimising the market for new locomotives. The result for private builders throughout the country was disastrous.

One of the casualties was Avonside, which was liquidated in November 1934. The company's assets were acquired by the Hunslet Engine Co of Leeds in July the following year, four months after completion of the last locomotive. Peckett's survived, but only just. World War 2 resulted in several government orders and between 1939 and 1945 31 of the 65 locomotives to leave the works went either to Royal Ordnance factories or the Woolwich Arsenal. After the war production continued on a modest scale, but the

conservatism which had previously seen the firm survive steadily through thick and thin was to prove its undoing. While companies such as Hudswell Clarke and, ironically, Hunslet had secured their futures by progressing to the construction of diesel locomotives, Peckett's acceptance of the change in the face of British motive power came too late.

In 1956 Peckett built a pair of demonstration 200hp 0-4-0 diesel engines but it was July the following year before the company won a firm order for its first diesel locomotive. In 1958 one of the original demonstrators was sold and a replacement was built. 1959 saw an order for one 200hp 0-6-0 diesel and when it left the works in August that year, it became the last new locomotive to be constructed by the company. The

Below:
Much of Avonside's work was for the export market and this 2-8-0 (works No 2049) is for FC Guaqui La Paz, Peru. The locomotive was posed for a company publicity shot outside the workshop in 1930, just four years before the famous firm went into liquidation. Bristol Industrial Museum

demonstrator of 1958 was sold in April 1961. The last steam locomotive to be built by Peckett's had been completed in June 1958, a full 15 months after the penultimate one. That final steam engine was an outside cylindered 0-6-0T built to the 3ft gauge lines of the Sena Sugar Estates Ltd in Mozambique. It carried works number 2165.

Peckett's application of works numbers is interesting. When the family took over from Fox Walker in 1881, the predecessor's sequence was continued with No 421, a semi-portable engine for the Brendon Hills iron mines in West Somerset and this was, almost certainly, the completion of an order inherited from Fox Walker, as were the next three lots. The first locomotive built under the Peckett regime appeared in July 1882 and was works No 426. Occasional gaps appear in Peckett's numbering sequence until 1890, which can usually be explained by cancelled orders. However, from 1890, complete blocks of 10 numbers at a time are omitted from the lists at regular intervals.

For example, No 506 was built in August 1890 but the next to be built was, despite completion in the following month, allocated No 517. It is generally assumed that this practice was adopted to mislead competitors, in particular Edwin Walker's Avonside company, and this assumption is backed up by the fact that, after the demise of Avonside, only two blocks of works numbers are omitted. The first missing sequence would have slotted into the year 1936 but the second probably emphasises the company's

Table Four
Standard Peckett Locomotive Classes

Class	Wheel arr	Driving Wheels	Cylinders (in)	First built	Last built	For Britain SG	NG	Export†	Notes
B1/B2	0-6-0ST	3ft 7in	14x20(O)	FW	1931	92		7	(i)
B3	0-6-0ST	3ft 7in	14x22(O)	1931	1954	17		3	
C	0-6-0ST	3ft 2in	14x20(I)	1905	1927	10			
C1	0-6-0ST	3ft 0½in	14x20(I)	1927	1956	2			(ii)
E	0-4-0ST	3ft 7in	15x21(O)	1903	1940	52			
E1	0-4-0ST	3ft 7in	15x23(O)	1950	1954	3			
F/FA	0-6-0ST	3ft 7in	15x21(O)	1906	1943	14			(iii)
G	0-6-0ST	3ft 7in	15x21(I)	1908	1908	1			
M3/M4	0-4-0ST	2ft 6in	10x14(O)	FW	1912	61	11	4	(iv)
M5	0-4-0ST	2ft 9in	10x15(O)	1905	1946	63	1	11	(v)
OQ	0-6-0ST	4ft 0½in	18x26(O)	1951	1954	3			
OQT	0-8-0	4ft 6in	18x26(O)	1931	1931			1	
OX	0-6-0ST	3ft 10in	16x24(O)	1913	1954	24			(vi)
OY	0-4-0ST	3ft 10in	16x24(O)	1912	1955	25		1	(vii)
Q	0-6-0ST	4ft 0½in	18x24(I)	1899	1918	7			
R1/R2	0-4-0ST	3ft 0in*	12x18(O)	1891	1952	118	2	6	(viii)
R3	0-4-0ST	3ft 0in	12x20(O)	1929	1929	2			
R4	0-4-0ST	3ft 0½in	12x20(O)	1930	1952	48	1	4	(ix)
S1	0-4-0ST	3ft 0in	15x18(I)	FW	1883	1			
W2/W3	0-4-0ST	3ft 0½inin	13x20(O)	FW	1884	2			(x)
W4	0-4-0ST	3ft 2in	14x20(O)	1885	1906	143		1	
W5	0-4-0ST	3ft 2½in	14x20(O)	1906	1925	93		3	
W6/W7	0-4-0ST	3ft 2½in	14x22(O)	1926	1953	103		3	(xi)
X/X2	0-6-0ST	3ft 10in	16x22(I)	1888	1940	97	1	2	(xii)
XL	0-6-0ST	3ft 0½in	12x18(I)**	1890	1931	9			(xiii)
Y	0-4-0ST	3ft 10in	16x22(I)	1906	1938	7			

Notes:
† Export locomotives: all gauges included in this column.
* Wheels either 3ft 0in or 3ft 0½in.
** Cylinders either 12x18 or 13x18.
FW Design originated with Fox Walker.
(i) Last 'B1' built 1904, first B2 in 1905. Includes one oil-burner and three others with variations.
(ii) Includes one with 15in x 21in cylinders.
(iii) Last 'F' built 1918, first 'FA' in 1910.
(iv) Last 'M3' built 1891, first 'M4' in 1890. After 1905, the only 'M4s' built were non-standard gauge locos. Two 'M4s' built with 10in x 15in cylinders.
(v) Includes one oil-burner. Export locos include three built as 0-4-2Ts and three as 0-6-2Ts.
(vi) 'OX' class gradually updated as 'OX1', 'OX2', 'OX3' and then 'OX4'.
(vii) OY class gradually updated as 'OY1' then 'OY2'. Includes one with variations.
(viii) Last 'R1' built 1909, first 'R2' in 1910. Includes two locos of 1893 designated 'R' class, plus three with variations, including one 0-6-0ST.
(ix) Includes one with variations and one built as 0-6-0T.
(x) One loco of each class, both built in the same year.
(xi) Last 'W6' built 1945, first 'W7' in 1938. Includes six oil-burners and one with variations.
(xii) Last 'X' built 1906, first 'X2' in 1906. One X built as 0-4-0ST.
(xiii) Eight 'XLs' built 1887 to 1895, the other in 1931.

Left:
James Pearson's first passenger locomotive design for the Bristol & Exeter was turned into reality at Bristol works in 1870. B&E No 43 was built in 1871 for the broad gauge and, when the company passed to the GWR, the locomotive became No 2021. It was not converted for the standard gauge and therefore became redundant in 1892, and was consequently withdrawn.
Photomatic

embarrassment at having ignored the national trend towards the production of diesels. Peckett's diesels were treated to a separate numbering sequence and the first four were given works Nos 5000-03. The next diesel to be built, which turned out to be the last, was not numbered 5004 but 5014! The lists of the old rival, Avonside, are not without their quirks. It was only in 1861, part way through the Slaughter Gruning period, that works numbers were used consistently.

Peckett's Atlas Works lost its branch line connection to the outside world in 1958 and the then infrequent movement of locomotives to and from the works was subsequently undertaken by road. In 1961 Peckett's goodwill and stock of spares was acquired by the Reed Crane & Hoist Co of Yorkshire; in February the following year, the last repair job was completed and, soon after, the gates were closed for the last time.

The Peckett and Avonside companies, along with their predecessors, left significant legacies in the story of British locomotive development, but they were not alone in Bristol. The broad gauge

Bristol & Exeter Railway had its own works in the city and, between 1859 and 1876, constructed 35 locomotives. The B&E had, between 1840 and 1849, been worked by the Great Western but, on 1 May 1849, it reverted to full independence. The B&E's chief engineer, C.H.Gregory, was replaced, in May 1850, by James Pearson who had previously held the celebrated post of atmospheric superintendent on the South Devon Railway, a position paralleled, in later years, by the captaincy of the Titanic.

In its early years of independence, the Bristol & Exeter ordered its locomotives from outside suppliers, which included our old friends, Stothert & Slaughter. The B&E established its own workshop at Pylle Hill, just outside Temple Meads station, but the premises were intended, initially, to undertake only repairs and overhauls. Although Pearson was nominally responsible for the design of the B&E's early locomotives, the credit for much of the work is due to the draughtsmen employed by the various builders. The company eventually realised that it

had the basic facilities to construct locomotives from scratch, but it was September 1859 before the first home-built locomotive appeared. This was No 29, a 4-2-4T and, in April 1862, a similar engine was built at Bristol and given No 12. The first survived until 1880, the second until 1885 and, despite neither having been treated to rebuilding, their combined mileage was well over one million.

Four more 4-2-4Ts appeared, three in 1868 and the other in 1873, and these were renewals of earlier locomotives. The originals had 9ft 0in driving wheels and were used on the fastest expresses; one had been recorded as achieving 82mph down the Wellington Bank. The renewals had slightly smaller driving wheels of 8ft 10in but, with inside frames and both well- and back-tanks, were similar in many other respects to the predecessors.

Pearson's first tender engine to be built at Bristol was constructed in February 1870 and, by December 1872, nine similar engines had appeared from the works. As a class, they were similar to the Great Western's 'Hawthorns' of 1865 and, like their GWR counterparts, proved to be versatile locomotives. Throughout their lives, most were shedded at Bristol and worked through to Newton Abbot. Apart from four shunting tanks, the only other

Table Five
Non-Standard Peckett Locomotives

Gauge	0-4-0T	0-4-0ST	0-4-2ST	0-6-0T	0-6-0ST	2-4-2T	4-4-0T	0-6-0
1ft 9in					3			
2ft 0in		1	1	9				2
2ft 5½in								
60cm		1		6				
2ft 6in		8	1					
2ft 7½in					1			
2ft 8in			1					
2ft 8½in		2						
3ft 0in	9	28		2	1		2	
3ft 6in		3	4*		1		1	
Metre		1		1			2	
4ft 8½in	4	13				1		
5ft 6in		1						
Totals	13	59	7	3	21	1	5	2

Note:
* includes three 0-4-2Ts.

broad gauge locomotives to be built at Bristol works was a trio of 2-4-0s, two of which were built in 1874 and the other in 1875. The intention was that these 2-4-0s would be suitable candidates for eventual gauge conversion. Simultaneously with their construction, three almost identical 2-4-0s were built at Bristol for the standard gauge.

Of the Bristol & Exeter's standard gauge stock which was designed by Pearson, three 0-4-0Ts emerged from Bristol works in 1875 but were all condemned in the summer of 1880. A pair of 2-4-0Ts, which were completed at Bristol in 1876 just after the Great Western had taken over the B&E, fared a little better and lasted as Bristol-allocated engines until 1888 and 1890. By contrast, a longevity award must have been deserved by the two 0-6-0Ts which were built at Bristol, one in 1874, the other in 1875. Intended, originally, for the Culm Valley Railway in Devon, they both benefitted from being rebuilt at Swindon, once in 1881 and again in 1896. After the first rebuilding, both were despatched to Weymouth for work on the quayside trains where they remained until 1927. One of the pair, by then GWR No 1377, was withdrawn but the other, GWR No 1376, was allocated to Oswestry, the traditional home of GWR oddities, where it remained until retirement in January 1934.

There were two other locomotives which were built at Bristol works but these were neither broad nor standard gauge. The Bristol & Exeter worked the tramway between Westleigh Quarries and Burlescombe station in Devon, and this was built to 3ft gauge. For this duty, Bristol constructed a pair of diminutive 0-4-0WTs, one in 1874, the other in 1875, and they continued working the line until the lease on the quarry expired in 1898. Under Great Western ownership, the engines were numbered 1381 and 1382 and the obligatory Swindon-style cast iron numberplates all but dwarfed the tiny machines.

Pearson's reign at Bristol works was not only remembered for his designs. Until 1860, the Bristol & Exeter's locomotive livery was an impressively lined-out green but, with his staunch Quaker background, Pearson objected to such a vulgar display. As soon as he was able, he introduced a severe unadorned black as the standard livery.

Apart from the Clandown colliery locomotive which was mentioned at the start of this chapter, all of the other local locomotive building so far mentioned, broad or standard gauge, industrial or main line, was undertaken in Bristol itself. There were, however, three other engines which were constructed locally.

The unlikely source of this missing trio is Highbridge Works, the home of the Somerset & Dorset Railway. In 1885, additional shunting power was required on the colliery branches at Radstock and the S&D's superintendent, W.H.French, supervised the building of a 0-4-2ST at the company's works. The locomotive was intended to assist the existing shunter, a 0-4-0ST named *Bristol* which, coincidentally, had been built by Slaughter Gruning in 1852 for a company in Essex. *Bristol* had seen service with several contractors before being bought by the S&D for all of £385, the bargain price reflecting the fact that it was in need of extensive rebuilding before being let loose on the colliery slopes. The S&D-built 0-4-2ST had 3ft 6in driving wheels, outside cylinders of 10in x 14in and weighed in at 17¼ tons. Numbered in the duplicate list as 25A, it was rebuilt in 1896 and again in 1906, the second rebuild providing it with vacuum brakes for the unlikely task of working the branch to Burnham-on-Sea. Unsurprisingly, No 25A was not the ideal locomotive for branch passenger duties and it was returned to Radstock for shunting work, where it lasted until 1929.

Alfred Whitaker replaced French in the chair at Highbridge in 1889 and, not to be outdone by his predecessor, Whitaker built not one, but two, engines at Highbridge in 1895. Both were 0-4-0STs with 3ft drivers and 10in x 14in outside cylinders, dimensions not dissimilar to the antiquarian Slaughter Gruning locomotive *Bristol* which was, by 1895, considered past its sell-by date. The Whitaker engines became Nos 26A and 45A in the duplicate list and, although the latter was retired in 1929, the former survived until the LMS take-over of 1930. Despite being allotted LMS No 1509, it was withdrawn in December the same year without having had the dignity of carrying its new number.

None of the four Somerset-built engines lasted until the preservation era, but many Bristol-built locomotives are now in regular use on restored lines all over the country. Appropriately, the local preservation organisations have their fair share.

Table Six
Bristol & Exeter Locomotives built at Bristol Works
Broad Gauge

Built	Nos	Wheel Arr	Driving wheels	Cylinders (in)	Total	GWR Nos	Last wdn
1859/62	12/29	4-2-4T	7ft 6in	17x24(I)	2	2005/06	1885
1866/67	75/76	0-6-0ST	3ft 6in	17x24(I)	2	2092/93	1890
1868/73	39-42	4-2-4T	8ft 10in	18x24(I)	4	2001-04	1890*
1870-72	2/4-6/8/14/43-46	2-4-0	6ft 7½in	17x24(I)	10	2015-24	1892
1872/74	91/92	0-4-0WT	3ft 6in	14x18(O)	2	2094/95	1881
1874/75	11/20/34	2-4-0	6ft 4in	17x24(I)	3	2025-27	1886

* Converted to tender engines in 1877.

Standard Gauge

Built	Nos	Wheel Arr	Driving wheels	Cylinders (in)	Total	GWR Nos	Last wdn
1874/75	1/3/16	2-4-0	6ft 4in	17x24(I)	3	1355-57	1884
1874/75	114/15	0-6-0T	3ft 6in	12x18(I)	2	1376/77	1934
1875	93-95	0-4-0T	4ft 0in	14x18(O)	3	1378-80	1880
1876	30/33	2-4-0T	5ft 0in	16x24(I)	2	1358/59	1890

Westleigh Quarries 3ft 0in gauge

Built	Nos	Wheel Arr	Driving wheels	Cylinders (in)	Total	GWR Nos	Last wdn
1874/75	112/13	0-4-0WT	2ft 0in	8x12(O)	2	1381/82	1899

9 The Preservationists

Of all the railways which once homed in on Bristol or criss-crossed Somerset, just the basic framework of the system now survives under the tender, loving care of British Rail. The only branch line not to have disappeared from the local BR maps is the one to Severn Beach and, ironically, the original section of that branch started life as part of one of the small independent companies, the Bristol Port Railway & Pier. A few of the other minnows were absorbed by bigger companies and survive today, albeit totally incognito, but most of the respected names in local railway history have all but vanished.

Throughout Britain, the efforts of preservationists have helped to save some of the country's railway heritage and, fortunately, Bristol and Somerset have their fair share of dedicated enthusiasts. Today there are four locations in the area where standard gauge steam railways operate and a fifth is in the formative stage. Quite appropriately, three of the area's preserved lines reflect local or regional history and this is in contrast to some organisations elsewhere. Purists have often been heard to comment that it is 'not quite right' to see a Southern Pacific negotiating Yorkshire hills or a GWR 'Dukedog' meandering through Sussex. On the whole, the steam locomotives which work in Bristol and Somerset today have distinct local links.

The Somerset and Dorset Museum Trust

The first preservation organisation to emerge in Somerset was the Somerset & Dorset Railway Museum Trust which established its headquarters at the former S&D station and yard at Radstock North in 1970. The Trust rescued one of the ex-S&D 2-8-0s, No 53808 (S&D No 88), from Dai Woodham's scrapyard at Barry in 1970 and, soon after, acquired ex-LMS 'Jinty' No 47493. Sadly, all seven of the 'Jinties' which had once sported S&D numbers were scrapped but, although No 47493 had spent some of its last years at Wigan and was hardly a local engine, it was one of only 10 representatives of the

type to escape cutting up. Fellow 'Jinty' No 47313 became the last ex-S&D locomotive to remain in service with British Railways; originally S&D No 22, it had spent its last years on colliery work in Derbyshire and was retired in June 1967.

The Somerset & Dorset Trust acquired a number of industrial tank engines. One was Peckett 'R3' 0-4-0ST (works No 1788) which had been delivered new in 1929 to Kilmersdon colliery and went on to become the last NCB colliery locomotive to work in North Somerset. The Peckett's final duties involved the clearance of the colliery site after closure. When the locomotive was withdrawn in 1974, the National Coal Board presented it to the S&D Trust.

It is quite remarkable that, despite the unquestionable charisma of the Somerset & Dorset Railway, just two of its locomotives passed into the hands of preservationists. Apart from No 53808, only sister 2-8-0 No 53809 (ex-S&D No 89) eluded the cutter's torch; it now lives at the Midland Railway Centre at Butterley. The tender of a further 2-8-0, No 53805 (ex-S&D No 85) also survives, but its pedigree is not publicised; it is attached to the first Midland Compound, now No 1000, which resides at the National Railway Museum.

The West Somerset Railway

The Somerset & Dorset Museum Trust held occasional steam days at Radstock but the site, although traditional, was not to be a permanent one. The Trust eventually moved its headquarters to Washford station on the Taunton-Minehead line which was taken over by the West Somerset Railway in 1973. The WSR was formed in 1971, just four months after British Rail had closed the Minehead branch and, after negotiations, Somerset County Council bought the branch, complete with track still in position, and leased the whole lot to the preservation company. The first section reopened in 1976 from Minehead to Blue Anchor and, by June 1979, the line had been extended to Bishop's Lydeard. With a

20-mile run, the West Somerset now boasts the distinction of being the longest privately-owned passenger-carrying railway line in Britain.

The move to Washford and the use of the West Somerset's facilities proved beneficial for the Somerset & Dorset Trust. Serious restoration work on 2-8-0 No 53808 was able to be undertaken and, in August 1987, the locomotive was steamed once again. At Washford, the Trust has established a workshop in the station yard, and most of the rolling stock on display has a connection with the S&D. The station houses an S&D museum and the signalbox has been restored as a working replica of Midford box. The next station along the line from Washford is at Blue Anchor, where an excellent museum is housed on the down platform. The museum's exhibits are, in the main, Bristol & Exeter- and Great Western-orientated, and visitors are encouraged to wrestle with a quill pen when signing the register. A nice touch!

Although the West Somerset's museum is at Blue Anchor, the administrative centre of the company is at Minehead. The locomotive department adjacent to the station takes care of the working steam engines which are the ex-S&D 2-8-0, ex-GWR '6400' 0-6-0PT No 6412, '4500' 2-6-2T No 4561 and '2251' class 0-6-0 No 3205. The Pannier tank was a Swansea engine for much of its life but, at the time of withdrawal in 1964, was shedded at Gloucester. The Prairie tank was retired in 1962, having spent much of its later life in Devon and Cornwall and, like the Pannier, it is owned by the WSR. The Collett 0-6-0, which is in private ownership, ended its British Rail days in 1965 at the old Somerset & Dorset shed at Templecombe, and after preservation, had spells working on the Dart Valley and Severn Valley Railways before arriving in Somerset in 1987. Surprisingly, No 3205 is the only representative of its versatile class which escaped scrapping.

The West Somerset Railway provides accommodation for four other locomotives which are in varying stages of restoration. At the heavy end there is ex-

GWR 2-8-0 No 3850, once a Bristol-based locomotive, while two different classes of Prairie tanks are represented by Nos 4160 and 5542. The former is the heavier of the pair, but spent most of its working life in South-East Wales while the latter often appeared in the Taunton and Frome areas until its retirement in 1961. No 7820 *Dinmore Manor* is the other locomotive which has been found digs on the WSR during restoration.

From the outset, the West Somerset considered that it would be a financial necessity to operate diesels on off-peak services and the company's diesel depot is located at Williton. Passenger services are handled by a stud of two-car DMUs, two of Park Royal origin, two from Gloucester and the other from Craven. A pair of Class 35 'Hymeks', Nos 7017 and 7018, three Class 14s, Nos 9500/26/51, 'Western' class No D1035 *Western Yeoman* (formerly No D1010 *Western Campaigner*) and four diesel shunters are also resident at Williton.

The restoration of the stations along the West Somerset line has been very well done, and when the 0-6-0PT or 2-6-2T is in action at the head of a rake of chocolate and cream coaches, the scene is pure Great Western. The spacious station at Bishop's Lydeard is the official terminus of the West Somerset Railway but negotiations with both British Rail and the Taunton Cider Co eventually resulted in an agreement for the occasional through running to and from Taunton. The involvement of Taunton Cider was required because access to the WSR from the main line could only be gained via the Cider Co's yard. The first through train to Minehead for 19 years ran on 16 June 1990, and the exercise has since been repeated for a handful of specials.

The East Somerset Railway

At the opposite end of the county, the East Somerset Railway came into existence out of necessity. Wildlife artist David Shepherd bought two steam locomotives in 1967 but found himself with the little problem of having nowhere to put them. The engines were given temporary accommodation on the Longmoor Military Railway in Hampshire until the line's closure, and afterwards they were relegated to an undignified existence on an overgrown storage siding near Southampton. After much searching, Shepherd stumbled on Cranmore station between Witham and Shepton Mallet which, although it had been left to rot since 1963, had retained its rail connection to the outside world as the bitumen

yard adjoining the station was still in daily use. Shepherd bought the site with the intention of establishing a preservation centre. The decision to call the company the East Somerset Railway did not take too much deliberation as that was the name of the company which had originally built the line from Witham, through Cranmore and into Shepton Mallet in 1858.

The two locomotives which were eventually to end up at Cranmore were both British Railways Standard classes. One was '9F' 2-10-0 No 92203 which, when purchased by David Shepherd for £3,000, was only eight years old; the other was '4MT' 4-6-0 No 75029. Shepherd named both the engines, the '9F' becoming *Black Prince* and the '4MT' *The Green Knight*. Further locomotives have since arrived and these comprise ex-LMS 'Jinty' No 47493 which had previously lived at Radstock, ex-GWR '5600' class 0-6-2T No 6634, Stroudley 'E1' 0-6-0T No B110 and two Andrew Barclay industrial saddle tanks. A most useful early acquisition by the East Somerset was a Dubs 0-4-0 crane tank of 1901, which was restored at Cranmore in 1977; it has more than earned its keep on permanent way duties.

Despite a stock list which includes five former main line locomotives, the East Somerset's schedule for overhauls and restoration seems a little out of synch as most of them have spent much of the last two seasons in the workshops. The majority of workings during this period have been performed by hired motive power with the North Eastern Locomotive Preservation Group's 'J72' class 0-6-0T No 69023 in action in 1990 and an East Lancashire Railway ex-industrial 0-6-0T in 1991.

From Cranmore, the East Somerset Railway runs for just under three miles to a purpose-built platform called Mendip Vale. Until 1985 the line ran for only about half the present distance and terminated at Merryfield Lane halt, which has been retained as an intermediate station. A further halt, Cranmore West, was constructed on the opposite side of the line to the engine shed and workshop primarily for the benefit of passengers who wanted to break their return journeys for an inspection of the locomotives. The proprietors of the ESR readily admit that their line is hardly the longest preserved railway in existence, but they are quick to point out that it is one of the very few in the country which is 100% steam-operated.

Despite that proud claim, pedantic purists might grumble that the motive power and rolling stock of the East Somerset fails to give the railway a positive identity, but this is not something that

causes undue concern at Cranmore. The company has completed some first class renovation work with tasteful new buildings at the station, and a highly-convincing Victorian-style engine shed and workshop. Early in 1991, the new visitor centre, complete with restaurant and shops, was opened at the station, and the new premises also provide an outlet for David Shepherd's paintings. The natural history link is well-promoted and details of specialised local walks are readily available. On the railway front, a noteworthy addition during 1991 was a British-built 4-8-0 which had been constructed in 1896 for sevice in the Belgian Congo (now Zaire). The locomotive had been presented to David Shepherd by President Kaunda of Zambia in 1974, and it had been given a home at Whipsnade Zoo until being dispatched to Cranmore as a static exhibit.

Development of land to the west of Mendip Vale has put paid to any hopes of ever extending the East Somerset in that direction but, to the east of Cranmore, the link to British Rail at Witham is still maintained and through trains can be accommodated. In November 1990, an InterCity 125 ran through to Cranmore and, in the Spring of 1991, a Class 47 diesel and its train of nine Pullman sleeping cars was stabled overnight at Cranmore. The Pullman's 20 passengers were Americans who had paid the sum of $3,000 a head for a rail-tour of Britain and it was remarked that, for that price, they could at least have been hauled by a proper steam engine.

The Avon Valley Railway

At Bitton station, on the ex-Midland line between Bristol and Bath, the Bristol Suburban Railway Society was established in the early 1970s. At the time, the line was still used by two daily coal trains bound for Bath gas works but the gas works closed in 1971 and the rails were lifted the following year. This left the society with a bit of a void as, not only had it yet to obtain its first locomotive, but it had also lost its track. Undeterred, the engineless and trackless society formally leased the entire Bitton station and yard in 1973 and members started work on the site which, although unused by the public for only seven years, had already fallen into a state approaching dereliction.

The first rails were obtained from Fry's factory in nearby Keynsham and this enabled the sole locomotive to be brought out of storage. It was an Avonside 0-6-0T (works No 1798) which had been built in 1918 for the Imperial Smelting Works at Avonmouth, and on its withdrawal in 1972, had been purchased by the society. It was first steamed at Bitton in 1974 and was named *Edwin Hulse* after a former chairman of the society. The society's fortunes wavered through the 1970s, and the initial optimism gave way to stagnation but a major reconstitution in the early 1980s, from which the Bitton Railway Co emerged, acted as a catalyst for renewed enthusiasm.

The newly-constituted company adopted the banner of the Avon Valley Railway and, with a greater degree of professionalism than before, it set its sights on relaying track both to the north and the south of Bitton station. The necessary Light Railway Order was obtained and the 1-mile stretch northwards from Bitton to Oldland Common was reopened in 1989. The order also approved an extension of 1¼ miles southwards from Bitton towards the River Avon and this is currently awaiting construction; the company's ultimate dream is to extend into Bath.

As Bitton station stands on what was once the Midland line, the locomotive stock of the Avon Valley Railway understandably shows strong LMS influence. Four standard LMS classes are represented but, as yet, the locomotives are far from ready for action. Fowler '4F' 0-6-0 No 44123, 'Black Five' No 45379, 'Jinty' No 47324 and '8F' 2-8-0 No 48173 all finished their days side by side at Barry scrapyard. The '4F' and the 'Jinty' were initially rescued for the Mid-Hants Railway but were moved to Bitton in 1986 to join the other two senior residents. Although none of the quartet was ever officially allocated to either Bristol or Bath sheds, all but the 'Jinty' performed duties which brought them to the area on many occasions.

Two other main line locomotives are awaiting attention at Bitton. One is Bulleid Pacific No 34058 *Sir Frederick Pile* which was, for much of its life, an Exmouth Junction locomotive and, therefore, well acquainted with the line through southern Somerset. The other is Standard '4MT' 2-6-4T No 80104. The Avon Valley Railway also has its share of industrial tank engines and, apart from *Edwin Hulse*, there is a Manning Wardle 0-6-0ST, a Hawthorn 0-6-0T and a Bagnall 0-4-0ST. Flying the local flag is Peckett 'B2' class 0-6-0ST named *Fonmon* (works No 1636) which was built in 1924.

The fleet of three small diesel locomotives includes a Barclay 0-4-0 named *Grumpy* which was ordered by the Ministry of Supply in 1940. It spent its entire career until retirement in 1978 in military service and it had gained its name in

Above:
The Avon Valley Railway's Manning Wardle 0-6-0ST **Littleton No 5** *provided the mainstay of motive power during 1991. Built in 1922 for colliery duties in South Staffordshire, it survived into NCB days, and was sold in working order in 1972. The Avon Valley bought it from its previous private owners in 1980 and, with its tractive effort of 22,500lb, it has proved to be a very useful acquisition. On the right of this picture, the locomotive and its train are seen leaving Bitton station for Oldland Common on 26 August 1991. Various restoration projects are underway in the workshop yard alongside the station.* Author

1952, when it was one of seven locomotives shipped to Suez. In case the link between the number seven and the name *Grumpy* seems rather cryptic, the clue is that other members of the seven included *Doc*, *Sneezy* and *Happy*.

The Bristol Industrial Museum

The remaining steam operation in the area is the smallest but, nevertheless, has the strongest local links. The Bristol Harbour Railway runs between the Bristol Industrial Museum at Princes Wharf and the Maritime Heritage Centre, close to Brunel's famous SS *Great Britain*, a distance of less than one mile. The railway is under the control of the Industrial Museum and is treated as an extension of the museum rather than as a preserved line; considering that the harbour lines

were used only for freight, there is no tradition of passenger usage to preserve.

Two locomotives are active on the Bristol Harbour Railway and both were constructed locally and used at Avonmouth Docks. The senior member is Avonside 'B4' class 0-6-0ST *Portbury* (works No 1764) which was built in 1917 for work on the site of Portbury Shipyard. In 1920, the engine was acquired by Bristol Docks Committee and transferred to Avonmouth where it continued to work until withdrawn in 1958. After 12 years in storage it was moved to Radstock, where the Somerset & Dorset Trust hoped to embark on restoration but, despite the Trust's move to Washford, work on *Portbury* was never started. Bristol City Museum rescued the locomotive in 1985 and took less than three years to restore it to working order.

The museum's other working locomotive is a 1937 Peckett 'FA' class 0-6-0ST (works No 1940). Named *Henbury*, it was built for the Port of Bristol Authority for service at Avonmouth Docks, and went on to become one of the last steam

Below:
Avonside 0-6-0ST **Portbury** *(works No 1764) was built in 1917 for duties at the Admiralty shipyard at Portbury, and was acquired for work at Avonmouth docks three years later. It has been well restored by the Bristol Industrial Museum and is now a regular performer at the museum's steam days. In this view it is seen at work on 26 August 1991.* Author

engines in use at Avonmouth. When withdrawn and mothballed in 1964, *Henbury* had had the benefit of a major overhaul just two years previously and so, when the Somerset & Dorset Trust took charge of the locomotive in 1972, it did not take extensive work to restore it to working condition. *Henbury* returned to Bristol in 1978, and had its moment of glory three years later when it deputised for Western Fuel's 0-6-0 diesel on shunting duties between Ashton and Wapping Wharf. The loading of Western Fuel's trains was regularly in excess of 400 tons, but any locomotive which had seen service at Avonmouth was more than capable of such labours.

Awaiting restoration at Bristol Industrial Museum is an ex-Mountain Ash Colliery 0-6-0ST, which was built by Fox Walker in 1874. The presence of this locomotive in Bristol is significant in that the museum has one representative from each of the three local builders.

Of the other museums in the area, none has working steam locomotives, but Radstock Museum can offer the next best thing: a model railway. Although not specifically railway-orientated, the museum at Haydon Hill on the outskirts of Radstock houses a fascinating collection of exhibits and photographs which chronicle the development of the mining industry and the railways in and around the town.

The Somerset & Avon Railway Association

A late arrival in the preservation stakes is the Somerset & Avon Railway Association, known affectionately as SARA. Formed in 1990, SARA has already made significant progress with its plan to reopen the railway between Frome and Radstock, the line which originally opened as a broad gauge mineral route in 1854. The Association had one major advantage in that the tracks between the two towns remained completely in situ, and at Radstock the locomotive shed remained intact despite being officially closed as far back as 1929.

Negotiations with British Rail resulted in SARA acquiring the shed and station site at Radstock for an affordable rent, and local quarry owners, ARC, provided the first locomotive for the organisation. Although that first engine is a Sentinel diesel, SARA intends to introduce steam haulage to the line at the earliest possible opportunity. A nominal subsidiary, the Vobster Light Railway Co, is currently embarking on a project to lay a 2ft gauge line from Mells Road station along the route of the old Newbury Railway towards Vobster.

Conclusion

The subject of preserved railways presents a tremendous irony, which is just as evident in Bristol and Somerset as elsewhere in Britain. Apart from lines such as the Bristol Harbour Railway which have been pressed into action to provide running space for restored locomotives, the other preserved railways operate over lines which were once categorised by the authorities as never having a chance of being viable. Take the case of the branch from Taunton to Minehead as an example. Less than five years after British Rail closed the line in order to cut its losses, the West Somerset Railway had reopened part of the same branch using older rolling stock and charging higher fares, but in complete contrast to BR the WSR showed a profit. Furthermore, could anyone explain to the unconverted why crowds flock to Bitton on summer Sundays to travel just 1-mile in elderly coaches to Oldland Common, which consists of little more than a stereotyped housing estate while, only five miles away, clean and comfortable InterCity 125s run only partly full.

Any self-respecting railway enthusiast would profess that Dr Richard Beeching's thoughts on railways were similar to how Vlad the Impaler viewed humanitarianism but, if it had not been for Beeching, the preservation movement would have had little to work on. Beeching himself was not totally unaware of that situation. When the Dart Valley Railway opened its restored line in South Devon in 1969, the directors' plucky choice of guest speaker was one Lord (formerly Dr Richard) Beeching. His Lordship's speech included the observation that, had he not closed the line, he would have been unable to reopen it. The reaction of his audience is not on record.

In the Bristol and Somerset area, railway history has been kept alive to a much greater degree than in most other parts of Britain. A combination of sympathetic preservation and local pride has helped to retain a number of the many different facets which contributed to the individuality of the local story. There is, however, one particular aspect of local railway history which falls into the category of missed opportunities and that is, of course, the legendary Somerset & Dorset Railway. Despite the commendable efforts of the Somerset & Dorset Trust at Washford, it's sad that it has been impossible to preserve anything of the actual route of one of Britain's most famous railways. Very little of the old line has been used for redevelopment, but at least it offers a lot of scope for taking the dog for a walk.

Preservation Organisations in Bristol and Somerset

Please note that none of the preserved railways in the area operates on every day of the year and so, if planning a visit, check the opening dates and times before making a special journey. Stock lists for each company have been excluded because working locomotives have a habit of being transferred from one railway to another, and so no list could be considered to be current.

Avon Valley Railway
Bitton Station, Willsbridge, Bristol BS15 6ED. Tel: (0272) 327926.
On A431 5 miles east of Bristol, 7 miles west of Bath.

Bristol Harbour Railway
Bristol Industrial Museum, Princes Wharf, City Docks, Bristol BS1 4RN. Tel: (0272) 251470.
Adjacent to Prince Street, ½-mile south of Bristol city centre.

East Somerset Railway
Cranmore Station, Shepton Mallet, Somerset BA4 4QP. Tel: (074 988) 417.
Just to south of A361 3 miles east of Shepton Mallet, 8 miles west of Frome.

Somerset & Avon Railway Association
Details from: Mr.Bill Sweet, 13 Tuddington Gardens, Wells, Somerset BA5 2EJ.
Radstock Station site by junction of A367 and A362 in town centre.

West Somerset Railway
The Railway Station, Minehead, Somerset TA24 5BG. Tel:(0643) 4996.
Adjacent to sea front.